1040

THIS BOOKLET DOES NOT CONTAIN INSTRUCTIONS FOR ANY FORM 1040 SCHEDULES

INSTRUCTIONS

2017

I0481169

freefile is the fast, safe, and free way to prepare and *e-file* your taxes. See *IRS.gov/FreeFile.*

Get a faster refund, reduce errors, and save paper. For more information on **IRS** Free File and *e-file*, see *Free Software Options for Doing Your Taxes* in these instructions or go to *IRS.gov/FreeFile.*

2017 TAX CHANGES

See *What's New* in these instructions.

FUTURE DEVELOPMENTS

For the latest information about developments related to Form 1040 and its instructions, such as legislation enacted after they were published, go to *IRS.gov/Form1040.*

IRS

Department of the Treasury **Internal Revenue Service** IRS.gov

Jan 16, 2018   Cat. No. 24811V

Table of Contents

Department
of the
Treasury

**Internal
Revenue
Service**

The Taxpayer Advocate Service Is Here To Help You

What is the Taxpayer Advocate Service?
The Taxpayer Advocate Service (TAS) is an *independent* organization within the Internal Revenue Service (IRS) that helps taxpayers and protects taxpayer rights. Our job is to ensure that every taxpayer is treated fairly and that you know and understand your rights under the *Taxpayer Bill of Rights*.

What can the Taxpayer Advocate Service do for you?
We can help you resolve problems that you can't resolve with the IRS. And our service is free. If you qualify for our assistance, you will be assigned to one advocate who will work with you throughout the process and will do everything possible to resolve your issue. TAS can help you if:
  • Your problem is causing financial difficulty for you, your family, or your business.
  • You face (or your business is facing) an immediate threat of adverse action.
  • You've tried repeatedly to contact the IRS but no one has responded, or the IRS hasn't responded by the date promised.

How can you reach us?
We have offices in *every state, the District of Columbia, and Puerto Rico*. Your local advocate's number is at *www.TaxpayerAdvocate.IRS.gov* and in your local directory. You can also call us at 1-877-777-4778.

How can you learn about your taxpayer rights?
The Taxpayer Bill of Rights describes ten basic rights that all taxpayers have when dealing with the IRS. Our Tax Toolkit at *www.TaxpayerAdvocate.IRS.gov* can help you understand *what these rights mean to you* and how they apply. These are **your** rights. Know them. Use them.

How else does the Taxpayer Advocate Service help taxpayers?
TAS works to resolve large-scale problems that affect many taxpayers. If you know of one of these broad issues, please report it to us at *IRS.gov/SAMS*.

Low Income Taxpayer Clinics Help Taxpayers

Low Income Taxpayer Clinics (LITCs) are independent from the IRS. Some serve individuals whose income is below a certain level and who need to resolve a tax problem. These clinics provide professional representation before the IRS or in court on audits, appeals, tax collection disputes, and other issues for free or for a small fee. Some clinics provide information about taxpayer rights and responsibilities in many different languages for individuals who speak English as a second language. For more information, and to find a clinic near you, read the LITC page on *IRS.gov/LITC* or IRS *Publication 4134, Low Income Taxpayer Clinic List*. You can also get this publication at your local IRS office or by calling 1-800-829-3676.

Suggestions for Improving the IRS

Taxpayer Advocacy Panel

Have a suggestion for improving the IRS and do not know who to contact? The Taxpayer Advocacy Panel (TAP) is a diverse group of citizen volunteers who listen to taxpayers, identify taxpayers' issues, and make suggestions for improving IRS service and customer satisfaction. The panel is demographically and geographically diverse, with at least one member from each state, the District of Columbia, and Puerto Rico. Contact TAP at *www.improveirs.org* or 1-888-912-1227 (toll-free).

Affordable Care Act—What You Need To Know

Requirement To Reconcile Advance Payments of the Premium Tax Credit

The premium tax credit helps pay premiums for health insurance purchased from the Marketplace. Eligible individuals may have advance payments of the premium tax credit made on their behalf directly to the insurance company.

If you or a family member enrolled in health insurance through the Marketplace and advance payments of the premium tax credit were made to your insurance company to reduce your monthly premium payment, you must attach **Form 8962** to your return to **reconcile** (compare) the advance payments with your premium tax credit for the year.

The Marketplace is required to send **Form 1095-A** by **January 31, 2018,** listing the advance payments and other information you need to complete **Form 8962.**

1. You will need **Form 1095-A** from the Marketplace.

2. Complete **Form 8962** to claim the credit and to reconcile your advance credit payments.

3. Include **Form 8962** with your **1040, 1040A,** or **1040NR.** (Don't include Form 1095-A.)

Health Coverage Individual Responsibility Payment

For 2017, you must:

 OR  OR

Report Health Care Coverage

Check the Full-year coverage box on **line 61** to indicate that you, your spouse (if filing jointly), and anyone you can or do claim as a dependent had qualifying health care coverage throughout 2017.

Claim a Coverage Exemption

Attach **Form 8965** to claim an exemption from the requirement to have health care coverage. For more information, go to *IRS.gov/Form8965.*

Make a Shared Responsibility Payment

Make a shared responsibility payment if, for any month in 2017, you, your spouse (if filing jointly), or anyone you can or do claim as a dependent didn't have coverage and doesn't qualify for a coverage exemption. For more information, go to *IRS.gov/SRP.*

Health Coverage Reporting

- If you or someone in your family had health coverage in 2017, the provider of that coverage is required to send you a **Form 1095-A, 1095-B,** or **1095-C** (with Part III completed), that lists individuals in your family who were enrolled in the coverage and shows their months of coverage. You may use this information to help complete **line 61.** You should receive the **Form 1095-A** by early **February 2018 and Form 1095-B** or **1095-C** by early **March 2018,** if applicable. You don't need to wait to receive your Form 1095-B or 1095-C to file your return. You may rely on other information about your coverage to complete line 61. Don't include Form 1095-A, Form 1095-B, or Form 1095-C with your tax return.

- If you or someone in your family was an employee in 2017, the employer may be required to send you a **Form 1095-C. Part II** of **Form 1095-C** shows whether your employer offered you health insurance coverage and, if so, information about the offer. You should receive **Form 1095-C** by early **March 2018.** This information may be relevant if you purchased health insurance coverage for 2017 through the Health Insurance Marketplace and wish to claim the premium tax credit on **line 69.** However, you don't need to wait to receive this form to file your return. You may rely on other information received from your employer. If you don't wish to claim the premium tax credit for 2017, you don't need the information in **Part II** of **Form 1095-C.** For more information on who is eligible for the premium tax credit, see the Instructions for Form 8962.

Free Software Options for Doing Your Taxes

Why have 49 million Americans used Free File?

- *Security*—Free File uses the latest encryption technology to safeguard your information.
- *Flexible Payments*—File early; pay by April 17, 2018.
- *Greater Accuracy*—Fewer errors mean faster processing.
- *Quick Receipt*—Get an acknowledgment that your return was received and accepted.
- *Go Green*—Reduce the amount of paper used.
- *It's Free*—through *IRS.gov/FreeFile*.
- *Faster Refunds*—Join the eight in 10 taxpayers who get their refunds faster by using direct deposit and *e-file*.

 **Do Your Taxes for Free**

If your adjusted gross income was $66,000 or less in 2017, you can use free tax software to prepare and *e-file* your tax return. Earned more? Use Free File Fillable Forms.

Free File. This public-private partnership, between the IRS and tax software providers, makes approximately a dozen brand name commercial software products and *e-file* available for free. Seventy percent of the nation's taxpayers are eligible.

Just visit *IRS.gov/FreeFile* for details. Free File combines all the benefits of *e-file* and easy-to-use software at no cost. Guided questions will help ensure you get all the tax credits and deductions you are due. It's fast, safe, and free.

You can review each software provider's criteria for free usage or use an online tool to find which free software products match your situation. Some software providers offer state tax return preparation for free.

Free File Fillable Forms. The IRS offers electronic versions of IRS paper forms that also can be *e-filed* for free. Free File Fillable Forms is best for people experienced in preparing their own tax returns. There are no income limitations. Free File Fillable Forms does basic math calculations. It supports only federal tax forms.

Free Tax Help Available Nationwide

Volunteers are available in communities nationwide providing free tax assistance to low-to-moderate income (generally under $54,000 in adjusted gross income) and elderly taxpayers (age 60 and older). At selected sites, taxpayers can input and electronically file their own tax return with the assistance of an IRS-certified volunteer.

See *How To Get Tax Help* near the end of these instructions for additional information or visit IRS.gov (Keyword: VITA) for a VITA/TCE site near you!

IRS.gov is the gateway to all electronic services offered by the IRS, as well as the spot to download forms at *IRS.gov/Forms*.

Make your tax payments electronically—it's easy.

You can make electronic payments online, by phone, or from a mobile device. Paying electronically is safe and secure. The IRS uses the latest encryption technology and doesn't store the bank account number you use to submit your payment. When you use any of the IRS electronic payment options, it puts you in control of paying your tax bill and gives you peace of mind. You determine the payment date, and you will receive an immediate confirmation from the IRS. It's easy, secure, and much quicker than mailing in a check or money order. Go to *IRS.gov/Payments* to see all your electronic payment options.

What's New

For information about any additional changes to the 2017 tax law or any other developments affecting Form 1040 or its instructions, go to *IRS.gov/Form1040* or *IRS.gov/Extenders*.

Due date of return. File Form 1040 by April 17, 2018. The due date is April 17, because April 15 is a Sunday and the Emancipation Day holiday in the District of Columbia is observed on April 16—even if you do not live in the District of Columbia.

Childless earned income credit (EIC). If your child meets the tests to be your qualifying child, but also meets the tests to be the qualifying child of another person, only one of you can actually treat the child as a qualifying child to claim the EIC. If the other person can claim the child as a qualifying child, you can't claim the EIC as a taxpayer with a qualifying child unless you have another qualifying child. However, you may be able to claim the EIC without a qualifying child. For more information, see Pub. 596.

Secure access. To combat identity fraud, the IRS has upgraded its identity verification process for certain self-help tools on IRS.gov. To find out what types of information new users will need, go to *IRS.gov/SecureAccess*.

Access your online account. You must authenticate your identity. To securely log in to your federal tax account go to *IRS.gov/Account*. View the amount you owe, review 18 months of payment history, access online payment options, and create or modify an online payment agreement. You can also access your tax records online.

New withholding tables. To reflect changes made by the tax reform legislation, the IRS has released updated income-tax withholding tables. The new withholding tables are designed to work with the Form(s) W-4 you have already filed with your employer. To see if you need to have your withholding increased or decreased, use the IRS Withholding Calculator at *IRS.gov/W4App*. The calculator is being revised to take into account these changes and should be available by the end of February.

Personal exemption phaseout amounts increased for certain taxpayers. Your personal exemption is $4,050 but the amount is reduced if your adjusted gross income is more than $156,900 if married filing separately; $261,500 if single; $287,650 if head of household; or $313,800 if married filing jointly or qualifying widow(er). See the instructions for line 42.

Medical and dental expenses. You can deduct the part of your medical and dental expenses that is more than 7.5% of your adjusted gross income. See the Instructions for Schedule A.

Limit on itemized deductions. You may not be able to deduct all of your itemized deductions if your adjusted gross income is more than $156,900 if married filing separately; $261,500 if single; $287,650 if head of household; or $313,800 if married filing jointly or qualifying widow(er).

Standard deduction amounts increased. For 2017, the standard deduction for married individuals filing a joint return and qualifying widow(er)s has increased to $12,700; for head of household filers the amount has increased to $9,350; and for single filers and married individuals filing separate returns the amount has increased to $6,350.

Tuition and fees deduction expired. At the time these instructions went to print, certain tax benefits had expired, including the tuition and fees deduction (line 34). That line is now shown as "Reserved for future use" in case Congress extends the tuition and fees deduction for 2017. You can find out if legislation extended this and other tax benefits to allow you to claim them on your 2017 return at *IRS.gov/Form1040* or *IRS.gov/Extenders*.

Mailing your return. If you live in Connecticut, District of Columbia, Maryland, Pennsylvania, Rhode Island, or West Virginia and you are mailing in your return, you will need to mail it to a different address this year. See *Where Do You File?* at the end of these instructions.

EIN needed to claim the American opportunity credit. To claim the American opportunity credit, you need to have the employer identification number (EIN) of the institution to which your qualified expenses were paid. See the Instructions for Form 8863.

W-2 verification code. A new "verification code" box will appear on Form W-2, but not all W-2s will have a 16-digit code in box 9. If you *e-file* and your W-2 has a verification code in box 9, enter it when prompted by your tax software. Don't enter the verification code if you file your return on paper.

Disaster tax relief. Disaster tax relief was enacted for those impacted by certain Presidentially declared disasters. The tax benefits provided by this relief include the following.

• An increased standard deduction based on your qualified disaster losses. See the instructions for line 40 and the Instructions for Schedule A for information on qualifying for and figuring the increased standard deduction.

• Election to use your 2016 earned income to figure your 2017 earned income credit. See the instructions for lines 66a and 66b for more information on this election.

• Election to use your 2016 earned income to figure your 2017 additional child tax credit. See the instructions for line 67 and the Instructions for Schedule 8812 for more information on this election.

 At the time these instructions went to print, Congress was considering legislation that would provide additional tax relief for individuals affected by certain 2017 disasters. For more information and to see if legislation was enacted, see Pub. 976.

Filing Requirements

These rules apply to all U.S. citizens, regardless of where they live, and resident aliens.

 Have you tried IRS *e-file*? It's the fastest way to get your refund and it's free if you are eligible. Visit IRS.gov for details.

Do You Have To File?

Use Chart A, B, or C to see if you must file a return. U.S. citizens who lived in or had income from a U.S. possession should see Pub. 570. Residents of Puerto Rico can use *Tax Topic 901* to see if they must file.

 Even if you do not otherwise have to file a return, you should file one to get a refund of any federal income tax withheld. You also should file if you are eligible for any of the following credits.

- *Earned income credit.*
- *Additional child tax credit.*
- *American opportunity credit.*
- *Credit for federal tax on fuels.*
- *Premium tax credit.*
- *Health coverage tax credit.*

See Pub. 501 for details. Also see Pub. 501 if you do not have to file but received a Form 1099-B (or substitute statement).

Requirement to reconcile advance payments of the premium tax credit. If you, your spouse with whom you are filing a joint return, or a dependent was enrolled in coverage through the Marketplace for 2017 and advance payments of the premium tax credit were made for this coverage, you must file a 2017 return and attach Form 8962. You (or whoever enrolled you) should have received Form 1095-A from the Marketplace with information about your coverage and any advance payments.

You must attach Form 8962 even if someone else enrolled you, your spouse, or your dependent. If you are a dependent who is claimed on someone else's 2017 return, you do not have to attach Form 8962.

Exception for certain children under age 19 or full-time students. If certain conditions apply, you can elect to include on your return the income of a child who was under age 19 at the end of 2017 or was a full-time student under age 24 at the end of 2017. To do so, use Form 8814. If you make this election, your child doesn't have to file a return. For details, use *Tax Topic 553* or see Form 8814.

A child born on January 1, 1994, is considered to be age 24 at the end of 2017. Do not use Form 8814 for such a child.

Resident aliens. These rules also apply if you were a resident alien. Also, you may qualify for certain tax treaty benefits. See Pub. 519 for details.

Nonresident aliens and dual-status aliens. These rules also apply if you were a nonresident alien or a dual-status alien and both of the following apply.
- You were married to a U.S. citizen or resident alien at the end of 2017.
- You elected to be taxed as a resident alien.

See Pub. 519 for details.

 Specific rules apply to determine if you are a resident alien, nonresident alien, or dual-status alien. Most nonresident aliens and dual-status aliens have different filing requirements and may have to file Form 1040NR or Form 1040NR-EZ. Pub. 519 discusses these requirements and other information to help aliens comply with U.S. tax law.

When and Where Should You File?

File Form 1040 by **April 17, 2018.** (The due date is April 17, instead of April 15, because April 15 falls on a Sunday and April 16 is the Emancipation Day holiday in the District of Columbia—even if you do not live in the District of Columbia.) If you file after this date, you may have to pay interest and penalties. See *Interest and Penalties,* later.

If you were serving in, or in support of, the U.S. Armed Forces in a designated combat zone or contingency operation, you may be able to file later. See Pub. 3 for details.

If you *e-file* your return, there is no need to mail it. However, if you choose to mail it, filing instructions and addresses are at the end of these instructions.

What if You Can't File on Time?

You can get an automatic 6-month extension if, no later than the date your return is due, you file Form 4868. For details, see Form 4868. Instead of filing Form 4868, you can apply for an automatic extension by making an electronic payment by the due date of your return.

 An automatic 6-month extension to file doesn't extend the time to pay your tax. If you don't pay your tax by the original due date of your return, you will owe interest on the unpaid tax and may owe penalties. See Form 4868.

If you are a U.S. citizen or resident alien, you may qualify for an automatic extension of time to file without filing Form 4868. You qualify if, on the due date of your return, you meet one of the following conditions.
- You live outside the United States and Puerto Rico and your main place of business or post of duty is outside the United States and Puerto Rico.
- You are in military or naval service on duty outside the United States and Puerto Rico.

This extension gives you an extra 2 months to file and pay the tax, but interest will be charged from the original due date of the return on any unpaid tax. You must include a statement showing that you meet the requirements. If you are still unable to file your return by the end of the 2-month period, you can get an additional 4 months if, no later than June 15, 2018, you file Form 4868. This

4-month extension of time to file doesn't extend the time to pay your tax. See Form 4868.

Private Delivery Services

If you choose to mail your return, you can use certain private delivery services designated by the IRS to meet the "timely mailing treated as timely filing/paying" rule for tax returns and payments. These private delivery services include only the following.

• UPS Next Day Air Early A.M., UPS Next Day Air, UPS Next Day Air Saver, UPS 2nd Day Air, UPS 2nd Day Air A.M., UPS Worldwide Express Plus, and UPS Worldwide Express.

• FedEx First Overnight, FedEx Priority Overnight, FedEx Standard Overnight, FedEx 2 Day, FedEx International Next Flight Out, FedEx International Priority, FedEx International First, and FedEx International Economy.

• DHL Express 9:00, DHL Express 10:30, DHL Express 12:00, DHL Express Worldwide, DHL Express Envelope, DHL Import Express 10:30, DHL Import Express 12:00, DHL Import Express Worldwide.

To check for any updates to the list of designated private delivery services, go to *IRS.gov/PDS*. For the IRS mailing address to use if you're using a private delivery service, go to *IRS.gov/PDSStreetAddresses*.

The private delivery service can tell you how to get written proof of the mailing date.

Chart A—For Most People

IF your filing status is . . .	AND at the end of 2017 you were* . . .	THEN file a return if your gross income** was at least . . .
Single (see the instructions for line 1)	under 65 65 or older	$10,400 11,950
Married filing jointly*** (see the instructions for line 2)	under 65 (both spouses) 65 or older (one spouse) 65 or older (both spouses)	$20,800 22,050 23,300
Married filing separately (see the instructions for line 3)	any age	$4,050
Head of household (see the instructions for line 4)	under 65 65 or older	$13,400 14,950
Qualifying widow(er) (see the instructions for line 5)	under 65 65 or older	$16,750 18,000

*If you were born on January 1, 1953, you are considered to be age 65 at the end of 2017. (If your spouse died in 2017 or if you are preparing a return for someone who died in 2017, see Pub. 501.)

**Gross income means all income you received in the form of money, goods, property, and services that isn't exempt from tax, including any income from sources outside the United States or from the sale of your main home (even if you can exclude part or all of it). Don't include any social security benefits unless (a) you are married filing a separate return and you lived with your spouse at any time in 2017 or (b) one-half of your social security benefits plus your other gross income and any tax-exempt interest is more than $25,000 ($32,000 if married filing jointly). If (a) or (b) applies, see the instructions for lines 20a and 20b to figure the taxable part of social security benefits you must include in gross income. Gross income includes gains, but not losses, reported on Form 8949 or Schedule D. Gross income from a business means, for example, the amount on Schedule C, line 7, or Schedule F, line 9. But, in figuring gross income, don't reduce your income by any losses, including any loss on Schedule C, line 7, or Schedule F, line 9.

***If you didn't live with your spouse at the end of 2017 (or on the date your spouse died) and your gross income was at least $4,050, you must file a return regardless of your age.

Chart B—For Children and Other Dependents (See the instructions for line 6c to find out if someone can claim you as a dependent.)

If your parent (or someone else) can claim you as a dependent, use this chart to see if you must file a return.

In this chart, **unearned income** includes taxable interest, ordinary dividends, and capital gain distributions. It also includes unemployment compensation, taxable social security benefits, pensions, annuities, and distributions of unearned income from a trust. **Earned income** includes salaries, wages, tips, professional fees, and taxable scholarship and fellowship grants. **Gross income** is the total of your unearned and earned income.

Single dependents. Were you **either** age 65 or older **or** blind?

☐ **No.** You must file a return if **any** of the following apply.
  - Your unearned income was over $1,050.
  - Your earned income was over $6,350.
  - Your gross income was more than the **larger** of—
    - $1,050, or
    - Your earned income (up to $6,000) plus $350.

☐ **Yes.** You must file a return if **any** of the following apply.
  - Your unearned income was over $2,600 ($4,150 if 65 or older **and** blind).
  - Your earned income was over $7,900 ($9,450 if 65 or older **and** blind).
  - Your gross income was more than the **larger** of—
    - $2,600 ($4,150 if 65 or older **and** blind), or
    - Your earned income (up to $6,000) plus $1,900 ($3,450 if 65 or older **and** blind).

Married dependents. Were you **either** age 65 or older **or** blind?

☐ **No.** You must file a return if **any** of the following apply.
  - Your unearned income was over $1,050.
  - Your earned income was over $6,350.
  - Your gross income was at least $5 and your spouse files a separate return and itemizes deductions.
  - Your gross income was more than the **larger** of—
    - $1,050, or
    - Your earned income (up to $6,000) plus $350.

☐ **Yes.** You must file a return if **any** of the following apply.
  - Your unearned income was over $2,300 ($3,550 if 65 or older **and** blind).
  - Your earned income was over $7,600 ($8,850 if 65 or older **and** blind).
  - Your gross income was at least $5 and your spouse files a separate return and itemizes deductions.
  - Your gross income was more than the **larger** of—
    - $2,300 ($3,550 if 65 or older **and** blind), or
    - Your earned income (up to $6,000) plus $1,600 ($2,850 if 65 or older **and** blind).

Chart C—Other Situations When You Must File

You must file a return if any of the six conditions below apply for 2017.

1. You owe any special taxes, including any of the following.
  a. Alternative minimum tax.
  b. Additional tax on a qualified plan, including an individual retirement arrangement (IRA), or other tax-favored account. But if you are filing a return only because you owe this tax, you can file **Form 5329** by itself.
  c. Household employment taxes. But if you are filing a return only because you owe this tax, you can file **Schedule H** by itself.
  d. Social security and Medicare tax on tips you didn't report to your employer or on wages you received from an employer who didn't withhold these taxes.
  e. Recapture of first-time homebuyer credit. See the instructions for line 60b.
  f. Write-in taxes, including uncollected social security and Medicare or RRTA tax on tips you reported to your employer or on group-term life insurance and additional taxes on health savings accounts. See the instructions for line 62.
  g. Recapture taxes. See the instructions for lines 44, 60b, and 62.

2. You (or your spouse, if filing jointly) received health savings account, Archer MSA, or Medicare Advantage MSA distributions.
3. You had net earnings from self-employment of at least $400.
4. You had wages of $108.28 or more from a church or qualified church-controlled organization that is exempt from employer social security and Medicare taxes.
5. Advance payments of the premium tax credit were made for you, your spouse, or a dependent who enrolled in coverage through the Marketplace. You or whoever enrolled you should have received Form(s) 1095-A showing the amount of the advance payments.
6. Advance payments of the health coverage tax credit were made for you, your spouse, or a dependent. You or whoever enrolled you should have received Form(s) 1099-H showing the amount of the advance payments.

Where To Report Certain Items From 2017 Forms W-2, 1095, 1097, 1098, and 1099

File electronically. You may be eligible for free tax software that will take the guesswork out of preparing your return. Free File makes available free brand-name software and free *e-file*. Visit *IRS.gov/FreeFile* for details.

If any federal income tax withheld is shown on these forms, include the tax withheld on Form 1040, line 64. If any state or local income tax withheld is shown on these forms and you deduct state and local income taxes on Schedule A, line 5, include the tax withheld in your deduction on that line.

Form	Item and Box in Which It Should Appear	Where To Report
W-2	Wages, tips, other compensation (box 1)	Form 1040, line 7
	Allocated tips (box 8)	See *Wages, Salaries, Tips, etc.*
	Dependent care benefits (box 10)	Form 2441, Part III
	Adoption benefits (box 12, code T)	Form 8839, line 20
	Employer contributions to an Archer MSA (box 12, code R)	Form 8853, line 1
	Employer contributions to a health savings account (box 12, code W)	Form 8889, line 9
	Uncollected social security and Medicare or RRTA tax (box 12, code A, B, M, or N)	See the instructions for Form 1040, line 62
W-2G	Reportable winnings (box 1)	Form 1040, line 21 (Schedule C or C-EZ for professional gamblers)
1095-A	Advance payment of premium tax credit (line 33, column c)	See Form 8962 and its instructions
1097-BTC	Bond tax credit	See Form 8912 and its instructions
1098	Mortgage interest (box 1)	Schedule A, line 10, but first see the instructions on Form 1098*
	Refund of overpaid interest (box 4)	Form 1040, line 21, but first see the instructions on Form 1098*
	Points (box 6)	Schedule A, line 10, but first see the instructions on Form 1098*
1098-C	Contributions of motor vehicles, boats, and airplanes	Schedule A, line 17
1098-E	Student loan interest (box 1)	See the instructions for Form 1040, line 33*
1098-MA	Homeowner mortgage payments (box 3)	Schedule A, but first see the instructions on Form 1098-MA
1099-A	Acquisition or abandonment of secured property	See Pub. 4681
1099-B	Sales price of stocks, bonds, etc. (box 1d), cost or other basis (box 1e), and adjustments (boxes 1f and 1g)	Form 8949 or Schedule D, whichever applies; see the Instructions for Form 8949
	Aggregate profit or (loss) on contracts (box 11)	Form 6781, line 1
	Bartering (box 13)	See Pub. 525
1099-C	Canceled debt (box 2)	See Pub. 4681
1099-DIV	Total ordinary dividends (box 1a)	Form 1040, line 9a
	Qualified dividends (box 1b)	See the instructions for Form 1040, line 9b
	Total capital gain distributions (box 2a)	Form 1040, line 13, or, if required, Schedule D, line 13
	Unrecaptured section 1250 gain (box 2b)	See the instructions for Schedule D, line 19
	Section 1202 gain (box 2c)	See *Exclusion of Gain on Qualified Small Business (QSB) Stock* in the instructions for Schedule D
	Collectibles (28%) gain (box 2d)	See the instructions for Schedule D, line 18
	Nondividend distributions (box 3)	See the instructions for Form 1040, line 9a
	Investment expenses (box 5)	Schedule A, line 23
	Foreign tax paid (box 6)	Form 1040, line 48, or Schedule A, line 8; but first see the instructions for line 48
	Exempt-interest dividends (box 10)	Form 1040, line 8b
	Specified private activity bond interest dividends (box 11)	Form 6251, line 12
1099-G	Unemployment compensation (box 1)	See the instructions for Form 1040, line 19
	State or local income tax refunds, credits, or offsets (box 2)	See the instructions for Form 1040, line 10, and if box 8 on Form 1099-G is checked, see the box 8 instructions
	RTAA payments (box 5)	Form 1040, line 21
	Taxable grants (box 6)	Form 1040, line 21*
	Agriculture payments (box 7)	See the Instructions for Schedule F or Pub. 225*
	Market gain (box 9)	See the Instructions for Schedule F

*If the item relates to an activity for which you are required to file Schedule C, C-EZ, E, or F or Form 4835, report the taxable or deductible amount allocable to the activity on that schedule or form instead.

Form	Item and Box in Which It Should Appear	Where To Report
1099-INT	Interest income (box 1)	See the instructions on Form 1099-INT
	Early withdrawal penalty (box 2)	Form 1040, line 30
	Interest on U.S. savings bonds and Treasury obligations (box 3)	See the instructions on Form 1099-INT and the instructions for Form 1040, line 8a
	Investment expenses (box 5)	Schedule A, line 23
	Foreign tax paid (box 6)	Form 1040, line 48, or Schedule A, line 8; but first see the instructions for line 48
	Tax-exempt interest (box 8)	Form 1040, line 8b
	Specified private activity bond interest (box 9)	Form 6251, line 12
	Market discount (box 10)	Form 1040, line 8a
	Bond premium (box 11), bond premium on Treasury obligations (box 12), and bond premium on tax-exempt bond (box 13)	See the instructions on Form 1099-INT and Pub. 550
1099-K	Payment card and third party network transactions	Schedule C, C-EZ, E, or F
1099-LTC	Long-term care and accelerated death benefits	See Pub. 525 and the Instructions for Form 8853
1099-MISC	Rents (box 1)	See the Instructions for Schedule E*
	Royalties (box 2)	See the Instructions for Schedule E* (for timber, coal, and iron ore royalties, see Pub. 544)*
	Other income (box 3)	Form 1040, line 21*
	Nonemployee compensation (box 7)	Schedule C, C-EZ, or F; but if you were not self-employed, see the instructions on Form 1099-MISC
	Excess golden parachute payments (box 13)	See the instructions for Form 1040, line 62
	Other (boxes 5, 6, 8, 9, 10, 14, and 15b)	See the instructions on Form 1099-MISC
1099-OID	Original issue discount (box 1) Other periodic interest (box 2)	See the instructions on Form 1099-OID
	Early withdrawal penalty (box 3)	Form 1040, line 30
	Market discount (box 5)	Form 1040, line 8a
	Acquisition premium (box 6)	See the instructions on Form 1099-OID and Pub. 550
	Original issue discount on U.S. Treasury obligations (box 8)	See the instructions on Form 1099-OID
	Investment expenses (box 9)	Schedule A, line 23
	Bond premium (box 10)	See the instructions on Form 1099-OID and Pub. 550
	Tax-exempt OID (box 11)	Form 1040, line 8b, but first see the instructions on Form 1099-OID
1099-PATR	Patronage dividends and other distributions from a cooperative (boxes 1, 2, 3, and 5)	Schedule C, C-EZ, or F or Form 4835; but first see the instructions on Form 1099-PATR
	Domestic production activities deduction (box 6)	Form 8903, line 23
	Credits and other deductions (boxes 7, 8, and 10)	See the instructions on Form 1099-PATR
	Patron's AMT adjustment (box 9)	Form 6251, line 27
1099-Q	Qualified education program payments	See the instructions for Form 1040, line 21
1099-QA	Distributions from ABLE accounts	See the instructions for line 21, Form 5329, and Pub. 907
1099-R	Distributions from IRAs**	See the instructions for Form 1040, lines 15a and 15b
	Distributions from pensions, annuities, etc.	See the instructions for Form 1040, lines 16a and 16b
	Capital gain (box 3)	See the instructions on Form 1099-R
	Disability income with code 3 in box 7	See the instructions for Form 1040, line 7
1099-S	Gross proceeds from real estate transactions (box 2)	Form 4797, Form 6252, Form 8824, or Form 8949
	Buyer's part of real estate tax (box 6)	See the instructions for Schedule A, line 6*
1099-SA	Distributions from health savings accounts (HSAs)	Form 8889, line 14a
	Distributions from MSAs***	Form 8853
SSA-1099	Social security benefits	See the instructions for lines 20a and 20b
RRB-1099	Railroad retirement benefits	See the instructions for lines 20a and 20b

*If the item relates to an activity for which you are required to file Schedule C, C-EZ, E, or F or Form 4835, report the taxable or deductible amount allocable to the activity on that schedule or form instead.

**This includes distributions from Roth, SEP, and SIMPLE IRAs.

***This includes distributions from Archer and Medicare Advantage MSAs.

Line Instructions for Form 1040

You may be eligible for free tax software that will take the guesswork out of preparing your return. Free File makes available free brand-name software and free *e-file*. Visit *IRS.gov/FreeFile* for details.

Section references are to the Internal Revenue Code.

Name and Address

Print or type the information in the spaces provided. If you are married filing a separate return, enter your spouse's name on line 3 instead of below your name.

 If you filed a joint return for 2016 and you are filing a joint return for 2017 with the same spouse, be sure to enter your names and SSNs in the same order as on your 2016 return.

Name Change

If you changed your name because of marriage, divorce, etc., be sure to report the change to the Social Security Administration (SSA) before filing your return. This prevents delays in processing your return and issuing refunds. It also safeguards your future social security benefits.

Address Change

If you plan to move after filing your return, use Form 8822 to notify the IRS of your new address.

P.O. Box

Enter your box number only if your post office doesn't deliver mail to your home.

Foreign Address

If you have a foreign address, enter the city name on the appropriate line. Don't enter any other information on that line, but also complete the spaces below that line. Don't abbreviate the country name. Follow the country's practice for entering the postal code and the name of the province, county, or state.

Death of a Taxpayer

See *Death of a Taxpayer* under *General Information,* later.

Social Security Number (SSN)

An incorrect or missing SSN can increase your tax, reduce your refund, or delay your refund. To apply for an SSN, fill in Form SS-5 and return it, along with the appropriate evidence documents, to the Social Security Administration (SSA). You can get Form SS-5 online at *SSA.gov*, from your local SSA office, or by calling the SSA at 1-800-772-1213. It usually takes about 2 weeks to get an SSN once the SSA has all the evidence and information it needs.

Check that both the name and SSN on your Forms 1040, W-2, and 1099 agree with your social security card. If they don't, certain deductions and credits on your Form 1040 may be reduced or disallowed and you may not receive credit for your social security earnings. If your Form W-2 shows an incorrect SSN or name, notify your employer or the form-issuing agent as soon as possible to make sure your earnings are credited to your social security record. If the name or SSN on your social security card is incorrect, call the SSA.

IRS Individual Taxpayer Identification Numbers (ITINs) for Aliens

If you are a nonresident or resident alien and you don't have and aren't eligible to get an SSN, you must apply for an ITIN. It takes about 7 weeks to get an ITIN.

If you already have an ITIN, enter it wherever your SSN is requested on your tax return.

Some ITINs must be renewed. If you haven't used your ITIN on a federal tax return at least once for tax years 2014, 2015, or 2016, or if your ITIN has the middle digits 70, 71, 72, or 80 (9NN-70-NNNN), it expired at the end of 2017 and must be renewed if you need to file a federal tax return in 2018. You don't need to renew your ITIN if you don't need to file a federal tax return. You can find more information at *IRS.gov/ITIN*.

An ITIN is for tax use only. It doesn't entitle you to social security benefits or change your employment or immigration status under U.S. law.

For more information on ITINs, including application, expiration, and renewal, see Form W-7 and its instructions.

If you receive an SSN after previously using an ITIN, stop using your ITIN. Use your SSN instead. Visit a local IRS office or write a letter to the IRS explaining that you now have an SSN and want all your tax records combined under your SSN. Details about what to include with the letter and where to mail it are at *IRS.gov/ITIN*.

Nonresident Alien Spouse

If your spouse is a nonresident alien, he or she must have either an SSN or an ITIN if:
- You file a joint return,
- You file a separate return and claim an exemption for your spouse, or
- Your spouse is filing a separate return.

Presidential Election Campaign Fund

This fund helps pay for Presidential election campaigns. The fund reduces candidates' dependence on large contributions from individuals and groups and places candidates on an equal financial footing in the general election. The fund also helps pay for pediatric medical research. If you want $3 to go to this fund, check the box. If you are filing a joint return, your spouse also can have $3 go

Need more information or forms? Visit IRS.gov.

to the fund. If you check a box, your tax or refund won't change.

Filing Status

Check only the filing status that applies to you. The ones that will usually give you the lowest tax are listed last.
- Married filing separately.
- Single.
- Head of household.
- Married filing jointly.
- Qualifying widow(er).

For information about marital status, see Pub. 501.

 More than one filing status can apply to you. You can choose the one that will give you the lowest tax.

Line 1

Single

You can check the box on line 1 if any of the following was true on December 31, 2017.
- You were never married.
- You were legally separated according to your state law under a decree of divorce or separate maintenance. But if, at the end of 2017, your divorce wasn't final (an interlocutory decree), you are considered married and can't check the box on line 1.
- You were widowed before January 1, 2017, and didn't remarry before the end of 2017. But if you have a child, you may be able to use the qualifying widow(er) filing status. See the instructions for line 5.

Line 2

Married Filing Jointly

You can check the box on line 2 if any of the following apply.
- You were married at the end of 2017, even if you didn't live with your spouse at the end of 2017.
- Your spouse died in 2017 and you didn't remarry in 2017.
- You were married at the end of 2017, and your spouse died in 2018 before filing a 2017 return.

A married couple filing jointly report their combined income and deduct their combined allowable expenses on one re-

turn. They can file a joint return even if only one had income or if they didn't live together all year. However, both persons must sign the return. Once you file a joint return, you can't choose to file separate returns for that year after the due date of the return.

Joint and several tax liability. If you file a joint return, both you and your spouse are generally responsible for the tax and interest or penalties due on the return. This means that if one spouse doesn't pay the tax due, the other may have to. Or, if one spouse doesn't report the correct tax, both spouses may be responsible for any additional taxes assessed by the IRS. You may want to file separately if:
- You believe your spouse isn't reporting all of his or her income, or
- You don't want to be responsible for any taxes due if your spouse doesn't have enough tax withheld or doesn't pay enough estimated tax.

See the instructions for line 3. Also see *Innocent Spouse Relief* under *General Information,* later.

Nonresident aliens and dual-status aliens. Generally, a married couple can't file a joint return if either spouse is a nonresident alien at any time during the year. However, if you were a nonresident alien or a dual-status alien and were married to a U.S. citizen or resident alien at the end of 2017, you can elect to be treated as a resident alien and file a joint return. See Pub. 519 for details.

Line 3

Married Filing Separately

If you are married and file a separate return, you generally report only your own income, exemptions, deductions, and credits. Generally, you are responsible only for the tax on your own income. Different rules apply to people in community property states; see Pub. 555.

However, you usually will pay more tax than if you use another filing status for which you qualify. Also, if you file a separate return, you can't take the student loan interest deduction, the education credits, or the earned income credit. You also can't take the standard deduction if your spouse itemizes deductions.

Be sure to enter your spouse's SSN or ITIN on Form 1040. If your spouse

doesn't have and isn't required to have an SSN or ITIN, enter "NRA."

 You may be able to file as head of household if you had a child living with you and you lived apart from your spouse during the last 6 months of 2017. See Married persons who live apart.

Line 4

Head of Household

This filing status is for unmarried individuals who provide a home for certain other persons. You are considered unmarried for this purpose if any of the following applies.
- You were legally separated according to your state law under a decree of divorce or separate maintenance at the end of 2017. But if, at the end of 2017, your divorce wasn't final (an interlocutory decree), you are considered married.
- You are married but lived apart from your spouse for the last 6 months of 2017 and you meet the other rules under *Married persons who live apart*.
- You are married to a nonresident alien at any time during the year and you don't choose to treat him or her as a resident alien.

Check the box on line 4 only if you are unmarried (or considered unmarried) and either *Test 1* or *Test 2* applies.

Test 1. You paid over half the cost of keeping up a home that was the main home for all of 2017 of your parent whom you can claim as a dependent on line 6c, except under a multiple support agreement (see the line 6c instructions). Your parent didn't have to live with you.

Test 2. You paid over half the cost of keeping up a home in which you lived and in which one of the following also lived for more than half of the year (if half or less, see *Exception to time lived with you*).

1. Any person whom you can claim as a dependent on line 6c. But don't include:

a. Your child whom you claim as your dependent because of the rule for *Children of divorced or separated parents* in the line 6c instructions,

b. Any person who is your dependent only because he or she lived with you for all of 2017, or

c. Any person you claimed as a dependent under a multiple support agreement. See the line 6c instructions.

2. Your unmarried qualifying child who isn't your dependent.

3. Your married qualifying child who isn't your dependent only because you can be claimed as a dependent on line 6c of someone else's 2017 return.

4. Your qualifying child who, even though you are the custodial parent, isn't your dependent because of the rule for *Children of divorced or separated parents* in the line 6c instructions.

‘

If the child isn't claimed as your dependent on line 6c, enter the child's name on line 4. If you don't enter the name, it will take us longer to process your return.

Qualifying child. To find out if someone is your qualifying child, see Step 1 of the line 6c instructions.

Dependent. To find out if someone is your dependent, see the instructions for line 6c.

Exception to time lived with you. Temporary absences by you or the other person for special circumstances, such as school, vacation, business, medical care, military service, or detention in a juvenile facility, count as time lived in the home. Also see *Kidnapped child* in the line 6c instructions, if applicable.

If the person for whom you kept up a home was born or died in 2017, you still may be able to file as head of household. If the person is your qualifying child, the child must have lived with you for more than half the part of the year he or she was alive. If the person is anyone else, see Pub. 501.

Keeping up a home. To find out what is included in the cost of keeping up a home, see Pub. 501.

Married persons who live apart. Even if you weren't divorced or legally separated at the end of 2017, you are considered unmarried if all of the following apply.

• You lived apart from your spouse for the last 6 months of 2017. Temporary absences for special circumstances, such as for business, medical care, school, or military service, count as time lived in the home.

• You file a separate return from your spouse.

• You paid over half the cost of keeping up your home for 2017.

• Your home was the main home of your child, stepchild, or foster child for more than half of 2017 (if half or less, see *Exception to time lived with you*, earlier).

• You can claim this child as your dependent or could claim the child except that the child's other parent can claim him or her under the rule for *Children of divorced or separated parents* in the line 6c instructions.

Adopted child. An adopted child is always treated as your own child. An adopted child includes a child lawfully placed with you for legal adoption.

Foster child. A foster child is any child placed with you by an authorized placement agency or by judgment, decree, or other order of any court of competent jurisdiction.

Line 5

Qualifying Widow(er)

You can check the box on line 5 and use joint return tax rates for 2017 if all of the following apply.

1. Your spouse died in 2015 or 2016 and you didn't remarry before the end of 2017.

2. You have a child or stepchild (not a foster child) whom you can claim as a dependent or could claim as a dependent except that, for 2017:

a. The child had gross income of $4,050 or more,

b. The child filed a joint return, or

c. You could be claimed as a dependent on someone else's return.

If the child isn't claimed as your dependent on line 6c, enter the child's name on line 4. If you don't enter the name, it will take us longer to process your return.

3. This child lived in your home for all of 2017. If the child didn't live with you for the required time, see *Exception to time lived with you*, later.

4. You paid over half the cost of keeping up your home.

5. You could have filed a joint return with your spouse the year he or she died, even if you didn't actually do so.

If your spouse died in 2017, you can't file as qualifying widow(er). Instead, see the instructions for line 2.

Adopted child. An adopted child is always treated as your own child. An adopted child includes a child lawfully placed with you for legal adoption.

Dependent. To find out if someone is your dependent, see the instructions for line 6c.

Exception to time lived with you. Temporary absences by you or the child for special circumstances, such as school, vacation, business, medical care, military service, or detention in a juvenile facility, count as time lived in the home. Also see *Kidnapped child* in the line 6c instructions, if applicable.

A child is considered to have lived with you for all of 2017 if the child was born or died in 2017 and your home was the child's home for the entire time he or she was alive.

Keeping up a home. To find out what is included in the cost of keeping up a home, see Pub. 501.

Exemptions

You usually can deduct $4,050 on line 42 for each exemption you can take.

Line 6b

Spouse

Check the box on line 6b if either of the following applies.

1. Your filing status is married filing jointly and your spouse can't be claimed as a dependent on another person's return.

2. You were married at the end of 2017, your filing status is married filing separately or head of household, and both of the following apply.

a. Your spouse had no income and isn't filing a return.

b. Your spouse can't be claimed as a dependent on another person's return.

If your filing status is head of household and you check the box on line 6b, enter the name of your spouse on the

Need more information or forms? Visit IRS.gov.

dotted line next to line 6b. Also, enter your spouse's social security number in the space provided at the top of your return. If you became divorced or legally separated during 2017, you can't take an exemption for your former spouse.

Death of your spouse. If your spouse died in 2017 and you didn't remarry by the end of 2017, check the box on line 6b if you could have taken an exemption for your spouse on the date of death. For other filing instructions, see *Death of a Taxpayer* under *General Information,* later.

Line 6c—Dependents

Dependents and Qualifying Child for Child Tax Credit

Follow the steps below to find out if a person qualifies as your dependent, qualifies you to take the child tax credit, or both. If you have more than four dependents, check the box to the left of line 6c and include a statement showing the information required in columns (1) through (4).

Step 1 Do You Have a Qualifying Child?

A qualifying child is a child who is your...

Son, daughter, stepchild, foster child, brother, sister, stepbrother, stepsister, half brother, half sister, or a descendant of any of them (for example, your grandchild, niece, or nephew)

AND

was ...

Under age 19 at the end of 2017 and younger than you
(or your spouse, if filing jointly)

or

Under age 24 at the end of 2017, a student (defined later), and younger than you
(or your spouse, if filing jointly)

or

Any age and permanently and totally disabled (defined later)

AND

Who didn't provide over half of his or her own support for 2017 (see Pub. 501)

AND

Who isn't filing a joint return for 2017
or is filing a joint return for 2017 only to claim a refund of withheld income tax or estimated tax paid (see Pub. 501 for details and examples)

AND

Who lived with you for more than half of 2017. If the child didn't live with you for the required time, see *Exception to time lived with you,* later.

If the child meets the conditions to be a qualifying child of any other person (other than your spouse if filing jointly) for 2017, see Qualifying child of more than one person, *later.*

1. Do you have a child who meets the conditions to be your qualifying child?
   ☐ **Yes.** Go to Step 2.   ☐ **No.** Go to Step 4.

Step 2 Is Your Qualifying Child Your Dependent?

1. Was the child a U.S. citizen, U.S. national, U.S. resident alien, or a resident of Canada or Mexico? (See Pub. 519 for the definition of a U.S. national or U.S. resident alien. If the child was adopted, see *Exception to citizen test,* later.)
   ☐ **Yes.** Continue   ☐ **No.** (STOP)
   You can't claim this child as a dependent.

2. Was the child married?
   ☐ **Yes.** See *Married person,* later.   ☐ **No.** Continue

3. Could you, or your spouse if filing jointly, be claimed as a dependent on someone else's 2017 tax return? See Steps 1, 2, and 4.
   ☐ **Yes.** You can't claim any dependents. Go to Form 1040, line 7.   ☐ **No.** You can claim this child as a dependent. Complete Form 1040, line 6c, columns (1) through (3) for this child. Then, go to Step 3.

Step 3 Does Your Qualifying Child Qualify You for the Child Tax Credit?

1. Was the child under age 17 at the end of 2017?
   ☐ **Yes.** Continue   ☐ **No.** (STOP)
   This child isn't a qualifying child for the child tax credit.

2. Was the child a U.S. citizen, U.S. national, or U.S. resident alien? (See Pub. 519 for the definition of a U.S. national or U.S. resident alien. If the child was adopted, see *Exception to citizen test,* later.)
   ☐ **Yes.** This child is a qualifying child for the child tax credit. Check the box on Form 1040, line 6c, column (4).   ☐ **No.** (STOP)
   This child isn't a qualifying child for the child tax credit.

Need more information or forms? Visit IRS.gov.

Step 4 Is Your Qualifying Relative Your Dependent?

A qualifying relative is a person who is your...

Son, daughter, stepchild, foster child, or a descendant of any of them (for example, your grandchild)

or

Brother, sister, half brother, half sister, or a son or daughter of any of them (for example, your niece or nephew)

or

Father, mother, or an ancestor or sibling of either of them (for example, your grandmother, grandfather, aunt, or uncle)

or

Stepbrother, stepsister, stepfather, stepmother, son-in-law, daughter-in-law, father-in-law, mother-in-law, brother-in-law, or sister-in-law

or

Any other person (other than your spouse) who lived with you all year as a member of your household if your relationship didn't violate local law. If the person didn't live with you for the required time, see *Exception to time lived with you*, later.

Who wasn't a qualifying child (see Step 1) of any taxpayer for 2017. For this purpose, a person isn't a taxpayer if he or she isn't required to file a U.S. income tax return **and** either doesn't file such a return or files only to get a refund of withheld income tax or estimated tax paid. See Pub. 501 for details and examples.

Who had gross income of less than $4,050 in 2017. If the person was permanently and totally disabled, see *Exception to gross income test*, later.

For whom you provided over half of his or her support in 2017. But see *Children of divorced or separated parents*, *Multiple support agreements*, and *Kidnapped child*, later.

1. Does any person meet the conditions to be your qualifying relative?

☐ **Yes.** Continue ⬎

☐ **No.** (STOP)

Go to Form 1040, line 7.

2. Was your qualifying relative a U.S. citizen, U.S. national, U.S. resident alien, or a resident of Canada or Mexico? (See Pub. 519 for the definition of a U.S. national or U.S.

resident alien. If your qualifying relative was adopted, see *Exception to citizen test*, later.)

☐ **Yes.** Continue

☐ **No.** (STOP) You can't claim this person as a dependent.

3. Was your qualifying relative married?

☐ **Yes.** See *Married person*, later.

☐ **No.** Continue ⬎

4. Could you, or your spouse if filing jointly, be claimed as a dependent on someone else's 2017 tax return? See Steps 1, 2, and 4.

☐ **Yes.** (STOP) You can't claim any dependents. Go to Form 1040, line 7.

☐ **No.** You can claim this person as a dependent. Complete Form 1040, line 6c, columns (1) through (3). Don't check the box on Form 1040, line 6c, column (4).

Definitions and Special Rules

Adopted child. An adopted child is always treated as your own child. An adopted child includes a child lawfully placed with you for legal adoption.

Adoption taxpayer identification numbers (ATINs). If you have a dependent who was placed with you for legal adoption and you don't know his or her SSN, you must get an ATIN for the dependent from the IRS. See Form W-7A for details. If the dependent isn't a U.S. citizen or resident alien, apply for an ITIN instead, using Form W-7.

If you didn't have an SSN (or ITIN) by the due date of your 2017 return (including extensions), you can't claim the child tax credit on either your original or an amended 2017 return, even if you later get an SSN (or ITIN). Also, no child tax credit is allowed on your original or an amended 2017 return with respect to a child who didn't have an SSN, ATIN, or ITIN by the due date of your return (including extensions), even if that child later gets one of those numbers.

If you apply for an ATIN or an ITIN on or before the due date of your 2017 return (including extensions) and the IRS issues you an ATIN or an ITIN as a result of the application, the IRS will consider your ATIN or ITIN as issued on or before the due date of your return.

Children of divorced or separated parents. A child will be treated as the qualifying child or qualifying relative of his or her noncustodial parent (defined later) if all of the following conditions apply.

1. The parents are divorced, legally separated, separated under a written separation agreement, or lived apart at all times during the last 6 months of 2017 (whether or not they are or were married).

2. The child received over half of his or her support for 2017 from the parents (and the rules on *Multiple support agreements*, later, don't apply). Support of a child received from a parent's spouse is treated as provided by the parent.

3. The child is in custody of one or both of the parents for more than half of 2017.

4. Either of the following applies.

a. The custodial parent signs Form 8332 or a substantially similar statement that he or she won't claim the child as a dependent for 2017, and the noncustodial parent includes a copy of the form or statement with his or her return. If the divorce decree or separation agreement went into effect after 1984 and before 2009, the noncustodial parent may be able to include certain pages from the decree or agreement instead of Form 8332. See *Post-1984 and pre-2009 decree or agreement* and *Post-2008 decree or agreement*.

b. A pre-1985 decree of divorce or separate maintenance or written separation agreement between the parents provides that the noncustodial parent can claim the child as a dependent, and the noncustodial parent provides at least $600 for support of the child during 2017.

If conditions (1) through (4) apply, only the noncustodial parent can claim the child for purposes of the dependency exemption (line 6c) and the child tax credits (lines 52 and 67). However, this doesn't allow the noncustodial parent to claim head of household filing status, the credit for child and dependent care expenses, the exclusion for dependent care benefits, the earned income credit, or the health coverage tax credit. See Pub. 501 for details.

Example. Even if conditions (1) through (4) are met and the custodial parent signs Form 8332 or a substantially similar statement that he or she won't claim the child as a dependent for 2017, this doesn't allow the noncustodial parent to claim the child as a qualifying child for the earned income credit. The custodial parent or another taxpayer, if eligible, can claim the child for the earned income credit.

Custodial and noncustodial parents. The custodial parent is the parent with whom the child lived for the greater number of nights in 2017. The noncustodial parent is the other parent. If the child was with each parent for an equal number of nights, the custodial parent is the parent with the higher adjusted gross income. See Pub. 501 for an exception for a parent who works at night, rules for a child who is emancipated under state law, and other details.

Post-1984 and pre-2009 decree or agreement. The decree or agreement must state all three of the following.

1 The noncustodial parent can claim the child as a dependent without regard to any condition, such as payment of support.

2. The other parent won't claim the child as a dependent.

3. The years for which the claim is released.

The noncustodial parent must include all of the following pages from the decree or agreement.
• Cover page (include the other parent's SSN on that page).
• The pages that include all the information identified in (1) through (3) above.
• Signature page with the other parent's signature and date of agreement.

 You must include the required information even if you filed it with your return in an earlier year.

Post-2008 decree or agreement. If the divorce decree or separation agreement went into effect after 2008, the noncustodial parent can't include pages from the decree or agreement instead of Form 8332. The custodial parent must sign either Form 8332 or a substantially similar statement the only purpose of which is to release the custodial parent's claim to an exemption for a child, and the noncustodial parent must include a copy with his or her return. The form or statement must release the custodial parent's claim to the child without any conditions. For example, the release must not depend on the noncustodial parent paying support.

Release of exemption revoked. A custodial parent who has revoked his or her previous release of a claim to exemption for a child must include a copy of the revocation with his or her return. For details, see Form 8332.

Exception to citizen test. If you are a U.S. citizen or U.S. national and your adopted child lived with you all year as a member of your household, that child meets the requirement to be a U.S. citizen in Step 2, question 1; Step 3, question 2; and Step 4, question 2.

Exception to gross income test. If your relative (including a person who lived with you all year as a member of your household) is permanently and totally disabled (defined later), certain income for services performed at a sheltered workshop may be excluded for this test. For details, see Pub. 501.

Exception to time lived with you. Temporary absences by you or the other person for special circumstances, such as school, vacation, business, medical care, military service, or detention in a juvenile facility, count as time the person lived with you. Also see *Children of divorced or separated parents*, earlier, or *Kidnapped child*, later.

If the person meets all other requirements to be your qualifying child but was born or died in 2017, the person is considered to have lived with you for more than half of 2017 if your home was this person's home for more than half the time he or she was alive in 2017.

Any other person is considered to have lived with you for all of 2017 if the person was born or died in 2017 and your home was this person's home for the entire time he or she was alive in 2017.

Foster child. A foster child is any child placed with you by an authorized placement agency or by judgment, decree, or other order of any court of competent jurisdiction

Kidnapped child. If your child is presumed by law enforcement authorities to have been kidnapped by someone who isn't a family member, you may be able to take the child into account in determining your eligibility for head of household or qualifying widow(er) filing status, the dependency exemption, the child tax credit, and the earned income credit (EIC). For details, see Pub. 501 (Pub. 596 for the EIC).

Married person. If the person is married and files a joint return, you can't claim that person as your dependent. However, if the person is married but doesn't file a joint return or files a joint return only to claim a refund of withheld income tax or estimated tax paid, you may be able to claim him or her as a dependent. (See Pub. 501 for details and examples.) In that case, go to Step 2, question 3 (for a qualifying child) or Step 4, question 4 (for a qualifying relative).

Multiple support agreements. If no one person contributed over half of the support of your relative (or a person who lived with you all year as a member of your household) but you and another person(s) provided more than half of your relative's support, special rules may apply that would treat you as having provided over half of the support. For details, see Pub. 501.

Permanently and totally disabled. A person is permanently and totally disabled if, at any time in 2017, the person can't engage in any substantial gainful activity because of a physical or mental condition and a doctor has determined that this condition has lasted or can be expected to last continuously for at least a year or can be expected to lead to death.

Public assistance payments. If you received payments under the Temporary Assistance for Needy Families (TANF) program or other public assistance program and you used the money to support another person, see Pub. 501.

Qualifying child of more than one person. Even if a child meets the conditions to be the qualifying child of more than one person, only one person can claim the child as a qualifying child for all of the following tax benefits, unless the special rule for *Children of divorced or separated parents,* described earlier, applies.

  1. Dependency exemption (line 6c).
  2. Child tax credits (lines 52 and 67).
  3. Head of household filing status (line 4).
  4. Credit for child and dependent care expenses (line 49).
  5. Exclusion for dependent care benefits (Form 2441, Part III).
  6. Earned income credit (lines 66a and 66b).

No other person can take any of the six tax benefits just listed based on the qualifying child. If you and any other person can claim the child as a qualifying child, the following rules apply.

  • If only one of the persons is the child's parent, the child is treated as the qualifying child of the parent.
  • If the parents file a joint return together and can claim the child as a qualifying child, the child is treated as the qualifying child of the parents.
  • If the parents don't file a joint return together but both parents claim the child as a qualifying child, the IRS will treat the child as the qualifying child of the parent with whom the child lived for the longer period of time in 2017. If the child lived with each parent for the same amount of time, the IRS will treat the child as the qualifying child of the parent who had the higher adjusted gross income (AGI) for 2017.
  • If no parent can claim the child as a qualifying child, the child is treated as the qualifying child of the person who had the highest AGI for 2017.
  • If a parent can claim the child as a qualifying child but no parent does so claim the child, the child is treated as the qualifying child of the person who had the highest AGI for 2017, but

only if that person's AGI is higher than the highest AGI of any parent of the child who can claim the child.

Example. Your daughter meets the conditions to be a qualifying child for both you and your mother. Your daughter doesn't meet the conditions to be a qualifying child of any other person, including her other parent. Under the rules just described, you can claim your daughter as a qualifying child for all of the six tax benefits just listed for which you otherwise qualify. Your mother can't claim any of those six tax benefits based on your daughter. However, if your mother's AGI is higher than yours and you do not claim your daughter as a qualifying child, your daughter is the qualifying child of your mother.

For more details and examples, see Pub. 501.

If you will be claiming the child as a qualifying child, go to Step 2. Otherwise, stop; you can't claim any benefits based on this child.

Social security number. You must enter each dependent's social security number (SSN). Be sure the name and SSN entered agree with the dependent's social security card. Otherwise, at the time we process your return, we may disallow the exemption claimed for the dependent and reduce or disallow any other tax benefits (such as the child tax credit) based on that dependent. If the name or SSN on the dependent's social security card isn't correct or you need to get an SSN for your dependent, contact the Social Security Administration. See *Social Security Number (SSN),* earlier. If your dependent won't have a number by the date your return is due, see *What if You Can't File on Time?* earlier.

If your dependent child was born and died in 2017 and you do not have an SSN for the child, enter "Died" in column (2) and include a copy of the child's birth certificate, death certificate, or hospital records. The document must show the child was born alive.

If you didn't have an SSN (or ITIN) by the due date of your 2017 return (including extensions), you can't claim the child tax credit on either your original or an amended 2017 return, even if you later get an SSN (or ITIN). Also, no child tax credit is allowed on your original or an amended 2017 return with respect to a child who didn't have an SSN, ATIN, or ITIN by the due date of your return (including extensions), even if that child later gets one of those numbers.

If you apply for an ATIN or an ITIN on or before the due date of your 2017 return (including extensions) and the IRS issues you an ATIN or an ITIN as a result of the application, the IRS will consider your ATIN or ITIN as issued on or before the due date of your return.

Student. A student is a child who during any part of 5 calendar months of 2017 was enrolled as a full-time student at a school, or took a full-time, on-farm training course given by a school or a state, county, or local government agency. A school includes a technical, trade, or mechanical school. It doesn't include an on-the-job training course, correspondence school, or school offering courses only through the Internet.

Income

Generally, you must report all income except income that is exempt from tax by law. For details, see the following instructions, especially the instructions for lines 7 through 21. Also see Pub. 525.

Foreign-Source Income

You must report unearned income, such as interest, dividends, and pensions, from sources outside the United States unless exempt by law or a tax treaty. You also must report earned income, such as wages and tips, from sources outside the United States.

If you worked abroad, you may be able to exclude part or all of your foreign earned income. For details, see Pub. 54 and Form 2555 or 2555-EZ.

Foreign retirement plans. If you were a beneficiary of a foreign retirement plan, you may have to report the undistributed income earned in your plan. However, if you were the beneficiary of a Canadian registered retirement plan, see Rev. Proc. 2014-55, 2014-44 I.R.B. 753, available at *IRS.gov//irb/2014-44_IRB/ar10.html*, to find out if you can elect to defer tax on the undistributed income.

Report distributions from foreign pension plans on lines 16a and 16b.

Foreign accounts and trusts. You must complete Part III of Schedule B if you:
- Had a foreign account, or
- Received a distribution from, or were a grantor of, or a transferor to, a foreign trust.

Foreign financial assets. If you had foreign financial assets in 2017, you may have to file Form 8938. See Form 8938 and its instructions.

Chapter 11 Bankruptcy Cases

If you are a debtor in a chapter 11 bankruptcy case, income taxable to the bankruptcy estate and reported on the estate's income tax return includes:
- Earnings from services you performed after the beginning of the case (both wages and self-employment income), and
- Income from property described in section 541 of title 11 of the U.S. Code

that you either owned when the case began or that you acquired after the case began and before the case was closed, dismissed, or converted to a case under a different chapter.

Because this income is taxable to the estate, don't include this income on your own individual income tax return. The only exception is for purposes of figuring your self-employment tax. For that purpose, you must take into account all your self-employment income for the year from services performed both before and after the beginning of the case. Also, you (or the trustee, if one is appointed) must allocate between you and the bankruptcy estate the wages, salary, or other compensation and withheld income tax reported to you on Form W-2. A similar allocation is required for income and withheld income tax reported to you on Forms 1099. You also must include a statement that indicates you filed a chapter 11 case and that explains how income and withheld income tax reported to you on Forms W-2 and 1099 are allocated between you and the estate. For more details, including acceptable allocation methods, see Notice 2006-83, 2006-40 I.R.B. 596, available at *IRS.gov/irb/2006-40_IRB/ar12.html*.

Community Property States

Community property states include Arizona, California, Idaho, Louisiana, Nevada, New Mexico, Texas, Washington, and Wisconsin. If you and your spouse lived in a community property state, you usually must follow state law to determine what is community income and what is separate income. For details, see Form 8958 and Pub. 555.

Nevada, Washington, and California domestic partners. A registered domestic partner in Nevada, Washington, or California generally must report half the combined community income of the individual and his or her domestic partner. See Form 8958 and Pub. 555.

Rounding Off to Whole Dollars

You can round off cents to whole dollars on your return and schedules. If you do round to whole dollars, you must round all amounts. To round, drop amounts under 50 cents and increase amounts from 50 to 99 cents to the next dollar. For example, $1.39 becomes $1 and $2.50 becomes $3.

If you have to add two or more amounts to figure the amount to enter on a line, include cents when adding the amounts and round off only the total.

Line 7

Wages, Salaries, Tips, etc.

Enter the total of your wages, salaries, tips, etc. If a joint return, also include your spouse's income. For most people, the amount to enter on this line should be shown in box 1 of their Form(s) W-2. But the following types of income also must be included in the total on line 7.

- All wages received as a household employee. An employer isn't required to provide a Form W-2 to you if he or she paid you wages of less then $2,000 in 2017. If you received wages as a household employee and you didn't receive a Form W-2 because an employer paid you less than $2,000 in 2017, enter "HSH" and the amount not reported to you on a Form W-2 in the space to the left of line 7. For information on employment taxes for household employees, see *Tax Topic 756*.

- Tip income you didn't report to your employer. This should include any allocated tips shown in box 8 on your Form(s) W-2 unless you can prove that your unreported tips are less than the amount in box 8. Allocated tips aren't included as income in box 1. See Pub. 531 for more details. Also include the value of any noncash tips you received, such as tickets, passes, or other items of value. Although you don't report these noncash tips to your employer, you must report them on line 7.

 You may owe social security and Medicare or railroad retirement (RRTA) tax on unreported tips. See the instructions for line 58.

- Dependent care benefits, which should be shown in box 10 of your Form(s) W-2. But first complete Form 2441 to see if you can exclude part or all of the benefits.

- Employer-provided adoption benefits, which should be shown in box 12 of your Form(s) W-2 with code T. But see the Instructions for Form 8839 to find out if you can exclude part or all of the benefits. You also may be able to exclude amounts if you adopted a child with special needs and the adoption became final in 2017.

• Scholarship and fellowship grants not reported on Form W-2. Also, enter "SCH" and the amount on the dotted line next to line 7. However, if you were a degree candidate, include on line 7 only the amounts you used for expenses other than tuition and course-related expenses. For example, amounts used for room, board, and travel must be reported on line 7.

• Excess elective deferrals. The amount deferred should be shown in box 12 of your Form W-2, and the "Retirement plan" box in box 13 should be checked. If the total amount you (or your spouse if filing jointly) deferred for 2017 under all plans was more than $18,000 (excluding catch-up contributions as explained later), include the excess on line 7. This limit is (a) $12,500 if you have only SIMPLE plans, or (b) $21,000 for section 403(b) plans if you qualify for the 15-year rule in Pub. 571. Although designated Roth contributions are subject to this limit, don't include the excess attributable to such contributions on line 7. They already are included as income in box 1 of your Form W-2.

A higher limit may apply to participants in section 457(b) deferred compensation plans for the 3 years before retirement age. Contact your plan administrator for more information.

If you were age 50 or older at the end of 2017, your employer may have allowed an additional deferral (catch-up contributions) of up to $6,000 ($3,000 for section 401(k)(11) and SIMPLE plans). This additional deferral amount isn't subject to the overall limit on elective deferrals.

 You can't deduct the amount deferred. It isn't included as income in box 1 of your Form W-2.

• Disability pensions shown on Form 1099-R if you haven't reached the minimum retirement age set by your employer. But see *Insurance Premiums for Retired Public Safety Officers* in the instructions for lines 16a and 16b. Disability pensions received after you reach minimum retirement age and other payments shown on Form 1099-R (other than payments from an IRA*) are repor-

ted on lines 16a and 16b. Payments from an IRA are reported on lines 15a and 15b.

• Corrective distributions from a retirement plan shown on Form 1099-R of excess elective deferrals and excess contributions (plus earnings). But don't include distributions from an IRA* on line 7. Instead, report distributions from an IRA on lines 15a and 15b.

• Wages from Form 8919, line 6.

This includes a Roth, SEP, or SIMPLE IRA.

Were You a Statutory Employee?

If you were, the "Statutory employee" box in box 13 of your Form W-2 should be checked. Statutory employees include full-time life insurance salespeople and certain agent or commission drivers, traveling salespeople, and homeworkers. If you have related business expenses to deduct, report the amount shown in box 1 of your Form W-2 on Schedule C or C-EZ along with your expenses.

Missing or Incorrect Form W-2?

Your employer is required to provide or send Form W-2 to you no later than January 31, 2018. If you don't receive it by early February, use *Tax Topic 154* to find out what to do. Even if you don't get a Form W-2, you still must report your earnings on line 7. If you lose your Form W-2 or it is incorrect, ask your employer for a new one.

Line 8a

Taxable Interest

Each payer should send you a Form 1099-INT or Form 1099-OID. Enter your total taxable interest income on line 8a. But you must fill in and attach Schedule B if the total is over $1,500 or any of the other conditions listed at the beginning of the Schedule B instructions apply to you.

For more details about reporting taxable interest, including market discount on bonds and adjustments for amortizable bond premium or acquisition premium, see Pub. 550.

Interest credited in 2017 on deposits that you couldn't withdraw because of the bankruptcy or insolvency of the financial institution may not have to be

included in your 2017 income. For details, see Pub. 550.

 If you get a 2017 Form 1099-INT for U.S. savings bond interest that includes amounts you reported before 2017, see Pub. 550.

Line 8b

Tax-Exempt Interest

If you received any tax-exempt interest (including any tax-exempt original issue discount (OID)), such as from municipal bonds, each payer should send you a Form 1099-INT or a Form 1099-OID. In general, your tax-exempt stated interest should be shown in box 8 of Form 1099-INT or, for a tax-exempt OID bond, in box 2 of Form 1099-OID and your tax-exempt OID should be shown in box 11 of Form 1099-OID. Enter the total on line 8b. However, if you acquired a tax-exempt bond at a premium, only report the net amount of tax-exempt interest on line 8b (that is, the excess of the tax-exempt interest received during the year over the amortized bond premium for the year). Also, if you acquired a tax-exempt OID bond at an acquisition premium, only report the net amount of tax-exempt OID on line 8b (that is, the excess of tax-exempt OID for the year over the amortized acquisition premium for the year). See Pub. 550 for more information about OID, bond premium, and acquisition premium.

Also include on line 8b any exempt-interest dividends from a mutual fund or other regulated investment company. This amount should be shown in box 10 of Form 1099-DIV.

Don't include interest earned on your IRA, health savings account, Archer or Medicare Advantage MSA, or Coverdell education savings account.

Line 9a

Ordinary Dividends

Each payer should send you a Form 1099-DIV. Enter your total ordinary dividends on line 9a. This amount should be shown in box 1a of Form(s) 1099-DIV.

You must fill in and attach Schedule B if the total is over $1,500 or you received, as a nominee, ordinary dividends that actually belong to someone else.

Nondividend Distributions

Some distributions are a return of your cost (or other basis). They won't be taxed until you recover your cost (or other basis). You must reduce your cost (or other basis) by these distributions. After you get back all of your cost (or other basis), you must report these distributions as capital gains on Form 8949. For details, see Pub. 550.

 Dividends on insurance policies are a partial return of the premiums you paid. Don't report them as dividends. Include them in income on line 21 only if they exceed the total of all net premiums you paid for the contract.

Line 9b

Qualified Dividends

Enter your total qualified dividends on line 9b. Qualified dividends also are included in the ordinary dividend total required to be shown on line 9a. Qualified dividends are eligible for a lower tax rate than other ordinary income. Generally, these dividends are shown in box 1b of Form(s) 1099-DIV. See Pub. 550 for the definition of qualified dividends if you received dividends not reported on Form 1099-DIV.

Exception. Some dividends may be reported as qualified dividends in box 1b of Form 1099-DIV but aren't qualified dividends. These include:

• Dividends you received as a nominee. See the Schedule B instructions.

• Dividends you received on any share of stock that you held for less than 61 days during the 121-day period that began 60 days before the ex-dividend date. The ex-dividend date is the first date following the declaration of a dividend on which the purchaser of a stock isn't entitled to receive the next dividend payment. When counting the number of days you held the stock, include the day you disposed of the stock but not the day you acquired it. See the examples that follow. Also, when counting the number of days you held the stock, you can't count certain days during which your risk of loss was diminished. See Pub. 550 for more details.

• Dividends attributable to periods totaling more than 366 days that you received on any share of preferred stock held for less than 91 days during the 181-day period that began 90 days before the ex-dividend date. When counting the number of days you held the stock, you can't count certain days during which your risk of loss was diminished. See Pub. 550 for more details. Preferred dividends attributable to periods totaling less than 367 days are subject to the 61-day holding period rule just described.

• Dividends on any share of stock to the extent that you are under an obligation (including a short sale) to make related payments with respect to positions in substantially similar or related property.

• Payments in lieu of dividends, but only if you know or have reason to know that the payments aren't qualified dividends.

Example 1. You bought 5,000 shares of XYZ Corp. common stock on July 8, 2017. XYZ Corp. paid a cash dividend of 10 cents per share. The ex-dividend date was July 16, 2017. Your Form 1099-DIV from XYZ Corp. shows $500 in box 1a (ordinary dividends) and in box 1b (qualified dividends). However, you sold the 5,000 shares on August 11, 2017. You held your shares of XYZ Corp. for only 34 days of the 121-day period (from July 9, 2017, through August 11, 2017). The 121-day period began on May 17, 2017 (60 days before the ex-dividend date), and ended on September 14, 2017. You have no qualified dividends from XYZ Corp. because you held the XYZ stock for less than 61 days.

Example 2. The facts are the same as in *Example 1* except that you bought the stock on July 15, 2017 (the day before the ex-dividend date), and you sold the stock on September 16, 2017. You held the stock for 63 days (from July 16, 2017, through September 16, 2017). The $500 of qualified dividends shown in box 1b of Form 1099-DIV are all qualified dividends because you held the stock for 61 days of the 121-day period (from July 16, 2017, through September 14, 2017).

Example 3. You bought 10,000 shares of ABC Mutual Fund common stock on July 8, 2017. ABC Mutual Fund paid a cash dividend of 10 cents a share. The ex-dividend date was July 16, 2017. The ABC Mutual Fund advises you that the part of the dividend eligible to be treated as qualified dividends equals 2 cents a share. Your Form 1099-DIV from ABC Mutual Fund shows total ordinary dividends of $1,000 and qualified dividends of $200. However, you sold the 10,000 shares on August 11, 2017. You have no qualified dividends from ABC Mutual Fund because you held the ABC Mutual Fund stock for less than 61 days.

 Use the Qualified Dividends and Capital Gain Tax Worksheet or the Schedule D Tax Worksheet, whichever applies, to figure your tax. See the instructions for line 44 for details.

Line 10

Taxable Refunds, Credits, or Offsets of State and Local Income Taxes

 None of your refund is taxable if, in the year you paid the tax, you either (a) didn't itemize deductions, or (b) elected to deduct state and local general sales taxes instead of state and local income taxes.

If you received a refund, credit, or offset of state or local income taxes in 2017, you may be required to report this amount. If you didn't receive a Form 1099-G, check with the government agency that made the payments to you. Your 2017 Form 1099-G may have been made available to you only in an electronic format, and you will need to get instructions from the agency to retrieve this document. Report any taxable refund you received even if you didn't receive Form 1099-G.

If you chose to apply part or all of the refund to your 2017 estimated state or local income tax, the amount applied is treated as received in 2017. If the refund was for a tax you paid in 2016 and you deducted state and local income taxes on line 5 of your 2016 Schedule A, use the State and Local Income Tax Refund Worksheet in these instructions to see if any of your refund is taxable.

Exception. See *Itemized Deduction Recoveries* in Pub. 525 instead of using the

Need more information or forms? Visit IRS.gov.

State and Local Income Tax Refund Worksheet—Line 10

Keep for Your Records

Before you begin: √ Be sure you have read the *Exception* in the instructions for this line to see if you can use this worksheet instead of Pub. 525 to figure if any of your refund is taxable.

1. Enter the income tax refund from **Form(s) 1099-G** (or similar statement). But **don't** enter more than the amount of your state and local income taxes shown on your 2016 Schedule A, line 5 . . . . **1.** _____

2. Enter your total itemized deductions from your 2016 Schedule A, line 29 . . . . **2.** _____

   Note. If the filing status on your 2016 Form 1040 was married filing separately and your spouse itemized deductions in 2016, skip lines 3 through 5, enter the amount from line 2 on line 6, and go to line 7.

3. Enter the amount shown below for the filing status claimed on your **2016** Form 1040.
   - Single or married filing separately—$6,300
   - Married filing jointly or qualifying widow(er)—$12,600
   - Head of household—$9,300 } **3.** _____

4. Did you fill in line 39a on your 2016 Form 1040?

   ☐ **No.** Enter -0-.

   ☐ **Yes.** Multiply the number in the box on line 39a of your 2016 Form 1040 by $1,250 ($1,550 if your 2016 filing status was single or head of household). } **4.** _____

5. Add lines 3 and 4 . . . . **5.** _____

6. Is the amount on line 5 less than the amount on line 2?

   ☐ **No.** (STOP) None of your refund is taxable.

   ☐ **Yes.** Subtract line 5 from line 2 . . . . **6.** _____

7. **Taxable part of your refund.** Enter the **smaller** of line 1 or line 6 here and on Form 1040, line 10 . . . . **7.** _____

State and Local Income Tax Refund Worksheet in these instructions if any of the following applies.

1. You received a refund in 2017 that is for a tax year other than 2016.

2. You received a refund other than an income tax refund, such as a general sales tax or real property tax refund, in 2017 of an amount deducted or credit claimed in an earlier year.

3. The amount on your 2016 Form 1040, line 42, was more than the amount on your 2016 Form 1040, line 41.

4. You had taxable income on your 2016 Form 1040, line 43, but no tax on your Form 1040, line 44, because of the 0% tax rate on net capital gain and qualified dividends in certain situations.

5. Your 2016 state and local income tax refund is more than your 2016 state and local income tax deduction minus the amount you could have deducted as your 2016 state and local general sales taxes.

6. You made your last payment of 2016 estimated state or local income tax in 2017.

7. You owed alternative minimum tax in 2016.

8. You couldn't use the full amount of credits you were entitled to in 2016 because the total credits were more than the amount shown on your 2016 Form 1040, line 47.

9. You could be claimed as a dependent by someone else in 2016.

10. You received a refund because of a jointly filed state or local income tax return, but you aren't filing a joint 2017 Form 1040 with the same person.

11. You had to use the Itemized Deductions Worksheet in the 2016 Instruc-tions for Schedule A and both of the fol-lowing apply.

a. You couldn't deduct all of the amount on the 2016 Itemized Deduc-tions Worksheet, line 1.

b. The amount on line 8 of that 2016 worksheet would be more than the amount on line 4 of that worksheet if the amount on line 4 were reduced by 80% of the refund you received in 2017.

Line 11

Alimony Received

Enter amounts received as alimony or separate maintenance. You must let the person who made the payments know your social security number. If you don't, you may have to pay a penalty. For more details, see Pub. 504.

Line 12

Business Income or (Loss)

If you operated a business or practiced your profession as a sole proprietor, report your income and expenses on Schedule C or C-EZ.

Line 13

Capital Gain or (Loss)

If you sold a capital asset, such as a stock or bond, you must complete and attach Form 8949 and Schedule D.

Exception 1. You do not have to file Form 8949 or Schedule D if both of the following apply.

1. You have no capital losses, and your only capital gains are capital gain distributions from Form(s) 1099-DIV, box 2a (or substitute statements).

2. None of the Form(s) 1099-DIV (or substitute statements) have an amount in box 2b (unrecaptured section 1250 gain), box 2c (section 1202 gain), or box 2d (collectibles (28%) gain).

Exception 2. You must file Schedule D but generally don't have to file Form 8949 if *Exception 1* doesn't apply and your only capital gains and losses are:
- Capital gain distributions;
- A capital loss carryover from 2016;
- A gain from Form 2439 or 6252 or Part I of Form 4797;
- A gain or loss from Form 4684, 6781, or 8824;
- A gain or loss from a partnership, S corporation, estate, or trust; or
- Gains and losses from transactions for which you received a Form 1099-B (or substitute statement) that shows basis was reported to the IRS and for which you don't need to make any adjustments in column (g) of Form 8949 or enter any codes in column (f) of Form 8949.

If *Exception 1* applies, enter your total capital gain distributions (from box 2a of Form(s) 1099-DIV) on line 13 and check the box on that line. If you received capital gain distributions as a nominee (that is, they were paid to you but actually belong to someone else), report on line 13 only the amount that belongs to you. Include a statement showing the full amount you received and the amount you received as a nominee. See the Schedule B instructions for filing requirements for Forms 1099-DIV and 1096.

 If you don't have to file Schedule D, use the Qualified Dividends and Capital Gain Tax Worksheet in the line 44 instructions to figure your tax.

Line 14

Other Gains or (Losses)

If you sold or exchanged assets used in a trade or business, see the Instructions for Form 4797.

Lines 15a and 15b

IRA Distributions

 Special rules may apply if you received a distribution from your individual retirement arrangement (IRA) and your main home was in one of the Presidentially declared disaster areas eligible for these special rules on the specified date. Special rules also may apply if you received a distribution to buy or construct a main home in one of the Presidentially declared disaster areas eligible for these special rules, but that home wasn't bought or constructed because of the disaster. See Pub. 976 for details.

You should receive a Form 1099-R showing the total amount of any distribution from your IRA before income tax or other deductions were withheld. This amount should be shown in box 1 of Form 1099-R. Unless otherwise noted in the line 15a and 15b instructions, an IRA includes a traditional IRA, Roth IRA (including a *my*RA), simplified employee pension (SEP) IRA, and a savings incentive match plan for employees (SIMPLE) IRA. Except as provided next, leave line 15a blank and enter the total distribution (from Form 1099-R, box 1) on line 15b.

Exception 1. Enter the total distribution on line 15a if you rolled over part or all of the distribution from one:
- Roth IRA to another Roth IRA, or
- IRA (other than a Roth IRA) to a qualified plan or another IRA (other than a Roth IRA).

Also, enter "Rollover" next to line 15b. If the total distribution was rolled over, enter -0- on line 15b. If the total distribution wasn't rolled over, enter the part not rolled over on line 15b unless *Exception 2* applies to the part not rolled over. Generally, a rollover must be made within 60 days after the day you received the distribution. For more details on rollovers, see Pub. 590-A and Pub. 590-B.

If you rolled over the distribution into a qualified plan other than an IRA or you made the rollover in 2018, include a statement explaining what you did.

Exception 2. If any of the following apply, enter the total distribution on line 15a and see Form 8606 and its instructions to figure the amount to enter on line 15b.

1. You received a distribution from an IRA (other than a Roth IRA) and you made nondeductible contributions to any of your traditional or SEP IRAs for 2017 or an earlier year. If you made nondeductible contributions to these IRAs for 2017, also see Pub. 590-A and Pub. 590-B.

2. You received a distribution from a Roth IRA. But if either (a) or (b) below applies, enter -0- on line 15b; you don't have to see Form 8606 or its instructions.

a. Distribution code T is shown in box 7 of Form 1099-R and you made a contribution (including a conversion) to a Roth IRA for 2012 or an earlier year.

b. Distribution code Q is shown in box 7 of Form 1099-R.

3. You converted part or all of a traditional, SEP, or SIMPLE IRA to a Roth IRA in 2017.

4. You had a 2016 or 2017 IRA contribution returned to you, with the related earnings or less any loss, by the due date (including extensions) of your tax return for that year.

5. You made excess contributions to your IRA for an earlier year and had them returned to you in 2017.

6. You recharacterized part or all of a contribution to a Roth IRA as a contribution to another type of IRA, or vice versa.

Exception 3. If all or part of the distribution is a qualified charitable distribution (QCD), enter the total distribution

Need more information or forms? Visit IRS.gov.

on line 15a. If the total amount distributed is a QCD, enter -0- on line 15b. If only part of the distribution is a QCD, enter the part that is not a QCD on line 15b unless *Exception 2* applies to that part. Enter "QCD" next to line 15b.

A QCD is a distribution made directly by the trustee of your IRA (other than an ongoing SEP or SIMPLE IRA) to an organization eligible to receive tax-deductible contributions (with certain exceptions). You must have been at least age 70½ when the distribution was made.

Generally, your total QCDs for the year can't be more than $100,000. (On a joint return, your spouse also can have a QCD of up to $100,000.) The amount of the QCD is limited to the amount that would otherwise be included in your income. If your IRA includes nondeductible contributions, the distribution is first considered to be paid out of otherwise taxable income. See Pub. 590-A for details.

 You can't claim a charitable contribution deduction for any QCD not included in your income.

Exception 4. If all or part of the distribution is a health savings account (HSA) funding distribution (HFD), enter the total distribution on line 15a. If the total amount distributed is an HFD and you elect to exclude it from income, enter -0- on line 15b. If only part of the distribution is an HFD and you elect to exclude that part from income, enter the part that isn't an HFD on line 15b unless *Exception 2* applies to that part. Enter "HFD" next to line 15b.

An HFD is a distribution made directly by the trustee of your IRA (other than an ongoing SEP or SIMPLE IRA) to your HSA. If eligible, you generally can elect to exclude an HFD from your income once in your lifetime. You can't exclude more than the limit on HSA contributions or more than the amount that would otherwise be included in your income. If your IRA includes nondeductible contributions, the HFD is first considered to be paid out of otherwise taxable income. See Pub. 969 for details.

 The amount of an HFD reduces the amount you can contribute to your HSA for the year. If you fail to maintain eligibility for an HSA for the 12 months following the month of the HFD, you may have to report the HFD as income and pay an additional tax. See Form 8889, Part III.

More than one exception applies. If more than one exception applies, include a statement showing the amount of each exception, instead of making an entry next to line 15b. For example: "Line 15b – $1,000 Rollover and $500 HFD." But you do not need to attach a statement if only *Exception 2* and one other exception apply.

More than one distribution. If you (or your spouse if filing jointly) received more than one distribution, figure the taxable amount of each distribution and enter the total of the taxable amounts on line 15b. Enter the total amount of those distributions on line 15a.

 You may have to pay an additional tax if (a) you received an early distribution from your IRA and the total wasn't rolled over, or (b) you were born before July 1, 1946, and received less than the minimum required distribution from your traditional, SEP, and SIMPLE IRAs. See the instructions for line 59 for details.

More information. For more information about IRAs, see Pub. 590-A and Pub. 590-B.

Lines 16a and 16b

Pensions and Annuities

 Special rules may apply if you received a distribution from a profit-sharing plan or retirement plan and your main home was in one of the Presidentially declared disaster areas eligible for these special rules on the specified date. Special rules also may apply if you received a distribution on certain dates to buy or construct a main home in one of the Presidentially declared disaster areas eligible for these special rules, but that home wasn't bought or constructed because of the disaster. See Pub. 976 for details.

You should receive a Form 1099-R showing the total amount of your pension and annuity payments before income tax or other deductions were withheld. This amount should be shown in box 1 of Form 1099-R. Pension and annuity payments include distributions from 401(k), 403(b), and governmental 457(b) plans. Rollovers and lump-sum distributions are explained later. Don't include the following payments on lines 16a and 16b. Instead, report them on line 7.

• Disability pensions received before you reach the minimum retirement age set by your employer.

• Corrective distributions (including any earnings) of excess elective deferrals or other excess contributions to retirement plans. The plan must advise you of the year(s) the distributions are includible in income.

 Attach Form(s) 1099-R to Form 1040 if any federal income tax was withheld.

Fully Taxable Pensions and Annuities

Your payments are fully taxable if (a) you didn't contribute to the cost (see *Cost,* later) of your pension or annuity, or (b) you got your entire cost back tax free before 2017. But see *Insurance Premiums for Retired Public Safety Officers,* later. If your pension or annuity is fully taxable, enter the total pension or annuity payments (from Form(s) 1099-R, box 1) on line 16b; don't make an entry on line 16a.

Fully taxable pensions and annuities also include military retirement pay shown on Form 1099-R. For details on military disability pensions, see Pub. 525. If you received a Form RRB-1099-R, see Pub. 575 to find out how to report your benefits.

Partially Taxable Pensions and Annuities

Enter the total pension or annuity payments (from Form 1099-R, box 1) on line 16a. If your Form 1099-R doesn't show the taxable amount, you must use the General Rule explained in Pub. 939 to figure the taxable part to enter on line 16b. But if your annuity starting date (defined later) was after July 1, 1986, see *Simplified Method,* later, to find out if you must use that method to figure the taxable part.

You can ask the IRS to figure the taxable part for you for a $1,000 fee. For details, see Pub. 939.

If your Form 1099-R shows a taxable amount, you can report that amount on line 16b. But you may be able to report a lower taxable amount by using the General Rule or the Simplified Method or if the exclusion for retired public safety officers, discussed next, applies.

Insurance Premiums for Retired Public Safety Officers

If you are an eligible retired public safety officer (law enforcement officer, firefighter, chaplain, or member of a rescue squad or ambulance crew), you can elect to exclude from income distributions made from your eligible retirement plan that are used to pay the premiums for coverage by an accident or health plan or a long-term care insurance contract. You can do this only if you retired because of disability or because you reached normal retirement age. The premiums can be for coverage for you, your spouse, or dependents. The distribution must be from a plan maintained by the employer from which you retired as a public safety officer. Also, the distribution must be made directly from the plan to the provider of the accident or health plan or long-term care insurance contract. You can exclude from income the smaller of the amount of the premiums or $3,000. You can make this election only for amounts that would otherwise be included in your income.

An eligible retirement plan is a governmental plan that is a qualified trust or a section 403(a), 403(b), or 457(b) plan.

If you make this election, reduce the otherwise taxable amount of your pension or annuity by the amount excluded. The amount shown in box 2a of Form 1099-R doesn't reflect the exclusion. Report your total distributions on line 16a and the taxable amount on line 16b. Enter "PSO" next to line 16b.

If you are retired on disability and reporting your disability pension on line 7, include only the taxable amount on that line and enter "PSO" and the amount excluded on the dotted line next to line 7.

Simplified Method

You must use the Simplified Method if either of the following applies.

1. Your annuity starting date was after July 1, 1986, and you used this method last year to figure the taxable part.

2. Your annuity starting date was after November 18, 1996, and both of the following apply.

a. The payments are from a qualified employee plan, a qualified employee annuity, or a tax-sheltered annuity.

b. On your annuity starting date, either you were under age 75 or the number of years of guaranteed payments was fewer than 5. See Pub. 575 for the definition of guaranteed payments.

If you must use the Simplified Method, complete the Simplified Method Worksheet in these instructions to figure the taxable part of your pension or annuity. For more details on the Simplified Method, see Pub. 575 (or Pub. 721 for U.S. Civil Service retirement benefits).

 If you received U.S. Civil Service retirement benefits and you chose the alternative annuity option, see Pub. 721 to figure the taxable part of your annuity. Do not use the Simplified Method Worksheet in these instructions.

Annuity Starting Date

Your annuity starting date is the later of the first day of the first period for which you received a payment or the date the plan's obligations became fixed.

Age (or Combined Ages) at Annuity Starting Date

If you are the retiree, use your age on the annuity starting date. If you are the survivor of a retiree, use the retiree's age on his or her annuity starting date. But if your annuity starting date was after 1997 and the payments are for your life and that of your beneficiary, use your combined ages on the annuity starting date.

If you are the beneficiary of an employee who died, see Pub. 575. If there is more than one beneficiary, see Pub. 575 or Pub. 721 to figure each beneficiary's taxable amount.

Cost

Your cost is generally your net investment in the plan as of the annuity starting date. It doesn't include pre-tax con-

tributions. Your net investment may be shown in box 9b of Form 1099-R.

Rollovers

Generally, a rollover is a tax-free distribution of cash or other assets from one retirement plan that is contributed to another plan within 60 days of receiving the distribution. However, a rollover to a Roth IRA or a designated Roth account is generally not a tax-free distribution. Use lines 16a and 16b to report a rollover, including a direct rollover, from one qualified employer's plan to another or to an IRA or SEP.

Enter on line 16a the distribution from Form 1099-R, box 1. From this amount, subtract any contributions (usually shown in box 5) that were taxable to you when made. From that result, subtract the amount of the rollover. Enter the remaining amount on line 16b. If the remaining amount is zero and you have no other distribution to report on line 16b, enter -0- on line 16b. Also, enter "Rollover" next to line 16b.

See Pub. 575 for more details on rollovers, including special rules that apply to rollovers from designated Roth accounts, partial rollovers of property, and distributions under qualified domestic relations orders.

Lump-Sum Distributions

If you received a lump-sum distribution from a profit-sharing or retirement plan, your Form 1099-R should have the "Total distribution" box in box 2b checked. You may owe an additional tax if you received an early distribution from a qualified retirement plan and the total amount wasn't rolled over. For details, see the instructions for line 59.

Enter the total distribution on line 16a and the taxable part on line 16b. For details, see Pub. 575.

 If you or the plan participant was born before January 2, 1936, you could pay less tax on the distribution. See Form 4972.

Line 19

Unemployment Compensation

You should receive a Form 1099-G showing in box 1 the total unemploy-

Simplified Method Worksheet—Lines 16a and 16b   *Keep for Your Records*

Before you begin: ✓   If you are the beneficiary of a deceased employee or former employee who died **before** August 21, 1996, include any death benefit exclusion that you are entitled to (up to $5,000) in the amount entered on line 2 below.

More than one pension or annuity. If you had more than one partially taxable pension or annuity, figure the taxable part of each separately. Enter the total of the taxable parts on Form 1040, line 16b. Enter the total pension or annuity payments received in 2017 on Form 1040, line 16a.

1. Enter the total pension or annuity payments from Form 1099-R, box 1. Also, enter this amount on Form 1040, line 16a . . . . **1.** _____

2. Enter your cost in the plan at the annuity starting date . . . . **2.** _____
   Note. If you completed this worksheet last year, skip line 3 and enter the amount from line 4 of last year's worksheet on line 4 below (even if the amount of your pension or annuity has changed). Otherwise, go to line 3.

3. Enter the appropriate number from **Table 1** below. **But** if your annuity starting date was **after** 1997 **and** the payments are for your life and that of your beneficiary, enter the appropriate number from **Table 2** below . . . . **3.** _____

4. Divide line 2 by the number on line 3 . . . . **4.** _____

5. Multiply line 4 by the number of months for which this year's payments were made. If your annuity starting date was **before** 1987, skip lines 6 and 7 and enter this amount on line 8. Otherwise, go to line 6 . . . . **5.** _____

6. Enter the amount, if any, recovered tax free in years after 1986. If you completed this worksheet last year, enter the amount from line 10 of last year's worksheet . . . . . **6.** _____

7. Subtract line 6 from line 2 . . . . **7.** _____

8. Enter the **smaller** of line 5 or line 7 . . . . **8.** _____

9. **Taxable amount.** Subtract line 8 from line 1. Enter the result, but not less than zero. Also, enter this amount on Form 1040, line 16b. If your Form 1099-R shows a larger amount, use the amount on this line instead of the amount from Form 1099-R. If you are a retired public safety officer, see *Insurance Premiums for Retired Public Safety Officers* before entering an amount on line 16b . . . . **9.** _____

10. Was your annuity starting date before 1987?

    ☐ **Yes.** (STOP) Do not complete the rest of this worksheet.

    ☐ **No.** Add lines 6 and 8. This is the **amount you have recovered tax free** through 2017. You will need this number if you need to fill out this worksheet next year . . . . **10.** _____

11. **Balance of cost to be recovered.** Subtract line 10 from line 2. If zero, you won't have to complete this worksheet next year. The payments you receive next year will generally be fully taxable . . . . **11.** _____

Table 1 for Line 3 Above

	AND your annuity starting date was—	
IF the age at annuity starting date was . . .	**before** November 19, 1996, enter on line 3 . . .	**after** November 18, 1996, enter on line 3 . . .
55 or under	300	360
56–60	260	310
61–65	240	260
66–70	170	210
71 or older	120	160

Table 2 for Line 3 Above

IF the combined ages at annuity starting date were . . .	**THEN enter on line 3 . . .**
110 or under	410
111–120	360
121–130	310
131–140	260
141 or older	210

ment compensation paid to you in 2017. Report this amount on line 19. However, if you made contributions to a governmental unemployment compensation program or to a governmental paid family leave program and you aren't itemizing deductions, reduce the amount you report on line 19 by those contributions. If you are itemizing deductions, see the instructions on Form 1099-G.

If you received an overpayment of unemployment compensation in 2017 and you repaid any of it in 2017, subtract the amount you repaid from the total amount you received. Enter the result on line 19. Also, enter "Repaid" and the amount you repaid on the dotted line next to line 19. If, in 2017, you repaid unemployment compensation that you included in gross income in an earlier year, you can deduct the amount repaid on Schedule A, line 23. But if you repaid more than $3,000, see *Repayments* in Pub. 525 for details on how to report the repayment.

Lines 20a and 20b

Social Security Benefits

You should receive a Form SSA-1099 showing in box 3 the total social security benefits paid to you. Box 4 will show the amount of any benefits you repaid in 2017. If you received railroad retirement benefits treated as social security, you should receive a Form RRB-1099.

Use the Social Security Benefits Worksheet in these instructions to see if any of your benefits are taxable.

Exception. Do not use the Social Security Benefits Worksheet in these instructions if any of the following applies.

• You made contributions to a traditional IRA for 2017 and you or your spouse were covered by a retirement plan at work or through self-employment. Instead, use the worksheets in Pub. 590-A to see if any of your social security benefits are taxable and to figure your IRA deduction.

• You repaid any benefits in 2017 and your total repayments (box 4) were more than your total benefits for 2017 (box 3). None of your benefits are taxable for 2017. Also, you may be able to take an itemized deduction or a credit for part of the excess repayments if they were for benefits you included in gross

income in an earlier year. For more details, see Pub. 915.

• You file Form 2555, 2555-EZ, 4563, or 8815, or you exclude employer-provided adoption benefits or income from sources within Puerto Rico. Instead, use the worksheet in Pub. 915.

 Benefits for earlier year received in 2017? *If any of your benefits are taxable for 2017 and they include a lump-sum benefit payment that was for an earlier year, you may be able to reduce the taxable amount. See* Lump-Sum Election *in Pub. 915 for details.*

Social security information. Social security beneficiaries can now get a variety of information from the SSA website with a *my Social Security* account, including getting a replacement Form SSA-1099 if needed. For more information and to set up an account, go to *SSA.gov/myaccount*.

Form RRB-1099. If you need a replacement Form RRB-1099, call the Railroad Retirement Board at 1-877-772-5772 or go to *www.rrb.gov*.

Line 21

Other Income

 Do not report on this line any income from self-employment or fees received as a notary public. Instead, you must use Schedule C, C-EZ, or F, even if you don't have any business expenses. Also, don't report on line 21 any nonemployee compensation shown on Form 1099-MISC (unless it isn't self-employment income, such as income from a hobby or a sporadic activity). Instead, see the instructions on Form 1099-MISC to find out where to report that income.

Taxable income. Use line 21 to report any taxable income not reported elsewhere on your return or other schedules. List the type and amount of income. If necessary, include a statement showing the required information. For more details, see *Miscellaneous Income* in Pub. 525.

Examples of income to report on line 21 include the following.

• Most prizes and awards. But see *Olympic and Paralympic medals and USOC prize money*, later.

• Jury duty pay. Also see the instructions for line 36.

• Alaska Permanent Fund dividends.

• Reimbursements or other amounts received for items deducted in an earlier year, such as medical expenses, real estate taxes, general sales taxes, or home mortgage interest. See *Recoveries* in Pub. 525 for details on how to figure the amount to report.

• Income from the rental of personal property if you engaged in the rental for profit but were not in the business of renting such property. Also see the instructions for line 36.

• Income from an activity not engaged in for profit. See Pub. 535.

• Amounts deemed to be income from a health savings account (HSA) because you didn't remain an eligible individual during the testing period. See Form 8889, Part III.

• Gambling winnings, including lotteries, raffles, a lump-sum payment from the sale of a right to receive future lottery payments, etc. For details on gambling losses, see the instructions for Schedule A, line 28.

 Attach Form(s) W-2G to Form 1040 if any federal income tax was withheld.

• Reemployment trade adjustment assistance (RTAA) payments. These payments should be shown in box 5 of Form 1099-G.

• Loss on certain corrective distributions of excess deferrals. See *Retirement Plan Contributions* in Pub. 525.

• Dividends on insurance policies if they exceed the total of all net premiums you paid for the contract.

• Recapture of a charitable contribution deduction relating to the contribution of a fractional interest in tangible personal property. See *Fractional Interest in Tangible Personal Property* in Pub. 526. Interest and an additional 10% tax apply to the amount of the recapture. See the instructions for line 62.

• Recapture of a charitable contribution deduction if the charitable organization disposes of the donated property within 3 years of the contribution. See *Recapture if no exempt use* in Pub. 526.

• Canceled debts. These amounts may be shown in box 2 of Form 1099-C. However, part or all of your income from the cancellation of debt may be nontaxable. See Pub. 4681 or go to

Social Security Benefits Worksheet—Lines 20a and 20b

Keep for Your Records

Before you begin:
- ✓ Complete Form 1040, lines 21 and 23 through 32, if they apply to you.
- ✓ Figure any write-in adjustments to be entered on the dotted line next to line 36 (see the instructions for line 36).
- ✓ If you are married filing separately and you lived apart from your spouse for all of 2017, enter "D" to the right of the word "benefits" on line 20a. If you don't, you may get a math error notice from the IRS.
- ✓ Be sure you have read the *Exception* in the line 20a and 20b instructions to see if you can use this worksheet instead of a publication to find out if any of your benefits are taxable.

1. Enter the total amount from **box 5** of **all** your **Forms SSA-1099** and **Forms RRB-1099.** Also, enter this amount on Form 1040, line 20a .... **1.** _____

2. Multiply line 1 by 50% (0.50) .... **2.** _____

3. Combine the amounts from Form 1040, lines 7, 8a, 9a, 10 through 14, 15b, 16b, 17 through 19, and 21 .... **3.** _____

4. Enter the amount, if any, from Form 1040, line 8b .... **4.** _____

5. Combine lines 2, 3, and 4 .... **5.** _____

6. Enter the total of the amounts from Form 1040, lines 23 through 32, plus any write-in adjustments you entered on the dotted line next to line 36 .... **6.** _____

7. Is the amount on line 6 less than the amount on line 5?

   ☐ **No.** (STOP) None of your social security benefits are taxable. Enter -0- on Form 1040, line 20b.

   ☐ **Yes.** Subtract line 6 from line 5 .... **7.** _____

8. If you are:
   - Married filing jointly, enter $32,000
   - Single, head of household, qualifying widow(er), or married filing separately and you **lived apart** from your spouse for all of 2017, enter $25,000
   - Married filing separately and you lived with your spouse at any time in 2017, skip lines 8 through 15; multiply line 7 by 85% (0.85) and enter the result on line 16. Then, go to line 17
   .... **8.** _____

9. Is the amount on line 8 less than the amount on line 7?

   ☐ **No.** (STOP) None of your social security benefits are taxable. Enter -0- on Form 1040, line 20b. If you are married filing separately and you **lived apart** from your spouse for all of 2017, be sure you entered "D" to the right of the word "benefits" on line 20a.

   ☐ **Yes.** Subtract line 8 from line 7 .... **9.** _____

10. Enter: $12,000 if married filing jointly; $9,000 if single, head of household, qualifying widow(er), or married filing separately and you **lived apart** from your spouse for all of 2017 .... **10.** _____

11. Subtract line 10 from line 9. If zero or less, enter -0- .... **11.** _____

12. Enter the **smaller** of line 9 or line 10 .... **12.** _____

13. Enter one-half of line 12 .... **13.** _____

14. Enter the **smaller** of line 2 or line 13 .... **14.** _____

15. Multiply line 11 by 85% (0.85). If line 11 is zero, enter -0- .... **15.** _____

16. Add lines 14 and 15 .... **16.** _____

17. Multiply line 1 by 85% (0.85) .... **17.** _____

18. **Taxable social security benefits.** Enter the **smaller** of line 16 or line 17. Also enter this amount on Form 1040, line 20b .... **18.** _____

TIP *If any of your benefits are taxable for 2017 and they include a lump-sum benefit payment that was for an earlier year, you may be able to reduce the taxable amount. See Lump-Sum Election in Pub. 915 for details.*

IRS.gov and enter "canceled debt" or "foreclosure" in the search box.

• Taxable part of disaster relief payments. See Pub. 525 to figure the taxable part, if any. If any of your disaster relief payment is taxable, attach a statement showing the total payment received and how you figured the taxable part.

• Taxable distributions from a Coverdell education savings account (ESA) or a qualified tuition program (QTP). Distributions from these accounts may be taxable if (a) in the case of distributions from a QTP, they are more than the qualified higher education expenses of the designated beneficiary in 2017 or, in the case of distributions from an ESA, they are more than the qualified education expenses of the designated beneficiary in 2017, and (b) they were not included in a qualified rollover. Nontaxable distributions from these accounts don't have to be reported on Form 1040. This includes rollovers and qualified higher education expenses refunded to a student from a QTP that were recontributed to a QTP with the same designated beneficiary within 60 days after the date of refund. See Pub. 970.

 You may have to pay an additional tax if you received a taxable distribution from a Coverdell ESA or a QTP. See the Instructions for Form 5329.

• Taxable distributions from a health savings account (HSA) or an Archer MSA. Distributions from these accounts may be taxable if (a) they are more than the unreimbursed qualified medical expenses of the account beneficiary or account holder in 2017, and (b) they were not included in a qualified rollover. See Pub. 969.

 You may have to pay an additional tax if you received a taxable distribution from an HSA or an Archer MSA. See the Instructions for Form 8889 for HSAs or the Instructions for Form 8853 for Archer MSAs.

• Taxable distributions from an ABLE account. Distributions from this type of account may be taxable if (a) they are more than the designated beneficiary's qualified disability expenses, and (b) they were not included in a qualified rollover. Enter "ABLE" and the taxable amount on the dotted line

next to line 21. See Pub. 907 for more information.

 You may have to pay an additional tax if you received a taxable distribution from an ABLE account. See the Instructions for Form 5329.

Nontaxable income. Don't report any nontaxable income on line 21. Examples of nontaxable income include the following.

• Child support.
• Payments you received to help you pay your mortgage loan under the HFA Hardest Hit Fund.
• Any Pay-for-Performance Success Payments that reduce the principal balance of your home mortgage under the Home Affordable Modification Program.
• Life insurance proceeds received because of someone's death (other than from certain employer-owned life insurance contracts).
• Gifts and bequests. However, if you received a gift or bequest from a foreign person of more than $15,797, you may have to report information about it on Form 3520, Part IV. See the Instructions for Form 3520.

Net operating loss (NOL) deduction. Include on line 21 any NOL deduction from an earlier year. Subtract it from any income on line 21 and enter the result. If the result is less than zero, enter it in parentheses. On the dotted line next to line 21, enter "NOL" and show the amount of the deduction in parentheses. See Pub. 536 for details.

Medicaid waiver payments to care provider. Certain Medicaid waiver payments you received for caring for someone living in your home with you may be nontaxable. If these payments were incorrectly reported to you in box 1 of Form(s) W-2, and you can't get a corrected Form W-2, include the amount on line 7. On line 21, subtract the nontaxable amount of the payments from any income on line 21 and enter the result. If the result is less than zero, enter it in parentheses. Enter "Notice 2014-7" and the nontaxable amount on the dotted line next to line 21. For more information about these payments, see Pub. 525.

Olympic and Paralympic medals and USOC prize money. The value of

Olympic and Paralympic medals and the amount of United States Olympic Committee prize money you receive on account of your participation in the Olympic or Paralympic Games may be nontaxable. These amounts should be reported to you in box 3 of Form 1099-MISC. To see if these amounts are nontaxable, first figure your adjusted gross income including the amount of your medals and prize money. If your adjusted gross income is not more than $1,000,000 ($500,000 if married filing separately), these amounts are nontaxable and you should include the amount in box 3 of Form 1099-MISC on line 21, then subtract it by including it on line 36 along with any other write-in adjustments. On the dotted line next to line 36, enter the nontaxable amount and identify as "USOC."

Adjusted Gross Income

Line 23
Educator Expenses

If you were an eligible educator in 2017, you can deduct on line 23 up to $250 of qualified expenses you paid in 2017. If you and your spouse are filing jointly and both of you were eligible educators, the maximum deduction is $500. However, neither spouse can deduct more than $250 of his or her qualified expenses on line 23. You may be able to deduct expenses that are more than the $250 (or $500) limit on Schedule A, line 21. An eligible educator is a kindergarten through grade 12 teacher, instructor, counselor, principal, or aide who worked in a school for at least 900 hours during a school year.

Qualified expenses include ordinary and necessary expenses paid:
• For professional development courses you have taken related to the curriculum you teach or to the students you teach, or
• In connection with books, supplies, equipment (including computer equipment, software, and services), and other materials used in the classroom.

An ordinary expense is one that is common and accepted in your educational field. A necessary expense is one that is helpful and appropriate for your profession as an educator. An expense doesn't have to be required to be considered necessary.

Qualified expenses don't include expenses for home schooling or for non-athletic supplies for courses in health or physical education.

You must reduce your qualified expenses by the following amounts.
• Excludable U.S. series EE and I savings bond interest from Form 8815.
• Nontaxable qualified tuition program earnings or distributions.
• Any nontaxable distribution of Coverdell education savings account earnings.
• Any reimbursements you received for these expenses that weren't reported to you in box 1 of your Form W-2.

For more details, use *Tax Topic 458* or see Pub. 529.

Line 24

Certain Business Expenses of Reservists, Performing Artists, and Fee-Basis Government Officials

Include the following deductions on line 24.
• Certain business expenses of National Guard and reserve members who traveled more than 100 miles from home to perform services as a National Guard or reserve member.
• Performing-arts-related expenses as a qualified performing artist.
• Business expenses of fee-basis state or local government officials.

For more details, see Form 2106 or 2106-EZ.

Line 25

Health Savings Account (HSA) Deduction

You may be able to take this deduction if contributions (other than employer contributions, rollovers, and qualified HSA funding distributions from an IRA) were made to your HSA for 2017. See Form 8889.

Line 26

Moving Expenses

If you moved in connection with your job or business or started a new job, you may be able to take this deduction. But your new workplace must be at least 50 miles farther from your old home than your old home was from your old workplace. If you had no former workplace, your new workplace must be at least 50 miles from your old home. Use *Tax Topic 455* or see Form 3903.

Line 27

Deductible Part of Self-Employment Tax

If you were self-employed and owe self-employment tax, fill in Schedule SE to figure the amount of your deduction. If you completed Section A of Schedule SE, the deductible part of your self-employment tax is on line 6. If you completed Section B of Schedule SE, it is on line 13.

Line 28

Self-Employed SEP, SIMPLE, and Qualified Plans

If you were self-employed or a partner, you may be able to take this deduction. See Pub. 560 or, if you were a minister, Pub. 517.

Line 29

Self-Employed Health Insurance Deduction

You may be able to deduct the amount you paid for health insurance for yourself, your spouse, and your dependents. The insurance also can cover your child who was under age 27 at the end of 2017, even if the child wasn't your dependent. A child includes your son, daughter, stepchild, adopted child, or foster child (defined in the line 6c instructions).

One of the following statements must be true.
• You were self-employed and had a net profit for the year reported on Schedule C, C-EZ, or F.
• You were a partner with net earnings from self-employment.

• You used one of the optional methods to figure your net earnings from self-employment on Schedule SE.
• You received wages in 2017 from an S corporation in which you were a more-than-2% shareholder. Health insurance premiums paid or reimbursed by the S corporation are shown as wages on Form W-2.

The insurance plan must be established under your business. Your personal services must have been a material income-producing factor in the business. If you are filing Schedule C, C-EZ, or F, the policy can be either in your name or in the name of the business.

If you are a partner, the policy can be either in your name or in the name of the partnership. You can either pay the premiums yourself or your partnership can pay them and report them as guaranteed payments. If the policy is in your name and you pay the premiums yourself, the partnership must reimburse you and report the premiums as guaranteed payments.

If you are a more-than-2% shareholder in an S corporation, the policy can be either in your name or in the name of the S corporation. You can either pay the premiums yourself or the S corporation can pay them and report them as wages. If the policy is in your name and you pay the premiums yourself, the S corporation must reimburse you. You can deduct the premiums only if the S corporation reports the premiums paid or reimbursed as wages in box 1 of your Form W-2 in 2017 and you also report the premium payments or reimbursements as wages on Form 1040, line 7.

But if you also were eligible to participate in any subsidized health plan maintained by your or your spouse's employer for any month or part of a month in 2017, amounts paid for health insurance coverage for that month can't be used to figure the deduction. Also, if you were eligible for any month or part of a month to participate in any subsidized health plan maintained by the employer of either your dependent or your child who was under age 27 at the end of 2017, don't use amounts paid for coverage for that month to figure the deduction.

Self-Employed Health Insurance Deduction Worksheet—Line 29

Keep for Your Records

Before you begin:	✓ If, during 2017, you were an eligible trade adjustment assistance (TAA) recipient, alternative TAA (ATAA) recipient, reemployment TAA (RTAA) recipient, or Pension Benefit Guaranty Corporation pension payee, see the Instructions for Form 8885 to figure the amount to enter on line 1 of this worksheet.
	✓ Be sure you have read the **Exceptions** in the instructions for this line to see if you can use this worksheet instead of Pub. 535 to figure your deduction.

1. Enter the total amount paid in 2017 for health insurance coverage established under your business (or the S corporation in which you were a more-than-2% shareholder) for 2017 for you, your spouse, and your dependents. Your insurance also can cover your child who was under age 27 at the end of 2017, even if the child wasn't your dependent. But don't include amounts for any month you were eligible to participate in an employer-sponsored health plan or amounts paid from retirement plan distributions that were nontaxable because you are a retired public safety officer . . . . **1.** _____

2. Enter your net profit* and any other earned income** from the business under which the insurance plan is established, minus any deductions on Form 1040, lines 27 and 28. Don't include Conservation Reserve Program payments exempt from self-employment tax . . . . **2.** _____

3. **Self-employed health insurance deduction.** Enter the **smaller** of line 1 or line 2 here and on Form 1040, line 29. **Don't** include this amount in figuring any medical expense deduction on Schedule A . . . . **3.** _____

*If you used either optional method to figure your net earnings from self-employment, don't enter your net profit. Instead, enter the amount from Schedule SE, Section B, line 4b.

**Earned income* includes net earnings and gains from the sale, transfer, or licensing of property you created. However, it doesn't include capital gain income. If you were a more-than-2% shareholder in the S corporation under which the insurance plan is established, earned income is your Medicare wages (box 5 of Form W-2) from that corporation.

 A qualified small employer health reimbursement arrangement (QSEHRA) is considered to be a subsidized health plan maintained by an employer.

Example. If you were eligible to participate in a subsidized health plan maintained by your spouse's employer from September 30 through December 31, you can't use amounts paid for health insurance coverage for September through December to figure your deduction.

Medicare premiums you voluntarily pay to obtain insurance in your name that is similar to qualifying private health insurance can be used to figure the deduction. Amounts paid for health insurance coverage from retirement plan distributions that were nontaxable because you are a retired public safety officer can't be used to figure the deduction.

For more details, see Pub. 535.

If you qualify to take the deduction, use the Self-Employed Health Insurance Deduction Worksheet to figure the amount you can deduct.

Exceptions. Use Pub. 535 instead of the Self-Employed Health Insurance Deduction Worksheet in these instructions to figure your deduction if any of the following applies.

- You had more than one source of income subject to self-employment tax.
- You file Form 2555 or 2555-EZ.
- You are using amounts paid for qualified long-term care insurance to figure the deduction.

Use Pub. 974 instead of the worksheet in these instructions if the insurance plan was considered to be established under your business and was obtained through the Marketplace, and advance payments of the premium tax credit were made or you are claiming the premium tax credit.

Line 30

Penalty on Early Withdrawal of Savings

The Form 1099-INT or Form 1099-OID you received will show the amount of any penalty you were charged.

Lines 31a and 31b

Alimony Paid

If you made payments to or for your spouse or former spouse under a divorce or separation instrument, you may be able to take this deduction. Use *Tax Topic 452* or see Pub. 504.

Line 32

IRA Deduction

 If you made any nondeductible contributions to a traditional individual retirement arrangement (IRA) for 2017, you must report them on Form 8606.

If you made contributions to a traditional IRA for 2017, you may be able to take an IRA deduction. But you, or your spouse if filing a joint return, must have had earned income to do so. For IRA purposes, earned income includes alimony and separate maintenance payments reported on line 11. If you were a member of the U.S. Armed Forces, earned in-

Need more information or forms? Visit IRS.gov.

come includes any nontaxable combat pay you received. If you were self-employed, earned income is generally your net earnings from self-employment if your personal services were a material income-producing factor. For more details, see Pub. 590-A. A statement should be sent to you by May 31, 2018, that shows all contributions to your traditional IRA for 2017.

Use the IRA Deduction Worksheet to figure the amount, if any, of your IRA deduction. But read the following 11-item list before you fill in the worksheet.

1. If you were age 70½ or older at the end of 2017, you can't deduct any contributions made to your traditional IRA for 2017 or treat them as nondeductible contributions.

2. You can't deduct contributions to a Roth IRA. But you may be able to take the retirement savings contributions credit (saver's credit). See the instructions for line 51.

3. If you are filing a joint return and you or your spouse made contributions to both a traditional IRA and a Roth IRA for 2017, don't use the IRA Deduction Worksheet in these instructions. Instead, see Pub. 590-A to figure the amount, if any, of your IRA deduction.

4. You can't deduct elective deferrals to a 401(k) plan, 403(b) plan, section 457 plan, SIMPLE plan, or the federal Thrift Savings Plan. These amounts aren't included as income in box 1 of your Form W-2. But you may be able to take the retirement savings contributions credit. See the instructions for line 51.

5. If you made contributions to your IRA in 2017 that you deducted for 2016, don't include them in the worksheet.

6. If you received income from a nonqualified deferred compensation plan or nongovernmental section 457 plan that is included in box 1 of your Form W-2, or in box 7 of Form 1099-MISC, don't include that income on line 8 of the worksheet. The income should be shown in (a) box 11 of your Form W-2, (b) box 12 of your Form W-2 with code Z, or (c) box 15b of Form 1099-MISC. If it isn't, contact your employer or the payer for the amount of the income.

7. You must file a joint return to deduct contributions to your spouse's IRA. Enter the total IRA deduction for you and your spouse on line 32.

8. Don't include rollover contributions in figuring your deduction. Instead, see the instructions for lines 15a and 15b.

9. Don't include trustees' fees that were billed separately and paid by you for your IRA. These fees can be deducted only as an itemized deduction on Schedule A.

10. Don't include any repayments of qualified reservist distributions. You can't deduct them. For information on how to report these repayments, see *Qualified reservist repayments* in Pub. 590-A.

11. If the total of your IRA deduction on line 32 plus any nondeductible contribution to your traditional IRAs shown on Form 8606 is less than your total traditional IRA contributions for 2017, see Pub. 590-A for special rules.

 By April 1 of the year after the year in which you turn age 70½, you must start taking minimum required distributions from your traditional IRA. If you don't, you may have to pay a 50% additional tax on the amount that should have been distributed. For details, including how to figure the minimum required distribution, see Pub. 590-B.

Were You Covered by a Retirement Plan?

If you were covered by a retirement plan (qualified pension, profit-sharing (including 401(k)), annuity, SEP, SIMPLE, etc.) at work or through self-employment, your IRA deduction may be reduced or eliminated. But you can still make contributions to an IRA even if you can't deduct them. In any case, the income earned on your IRA contributions isn't taxed until it is paid to you.

The "Retirement plan" box in box 13 of your Form W-2 should be checked if you were covered by a plan at work even if you weren't vested in the plan. You also are covered by a plan if you were self-employed and had a SEP, SIMPLE, or qualified retirement plan.

If you were covered by a retirement plan and you file Form 2555, 2555-EZ, or 8815, or you exclude employer-provided adoption benefits, see Pub. 590-A to figure the amount, if any, of your IRA deduction.

Married persons filing separately. If you weren't covered by a retirement plan but your spouse was, you are considered covered by a plan unless you lived apart from your spouse for all of 2017.

 You may be able to take the retirement savings contributions credit. See the line 51 instructions.

IRA Deduction Worksheet—Line 32

 *If you were age 70½ or older at the end of 2017, you can't deduct any contributions made to your traditional IRA or treat them as nondeductible contributions. **Don't** complete this worksheet for anyone age 70½ or older at the end of 2017. If you are married filing jointly and only one spouse was under age 70½ at the end of 2017, complete this worksheet only for that spouse.*

Before you begin:	✓ Be sure you have read the 11-item list in the instructions for this line. You may not be able to use this worksheet.
	✓ Figure any write-in adjustments to be entered on the dotted line next to line 36 (see the instructions for line 36).
	✓ If you are married filing separately and you lived apart from your spouse for all of 2017, enter "D" on the dotted line next to Form 1040, line 32. If you don't, you may get a math error notice from the IRS.

		Your IRA	**Spouse's IRA**

1a. Were you covered by a retirement plan (see *Were You Covered by a Retirement Plan?*)? . . . . **1a.** ☐ Yes ☐ No

b. If married filing jointly, was your spouse covered by a retirement plan? . . . . **1b.** ☐ Yes ☐ No

Next. If you checked "No" on line 1a (and "No" on line 1b if married filing jointly), skip lines 2 through 6, enter the applicable amount below on line 7a (and line 7b if applicable), and go to line 8.
- $5,500, if under age 50 at the end of 2017.
- $6,500, if age 50 or older but under age 70½ at the end of 2017.
Otherwise, go to line 2.

2. Enter the amount shown below that applies to you.
- Single, head of household, or married filing separately and you **lived apart** from your spouse for all of 2017, enter $72,000.
- Qualifying widow(er), enter $119,000.
- Married filing jointly, enter $119,000 in both columns. But if you checked "No" on either line 1a or 1b, enter $196,000 for the person who wasn't covered by a plan.
- Married filing separately and you lived with your spouse at any time in 2017, enter $10,000.

2a. _____ **2b.** _____

3. Enter the amount from Form 1040, line 22 . . . . **3.** _____

4. Enter the total of the amounts from Form 1040, lines 23 through 31a, plus any write-in adjustments you entered on the dotted line next to line 36 . . . . **4.** _____

5. Subtract line 4 from line 3. If married filing jointly, enter the result in both columns . . . . **5a.** _____ **5b.** _____

6. Is the amount on line 5 less than the amount on line 2?

☐ **No.** 🛑 None of your IRA contributions are deductible. For details on nondeductible IRA contributions, see Form 8606.

☐ **Yes.** Subtract line 5 from line 2 in each column. Follow the instruction below that applies to you.
- If single, head of household, or married filing separately, and the result is $10,000 or more, enter the applicable amount below on line 7 for that column and go to line 8.
  i. $5,500, if under age 50 at the end of 2017.
  ii. $6,500, if age 50 or older but under age 70½ at the end of 2017.
  If the result is less than $10,000, go to line 7.
- If married filing jointly or qualifying widow(er), and the result is $20,000 or more ($10,000 or more in the column for the IRA of a person who wasn't covered by a retirement plan), enter the applicable amount below on line 7 for that column and go to line 8.
  i. $5,500, if under age 50 at the end of 2017.
  ii. $6,500 if age 50 or older but under age 70½ at the end of 2017.
  Otherwise, go to line 7.

6a. _____ **6b.** _____

Need more information or forms? Visit IRS.gov.

IRA Deduction Worksheet—*Continued*

		Your IRA	Spouse's IRA

7. Multiply lines 6a and 6b by the percentage below that applies to you. If the result isn't a multiple of $10, increase it to the next multiple of $10 (for example, increase $490.30 to $500). If the result is $200 or more, enter the result. But if it is less than $200, enter $200.

    • Single, head of household, or married filing separately, multiply by 55% (0.55) (or by 65% (0.65) in the column for the IRA of a person who is age 50 or older at the end of 2017).

    • Married filing jointly or qualifying widow(er), multiply by 27.5% (0.275) (or by 32.5% (0.325) in the column for the IRA of a person who is age 50 or older at the end of 2017). But if you checked "No" on either line 1a or 1b, then in the column for the IRA of the person who wasn't covered by a retirement plan, multiply by 55% (0.55) (or by 65% (0.65) if age 50 or older at the end of 2017).

7a. _____ **7b.** _____

8. Enter the total of your (and your spouse's if filing jointly):

    • Wages, salaries, tips, etc. Generally, this is the amount reported in box 1 of Form W-2. Exceptions are explained earlier in these instructions for line 32.

    • Alimony and separate maintenance payments reported on Form 1040, line 11.

    • Nontaxable combat pay. This amount should be reported in box 12 of Form W-2 with code Q.

8. _____

9. Enter the earned income you (and your spouse if filing jointly) received as a self-employed individual or a partner. Generally, this is your (and your spouse's if filing jointly) net earnings from self-employment if your personal services were a material income-producing factor, minus any deductions on Form 1040, lines 27 and 28. If zero or less, enter -0-. For more details, see Pub. 590-A . . . . **9.** _____

10. Add lines 8 and 9 . . . . **10.** _____

⚠️ **CAUTION** *If married filing jointly and line 10 is less than $11,000 ($12,000 if one spouse is age 50 or older at the end of 2017; $13,000 if both spouses are age 50 or older at the end of 2017),* **stop here** *and use the worksheet in Pub. 590-A to figure your IRA deduction.*

11. Enter traditional IRA contributions made, or that will be made by April 17, 2018 for 2017 to your IRA on line 11a and to your spouse's IRA on line 11b . . . . **11a.** _____ **11b.** _____

12. On line 12a, enter the **smallest** of line 7a, 10, or 11a. On line 12b, enter the **smallest** of line 7b, 10, or 11b. This is the most you can deduct. Add the amounts on lines 12a and 12b and enter the total on Form 1040, line 32. Or, if you want, you can deduct a smaller amount and treat the rest as a nondeductible contribution (see Form 8606) . . . . **12a.** _____ **12b.** _____

Line 33

Student Loan Interest Deduction

You can take this deduction only if all of the following apply.

• You paid interest in 2017 on a qualified student loan (defined later).

• Your filing status is any status except married filing separately.

• Your modified adjusted gross income (AGI) is less than: $80,000 if single, head of household, or qualifying widow(er); $165,000 if married filing jointly. Use lines 2 through 4 of the worksheet in these instructions to figure your modified AGI.

• You, or your spouse if filing jointly, aren't claimed as a dependent on someone else's (such as your parent's) 2017 tax return.

Use the worksheet in these instructions to figure your student loan interest deduction.

Exception. Use Pub. 970 instead of the worksheet in these instructions to figure your student loan interest deduction if you file Form 2555, 2555-EZ, or 4563, or you exclude income from sources within Puerto Rico.

Qualified student loan. A qualified student loan is any loan you took out to pay the qualified higher education expenses for any of the following individuals who was an eligible student.

1. Yourself or your spouse.

2. Any person who was your dependent when the loan was taken out.

3. Any person you could have claimed as a dependent for the year the loan was taken out except that:

a. The person filed a joint return,

b. The person had gross income that was equal to or more than the exemption amount for that year ($4,050 for 2017), or

c. You, or your spouse if filing jointly, could be claimed as a dependent on someone else's return.

However, a loan isn't a qualified student loan if (a) any of the proceeds were used for other purposes, or (b) the loan was from either a related person or a person who borrowed the proceeds under a qualified employer plan or a contract purchased under such a plan. For details, see Pub. 970.

Qualified higher education expenses. Qualified higher education expenses generally include tuition, fees, room and board, and related expenses such as books and supplies. The expenses must be for education in a degree, certificate, or similar program at an eligible educational institution. An eligible educational institution includes most colleges, universities, and certain vocational schools. For details, see Pub. 970.

Student Loan Interest Deduction Worksheet—Line 33

Keep for Your Records

Before you begin: ✓ Figure any write-in adjustments to be entered on the dotted line next to line 36 (see the instructions for line 36).

✓ Be sure you have read the **Exception** in the instructions for this line to see if you can use this worksheet instead of Pub. 970 to figure your deduction.

1. Enter the total interest you paid in 2017 on qualified student loans (see the instructions for line 33). **Don't** enter more than $2,500 . . . . 1. _____

2. Enter the amount from Form 1040, line 22 . . . . 2. _____

3. Enter the total of the amounts from Form 1040, lines 23 through 32, plus any write-in adjustments you entered on the dotted line next to line 36 . . . . 3. _____

4. Subtract line 3 from line 2 . . . . 4. _____

5. Enter the amount shown below for your filing status.

• Single, head of household, or qualifying widow(er)—$65,000

• Married filing jointly—$135,000 } . . . . 5. _____

6. Is the amount on line 4 more than the amount on line 5?

☐ **No.** Skip lines 6 and 7, enter -0- on line 8, and go to line 9.

☐ **Yes.** Subtract line 5 from line 4 . . . . 6. _____

7. Divide line 6 by $15,000 ($30,000 if married filing jointly). Enter the result as a decimal (rounded to at least three places). If the result is 1.000 or more, enter 1.000 . . . . 7. __.____

8. Multiply line 1 by line 7 . . . . 8. _____

9. **Student loan interest deduction.** Subtract line 8 from line 1. Enter the result here and on Form 1040, line 33. **Don't** include this amount in figuring any other deduction on your return (such as on Schedule A, C, E, etc.) . . . . 9. _____

Need more information or forms? Visit IRS.gov.

Line 34

Reserved for Future Use

 At the time these instructions went to print, the tuition and fees deduction formerly claimed on line 34 had expired. You can't claim a deduction on line 34 for expenses paid or incurred after 2016. Line 34 is now shown as "Reserved for future use" in case Congress extends the deduction for 2017. To find out if legislation extended the deduction so you can claim it on your 2017 return, go to IRS.gov/Extenders or IRS.gov/Form1040.

If legislation doesn't extend the deduction for 2017, treat the amount on line 34 as zero when any form, worksheet, or instruction refers to line 34.

Line 35

Domestic Production Activities Deduction

You may be able to deduct up to 9% of your qualified production activities income from the following activities.

1. Construction of real property performed in the United States.

2. Engineering or architectural services performed in the United States for construction of real property in the United States.

3. Any lease, rental, license, sale, exchange, or other disposition of:

a. Tangible personal property, computer software, and sound recordings that you manufactured, produced, grew, or extracted in whole or in significant part in the United States,

b. Any qualified film you produced, or

c. Electricity, natural gas, or potable water you produced in the United States.

Your deduction may be reduced if you had oil-related qualified production activities income.

The deduction doesn't apply to income derived from:
• The sale of food and beverages you prepared at a retail establishment;
• Property you leased, licensed, or rented for use by any related person;
• The transmission or distribution of electricity, natural gas, or potable water; or
• The lease, rental, license, sale, exchange, or other disposition of land.

For details, see Form 8903 and its instructions.

Line 36

Include in the total on line 36 any of the following write-in adjustments. To find out if you can take the deduction, see the form or publication indicated. On the dotted line next to line 36, enter the amount of your deduction and identify it as indicated.
• Archer MSA deduction (see Form 8853). Identify as "MSA."
• Jury duty pay if you gave the pay to your employer because your employer paid your salary while you served on the jury. Identify as "Jury Pay."
• Deductible expenses related to income reported on line 21 from the rental of personal property engaged in for profit. Identify as "PPR."
• Nontaxable amount of the value of Olympic and Paralympic medals and USOC prize money reported on line 21. Identify as "USOC."
• Reforestation amortization and expenses (see Pub. 535). Identify as "RFST."
• Repayment of supplemental unemployment benefits under the Trade Act of 1974 (see Pub. 525). Identify as "Sub-Pay TRA."
• Contributions to section 501(c)(18)(D) pension plans (see Pub. 525). Identify as "501(c)(18)(D)."
• Contributions by certain chaplains to section 403(b) plans (see Pub. 517). Identify as "403(b)."
• Attorney fees and court costs for actions involving certain unlawful discrimination claims, but only to the extent of gross income from such actions (see Pub. 525). Identify as "UDC."
• Attorney fees and court costs you paid in connection with an award from the IRS for information you provided that helped the IRS detect tax law violations, up to the amount of the award includible in your gross income. Identify as "WBF."

Line 37

If line 37 is less than zero, you may have a net operating loss that you can carry to another tax year. See the Instructions for Form 1045 for details.

Tax and Credits

Line 39a

If you were born before January 2, 1953, or were blind at the end of 2017, check the appropriate box(es) on line 39a. If you were married and checked the box on Form 1040, line 6b, and your spouse was born before January 2, 1953, or was blind at the end of 2017, also check the appropriate box(es) for your spouse. Be sure to enter the total number of boxes checked. Don't check any box(es) for your spouse if your filing status is head of household.

Death of spouse in 2017. If your spouse was born before January 2, 1953, but died in 2017 before reaching age 65, don't check the box that says "Spouse was born before January 2, 1953."

A person is considered to reach age 65 on the day before his or her 65th birthday.

Example. Your spouse was born on February 14, 1952, and died on February 13, 2017. Your spouse is considered age 65 at the time of death. Check the appropriate box for your spouse on line 39a. However, if your spouse died on February 12, 2017, your spouse isn't considered age 65. Don't check the box.

Death of taxpayer in 2017. If you are preparing a return for someone who died in 2017, see Pub. 501 before completing line 39a.

Blindness

If you weren't totally blind as of December 31, 2017, you must get a statement certified by your eye doctor (ophthalmologist or optometrist) that:
• You can't see better than 20/200 in your better eye with glasses or contact lenses, or
• Your field of vision is 20 degrees or less.

If your eye condition isn't likely to improve beyond the conditions listed above, you can get a statement certified by your eye doctor (ophthalmologist or optometrist) to this effect instead.

You must keep the statement for your records.

Line 39b

If your filing status is married filing separately (box 3 is checked), and your spouse itemizes deductions on his or her return, check the box on line 39b. Also check that box if you were a dual-status alien. But if you were a dual-status alien and you file a joint return with your spouse who was a U.S. citizen or resident alien at the end of 2017 and you and your spouse agree to be taxed on your combined worldwide income, don't check the box.

Line 40

Itemized Deductions or Standard Deduction

In most cases, your federal income tax will be less if you take the larger of your itemized deductions or standard deduction.

Itemized Deductions

To figure your itemized deductions, fill in Schedule A.

Standard Deduction

Most people can find their standard deduction by looking at the amounts listed under "All others" to the left of line 40.

Exception 1—Dependent. If you, or your spouse if filing jointly, can be claimed as a dependent on someone else's 2017 return, use the Standard Deduction Worksheet for Dependents to figure your standard deduction.

Exception 2—Box on line 39a checked. If you checked any box on line 39a, figure your standard deduction using the Standard Deduction Chart for People Who Were Born Before January 2, 1953, or Were Blind.

Exception 3—Box on line 39b checked. If you checked the box on line 39b, your standard deduction is zero, even if you were born before January 2, 1953, or were blind.

Exception 4—Increased standard deduction for net qualified disaster loss. If you had a net qualified disaster loss and you elect to increase your standard deduction by the amount of your net qualified disaster loss, use Schedule A to figure your standard deduction. See the instructions for Form 4684 and Schedule A, line 28 for more information.

Line 42

Exemptions

If the amount on line 38 is over $156,900, use the Deduction for Exemptions Worksheet to figure your deduction for exemptions.

Standard Deduction Worksheet for Dependents—Line 40

Keep for Your Records

Use this worksheet **only** if someone can claim you, or your spouse if filing jointly, as a dependent.

1.	Is your **earned income*** more than $700?	
	☐ **Yes.** Add $350 to your earned income. Enter the total	1. _____
	☐ **No.** Enter $1,050	
2.	Enter the amount shown below for your filing status.	
	• Single or married filing separately—$6,350	
	• Married filing jointly—$12,700	2. _____
	• Head of household—$9,350	
3.	**Standard deduction.**	
a.	Enter the **smaller** of line 1 or line 2. If born after January 1, 1953, and not blind, **stop here** and enter this amount on Form 1040, line 40. Otherwise, go to line 3b	3a. _____
b.	If born before January 2, 1953, or blind, multiply the number on Form 1040, line 39a, by $1,250 ($1,550 if single or head of household)	3b. _____
c.	Add lines 3a and 3b. Enter the total here and on Form 1040, line 40	3c. _____

***Earned income** includes wages, salaries, tips, professional fees, and other compensation received for personal services you performed. It also includes any taxable scholarship or fellowship grant. Generally, your earned income is the total of the amount(s) you reported on Form 1040, lines 7, 12, and 18, minus the amount, if any, on line 27.*

Need more information or forms? Visit IRS.gov.

Standard Deduction Chart for People Who Were Born Before January 2, 1953, or Were Blind

Don't use this chart if someone can claim you, or your spouse if filing jointly, as a dependent. Instead, use the worksheet above.

Enter the number from the box on
Form 1040, line 39a .... ▶ ☐

⚠ **CAUTION**   Don't use the number of exemptions from line 6d.

IF your filing status is . . .	AND the number in the box above is . . .	THEN your standard deduction is . . .
Single	1	$7,900
	2	9,450
Married filing jointly or Qualifying widow(er)	1	$13,950
	2	15,200
	3	16,450
	4	17,700
Married filing separately	1	$7,600
	2	8,850
	3	10,100
	4	11,350
Head of household	1	$10,900
	2	12,450

Deduction for Exemptions Worksheet—Line 42

Keep for Your Records

1. Is the amount on Form 1040, line 38, more than the amount shown on line 4 below for your filing status?

   ☐ **No.** (STOP) Multiply $4,050 by the total number of exemptions claimed on Form 1040, line 6d, and enter the result on line 42.

   ☐ **Yes. Continue.**

2. Multiply $4,050 by the total number of exemptions claimed on Form 1040, line 6d .... 2. _____

3. Enter the amount from Form 1040, line 38 .... 3. _____

4. Enter the amount shown below for your filing status.
   - Single —$261,500
   - Married filing jointly or qualifying widow(er)—$313,800
   - Married filing separately—$156,900
   - Head of household—$287,650
   .... 4. _____

5. Subtract line 4 from line 3. If the result is more than $122,500 ($61,250 if married filing separately), (STOP) Enter -0- on line 42 .... 5. _____

6. Divide line 5 by $2,500 ($1,250 if married filing separately). If the result isn't a whole number, increase it to the next higher whole number (for example, increase 0.00004 to 1) .... 6. _____

7. Multiply line 6 by 2% (0.02) and enter the result as a decimal (rounded to at least three places) .... 7. _____

8. Multiply line 2 by line 7 .... 8. _____

9. **Deduction for exemptions.** Subtract line 8 from line 2. Enter the result here and on Form 1040, line 42 .... 9. _____

Line 44

Tax

Include in the total on line 44 all of the following taxes that apply.

- Tax on your taxable income. Figure the tax using one of the methods described here.
- Tax from Form(s) 8814 (relating to the election to report child's interest or dividends). Check the appropriate box.
- Tax from Form 4972 (relating to lump-sum distributions). Check the appropriate box.
- Tax due to making a section 962 election (the election made by a domestic shareholder of a controlled foreign corporation to be taxed at corporate rates). See section 962 for details. Check box c and enter the amount and "962" in the space next to that box. Attach a statement showing how you figured the tax.
- Recapture of an education credit. You may owe this tax if you claimed an education credit in an earlier year, and either tax-free educational assistance or a refund of qualified expenses was received in 2017 for the student. See Form 8863 for more details. Check box c and enter the amount and "ECR" in the space next to that box.
- Any tax from Form 8621, line 16e, relating to a section 1291 fund. Check box c and enter the amount of the tax and "1291TAX" in the space next to that box.
- Repayment of any excess advance payments of the health coverage tax credit from Form 8885. Check box c and enter the amount of the repayment and "HCTC" in the space next to that box.

Do you want the IRS to figure the tax on your taxable income for you?

☐ **Yes.** See chapter 30 of Pub. 17 for details, including who is eligible and what to do. If you have paid too much, we will send you a refund. If you didn't pay enough, we will send you a bill.

☐ **No.** Use one of the following methods to figure your tax.

Tax Table or Tax Computation Worksheet. If your taxable income is less than $100,000, you must use the Tax Table, later in these instructions, to figure your tax. Be sure you use the correct column. If your taxable income is $100,000 or more, use the Tax Computation Worksheet right after the Tax Table.

However, don't use the Tax Table or Tax Computation Worksheet to figure your tax if any of the following applies.

Form 8615. Form 8615 generally must be used to figure the tax for any child who had more than $2,100 of unearned income, such as taxable interest, ordinary dividends, or capital gains (including capital gain distributions), and who either:

1. Was under age 18 at the end of 2017,

Need more information or forms? Visit IRS.gov.

2. Was age 18 at the end of 2017 and didn't have earned income that was more than half of the child's support, or

3. Was a full-time student at least age 19 but under age 24 at the end of 2017 and didn't have earned income that was more than half of the child's support.

But if the child files a joint return for 2017 or if neither of the child's parents was alive at the end of 2017, don't use Form 8615 to figure the child's tax.

A child born on January 1, 2000, is considered to be age 18 at the end of 2017; a child born on January 1, 1999, is considered to be age 19 at the end of 2017; a child born on January 1, 1994, is considered to be age 24 at the end of 2017.

Schedule D Tax Worksheet. If you have to file Schedule D, and line 18 or 19 of Schedule D is more than zero, use the Schedule D Tax Worksheet in the Instructions for Schedule D to figure the amount to enter on Form 1040, line 44. But if you are filing Form 2555 or 2555-EZ, you must use the Foreign Earned Income Tax Worksheet instead.

Qualified Dividends and Capital Gain Tax Worksheet. Use the Qualified Dividends and Capital Gain Tax Worksheet, later, to figure your tax if you don't have to use the Schedule D Tax Worksheet and if any of the following applies.

• You reported qualified dividends on Form 1040, line 9b.

• You don't have to file Schedule D and you reported capital gain distributions on Form 1040, line 13.

• You are filing Schedule D and Schedule D, lines 15 and 16, are both more than zero.

But if you are filing Form 2555 or 2555-EZ, you must use the Foreign Earned Income Tax Worksheet instead.

Schedule J. If you had income from farming or fishing (including certain amounts received in connection with the Exxon Valdez litigation), your tax may be less if you choose to figure it using income averaging on Schedule J.

Foreign Earned Income Tax Worksheet. If you claimed the foreign earned income exclusion, housing exclusion, or housing deduction on Form 2555 or 2555-EZ, you must figure your tax using the Foreign Earned Income Tax Worksheet.

Foreign Earned Income Tax Worksheet—Line 44

Keep for Your Records

> ⚠️ **CAUTION** If Form 1040, line 43, is zero, don't complete this worksheet.

1. Enter the amount from Form 1040, line 43 .... **1.** _____

2a. Enter the amount from your (and your spouse's, if filing jointly) Form 2555, lines 45 and 50, or Form 2555-EZ, line 18 .... **2a.** _____

  b. Enter the total amount of any itemized deductions or exclusions you couldn't claim because they are related to excluded income .... **b.** _____

  c. Subtract line 2b from line 2a. If zero or less, enter -0- .... **c.** _____

3. Add lines 1 and 2c .... **3.** _____

4. **Figure the tax on the amount on line 3.** Use the Tax Table, Tax Computation Worksheet, Qualified Dividends and Capital Gain Tax Worksheet*, Schedule D Tax Worksheet*, or Form 8615, whichever applies. See the instructions for line 44 to see which tax computation method applies. (Don't use a second Foreign Earned Income Tax Worksheet to figure the tax on this line.) .... **4.** _____

5. **Figure the tax on the amount on line 2c.** If the amount on line 2c is less than $100,000, use the Tax Table to figure this tax. If the amount on line 2c is $100,000 or more, use the Tax Computation Worksheet .... **5.** _____

6. Subtract line 5 from line 4. Enter the result. If zero or less, enter -0-. Also include this amount on Form 1040, line 44 .... **6.** _____

Enter the amount from line 3 above on line 1 of the Qualified Dividends and Capital Gain Tax Worksheet or Schedule D Tax Worksheet if you use either of those worksheets to figure the tax on line 4 above. Complete the rest of that worksheet through line 6 (line 10 if you use the Schedule D Tax Worksheet). Next, you must determine if you have a capital gain excess. To find out if you have a capital gain excess, subtract Form 1040, line 43, from line 6 of your Qualified Dividends and Capital Gain Tax Worksheet (line 10 of your Schedule D Tax Worksheet). If the result is more than zero, that amount is your capital gain excess.

If you don't have a capital gain excess, complete the rest of either of those worksheets according to the worksheet's instructions. Then complete lines 5 and 6 above.

If you have a capital gain excess, complete a second Qualified Dividends and Capital Gain Tax Worksheet or Schedule D Tax Worksheet (whichever applies) as instructed above but in its entirety and with the following additional modifications. Then complete lines 5 and 6 above. These modifications are to be made only for purposes of filling out the Foreign Earned Income Tax Worksheet above.

1. Reduce (but not below zero) the amount you would otherwise enter on line 3 of your Qualified Dividends and Capital Gain Tax Worksheet or line 9 of your Schedule D Tax Worksheet by your capital gain excess.

2. Reduce (but not below zero) the amount you would otherwise enter on line 2 of your Qualified Dividends and Capital Gain Tax Worksheet or line 6 of your Schedule D Tax Worksheet by any of your capital gain excess not used in (1) above.

3. Reduce (but not below zero) the amount on your Schedule D (Form 1040), line 18, by your capital gain excess.

4. Include your capital gain excess as a loss on line 16 of your Unrecaptured Section 1250 Gain Worksheet in the Instructions for Schedule D (Form 1040).

Need more information or forms? Visit IRS.gov.

Qualified Dividends and Capital Gain Tax Worksheet—Line 44   *Keep for Your Records*

Before you begin:	✓ See the earlier instructions for line 44 to see if you can use this worksheet to figure your tax. ✓ Before completing this worksheet, complete Form 1040 through line 43. ✓ If you don't have to file Schedule D and you received capital gain distributions, be sure you checked the box on line 13 of Form 1040.

1. Enter the amount from Form 1040, line 43. However, if you are filing Form 2555 or 2555-EZ (relating to foreign earned income), enter the amount from line 3 of the Foreign Earned Income Tax Worksheet . . . . **1.** _____

2. Enter the amount from Form 1040, line 9b* . . . . **2.** _____

3. Are you filing Schedule D?*
    ☐ **Yes.** Enter the **smaller** of line 15 or 16 of Schedule D. If either line 15 or 16 is blank or a loss, enter -0-.
    ☐ **No.** Enter the amount from Form 1040, line 13. **3.** _____

4. Add lines 2 and 3 . . . . **4.** _____

5. If filing Form 4952 (used to figure investment interest expense deduction), enter any amount from line 4g of that form. Otherwise, enter -0- . . . . **5.** _____

6. Subtract line 5 from line 4. If zero or less, enter -0- . . . . **6.** _____

7. Subtract line 6 from line 1. If zero or less, enter -0- . . . . **7.** _____

8. Enter:
    $37,950 if single or married filing separately,
    $75,900 if married filing jointly or qualifying widow(er),
    $50,800 if head of household. . . . . **8.** _____

9. Enter the smaller of line 1 or line 8 . . . . **9.** _____

10. Enter the smaller of line 7 or line 9 . . . . **10.** _____

11. Subtract line 10 from line 9. This amount is taxed at 0% . . . . **11.** _____

12. Enter the smaller of line 1 or line 6 . . . . **12.** _____

13. Enter the amount from line 11 . . . . **13.** _____

14. Subtract line 13 from line 12 . . . . **14.** _____

15. Enter:
    $418,400 if single,
    $235,350 if married filing separately,
    $470,700 if married filing jointly or qualifying widow(er),
    $444,550 if head of household. . . . . **15.** _____

16. Enter the smaller of line 1 or line 15 . . . . **16.** _____

17. Add lines 7 and 11 . . . . **17.** _____

18. Subtract line 17 from line 16. If zero or less, enter -0- . . . . **18.** _____

19. Enter the smaller of line 14 or line 18 . . . . **19.** _____

20. Multiply line 19 by 15% (0.15) . . . . **20.** _____

21. Add lines 11 and 19 . . . . **21.** _____

22. Subtract line 21 from line 12 . . . . **22.** _____

23. Multiply line 22 by 20% (0.20) . . . . **23.** _____

24. Figure the tax on the amount on line 7. If the amount on line 7 is less than $100,000, use the Tax Table to figure the tax. If the amount on line 7 is $100,000 or more, use the Tax Computation Worksheet . . . . **24.** _____

25. Add lines 20, 23, and 24 . . . . **25.** _____

26. Figure the tax on the amount on line 1. If the amount on line 1 is less than $100,000, use the Tax Table to figure the tax. If the amount on line 1 is $100,000 or more, use the Tax Computation Worksheet . . . . **26.** _____

27. **Tax on all taxable income.** Enter the **smaller** of line 25 or 26. Also include this amount on Form 1040, line 44. If you are filing Form 2555 or 2555-EZ, don't enter this amount on Form 1040, line 44. Instead, enter it on line 4 of the Foreign Earned Income Tax Worksheet . . . . **27.** _____

If you are filing Form 2555 or 2555-EZ, see the footnote in the Foreign Earned Income Tax Worksheet before completing this line.

Line 45

Alternative Minimum Tax (AMT)

If you aren't sure whether you owe the AMT, complete the Worksheet To See if You Should Fill in Form 6251.

Exception. Fill in Form 6251 instead of using the worksheet if you claimed or received any of the following items.

- Accelerated depreciation.
- Tax-exempt interest from private activity bonds.
- Intangible drilling, circulation, research, experimental, or mining costs.
- Amortization of pollution-control facilities or depletion.
- Income or (loss) from tax-shelter farm activities, passive activities, partnerships, S corporations, or activities for which you aren't at risk.
- Income from long-term contracts not figured using the percentage-of-completion method.
- Interest paid on a home mortgage not used to buy, build, or substantially improve your home.
- Investment interest expense reported on Form 4952.
- Net operating loss deduction.
- Alternative minimum tax adjustments from an estate, trust, electing large partnership, or cooperative.
- Section 1202 exclusion.
- Stock by exercising an incentive stock option and you didn't dispose of the stock in the same year.
- Any general business credit claimed on Form 3800 if either line 6 (in Part I) or line 25 of Form 3800 is more than zero.
- Qualified electric vehicle credit.
- Credit for prior year minimum tax.
- Foreign tax credit.
- Net qualified disaster loss and you are reporting your standard deduction on Schedule A, line 28. See the instructions for Form 4684 for more information.

 Form 6251 should be filled in for certain children who are under age 24 at the end of 2017. See the Instructions for Form 6251 for more information.

For help with the alternative minimum tax, go to *IRS.gov/AMT*.

Line 46

Excess Advance Premium Tax Credit Repayment

The premium tax credit helps pay premiums for health insurance purchased from the Marketplace. Eligible individuals may have advance payments of the premium tax credit paid on their behalf directly to the insurance company. If you, your spouse with whom you are filing a joint return, or your dependent was enrolled in coverage purchased from the Marketplace and advance payments of the premium tax credit were made for the coverage, complete Form 8962 to reconcile (compare) the advance payments with your premium tax credit. You (or whoever enrolled you) should have received Form 1095-A from the Marketplace with information about your coverage and any advance credit payments. If the advance credit payments were more than the premium tax credit you can claim, the amount you must repay will be shown on Form 8962, line 29. Enter that amount, if any, on Form 1040, line 46.

You may have to repay excess advance payments of the premium tax credit even if someone else enrolled you, your spouse, or your dependent in Marketplace coverage. In that case, another individual may have received the Form 1095-A for the coverage. You also may have to repay excess advance payments of the premium tax credit if you enrolled an individual in coverage through the Marketplace, you don't claim the individual as a dependent on your return, and no one else claims that individual as a dependent. For more information, see the Instructions for Form 8962.

Line 48

Foreign Tax Credit

If you paid income tax to a foreign country or U.S. possession, you may be able to take this credit. Generally, you must complete and attach Form 1116 to do so.

Exception. You don't have to complete Form 1116 to take this credit if all of the following apply.

1. All of your foreign source gross income was from interest and dividends and all of that income and the foreign tax paid on it were reported to you on Form 1099-INT, Form 1099-DIV, or Schedule K-1 (or substitute statement).

2. The total of your foreign taxes wasn't more than $300 (not more than $600 if married filing jointly).

3. You held the stock or bonds on which the dividends or interest were paid for at least 16 days and weren't obligated to pay these amounts to someone else.

4. You aren't filing Form 4563 or excluding income from sources within Puerto Rico.

5. All of your foreign taxes were:

a. Legally owed and not eligible for a refund or reduced tax rate under a tax treaty, and

b. Paid to countries that are recognized by the United States and don't support terrorism.

For more details on these requirements, see the Instructions for Form 1116.

Do you meet all five requirements just listed?

☐ **Yes.** Enter on line 48 the smaller of (a) your total foreign taxes, or (b) the total of the amounts on Form 1040, lines 44 and 46.

☐ **No.** See Form 1116 to find out if you can take the credit and, if you can, if you have to file Form 1116.

Line 49

Credit for Child and Dependent Care Expenses

You may be able to take this credit if you paid someone to care for:

- Your qualifying child under age 13 whom you claim as your dependent,
- Your disabled spouse or any other disabled person who couldn't care for himself or herself, or
- Your child whom you couldn't claim as a dependent because of the rules for *Children of divorced or separated parents* in the instructions for line 6c.

For details, use *Tax Topic 602* or see Form 2441.

Worksheet To See if You Should Fill in Form 6251—Line 45

 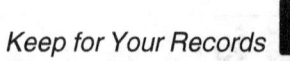

Before you begin: √ Be sure you have read the **Exception** in the instructions for this line to see if you must fill in Form 6251 instead of using this worksheet.

1. Are you filing **Schedule A**?

☐ **No.**   Skip lines 1 through 3; enter on line 4 the amount from Form 1040, line 38, and go to line 5.

☐ **Yes.**   Enter the amount from Form 1040, line 41 ....   **1.** _____

2. Enter the total of the amounts from Schedule A, lines 9 and 27 ....   **2.** _____

3. Add lines 1 and 2 ....   **3.** _____

4. Enter any tax refund from Form 1040, lines 10 and 21 ....   **4.** _____

5. If you completed the Itemized Deductions Worksheet in the Instructions for Schedule A, enter the amount from line 9 of that worksheet ....   **5.** _____

6. Add lines 4 and 5 ....   **6.** _____

7. Subtract line 6 from line 3 ....   **7.** _____

8. Enter the amount shown below for your filing status.

  • Single or head of household—$54,300
  • Married filing jointly or qualifying widow(er)—$84,500   } ....   **8.** _____
  • Married filing separately—$42,250

9. Is the amount on line 7 more than the amount on line 8?

☐ **No.** (STOP)   Don't complete the rest of this worksheet. You don't owe alternative minimum tax and don't need to fill out Form 6251. Leave line 45 blank.

☐ **Yes.**   Subtract line 8 from line 7 ....   **9.** _____

10. Enter the amount shown below for your filing status.

  • Single or head of household—$120,700
  • Married filing jointly or qualifying widow(er)—$160,900   } ....   **10.** _____
  • Married filing separately—$80,450

11. Is the amount on line 7 more than the amount on line 10?

☐ **No.**   Enter -0-. Skip line 12. Enter on line 13 the amount from line 9, and go to line 14.

☐ **Yes.**   Subtract line 10 from line 7 ....   **11.** _____

12. Multiply line 11 by 25% (0.25) and enter the **smaller** of the result or line 8 ....   **12.** _____

13. Add lines 9 and 12 ....   **13.** _____

14. Is the amount on line 13 more than $187,800 ($93,900 if married filing separately)?

☐ **Yes.** (STOP)   Fill in Form 6251 to see if you owe the alternative minimum tax.

☐ **No.**   Multiply line 13 by 26% (0.26) ....   **14.** _____

15. Add Form 1040, line 44 (minus any tax from Form 4972), and Form 1040, line 46. (If you used Schedule J to figure your tax on Form 1040, line 44, refigure that tax without using Schedule J before including it in this calculation) ....   **15.** _____

Next. Is the amount on line 14 more than the amount on line 15?

☐ **Yes.**   Fill in Form 6251 to see if you owe the alternative minimum tax.

☐ **No.**   You don't owe alternative minimum tax and don't need to fill out Form 6251. Leave line 45 blank.

Line 50

Education Credits

If you (or your dependent) paid qualified expenses in 2017 for yourself, your spouse, or your dependent to enroll in or attend an eligible educational institution, you may be able to take an education credit. See Form 8863 for details. However, you can't take an education credit if any of the following applies.

- You, or your spouse if filing jointly, are claimed as a dependent on someone else's (such as your parent's) 2017 tax return.
- Your filing status is married filing separately.
- The amount on Form 1040, line 38, is $90,000 or more ($180,000 or more if married filing jointly).
- You, or your spouse, were a nonresident alien for any part of 2017 unless your filing status is married filing jointly.

You may be able to increase an education credit if the student chooses to include all or part of a Pell grant or certain other scholarships or fellowships in income.

For more information, see Pub. 970, the instructions for line 68, and *IRS.gov/EdCredit*.

Line 51

Retirement Savings Contributions Credit (Saver's Credit)

You may be able to take this credit if you, or your spouse if filing jointly, made (a) contributions, other than rollover contributions, to a traditional or Roth IRA (including a *my*RA); (b) elective deferrals to a 401(k) or 403(b) plan (including designated Roth contributions) or to a governmental 457, SEP, or SIMPLE plan; (c) voluntary employee contributions to a qualified retirement plan (including the federal Thrift Savings Plan); or (d) contributions to a 501(c)(18)(D) plan.

However, you can't take the credit if either of the following applies.

1. The amount on Form 1040, line 38, is more than $31,000 ($46,500 if head of household; $62,000 if married filing jointly).

2. The person(s) who made the qualified contribution or elective deferral (a) was born after January 1, 2000, (b) is claimed as a dependent on someone else's 2017 tax return, or (c) was a student (defined next).

You were a student if during any part of 5 calendar months of 2017 you:
- Were enrolled as a full-time student at a school, or
- Took a full-time, on-farm training course given by a school or a state, county, or local government agency.

A school includes a technical, trade, or mechanical school. It doesn't include an on-the-job training course, correspondence school, or school offering courses only through the Internet.

For more details, use *Tax Topic 610* or see Form 8880.

Line 52

Child Tax Credit

Form 8862 required. If your 2016 child tax credit was denied or reduced for any reason other than a math or clerical error, you must attach a completed Form 8862 to your 2017 tax return to claim the credit in 2017. See Form 8862 and its instructions for details.

 If you take the child tax credit even though you aren't eligible and it is determined that your error is due to reckless or intentional disregard of the child tax credit rules, you won't be allowed to take the child tax credit or the additional child tax credit for 2 years even if you're otherwise eligible to do so. If you fraudulently take the child tax credit, you won't be allowed to take either credit for 10 years. You also may have to pay penalties.

Need more information or forms? Visit IRS.gov.

2017 Child Tax Credit Worksheet—Line 52

 Keep for Your Records

1. To be a qualifying child for the child tax credit, the child must be your dependent, **under age 17** at the end of 2017, and meet all the conditions in Steps 1 through 3 in the instructions for line 6c. Make sure you checked the box on Form 1040, line 6c, column (4), for each qualifying child.

2. If you don't have a qualifying child, you can't claim the child tax credit.

3. Be sure to see "Social security number" in the instructions for line 6c. If your qualifying child has an ITIN instead of an SSN, file Schedule 8812.

4. Do **not** use this worksheet, but use Pub. 972 instead, if:

    a. You are claiming the adoption credit, mortgage interest credit, District of Columbia first-time homebuyer credit, or residential energy efficient property credit;

    b. You are excluding income from Puerto Rico; or

    c. You are filing Form 2555, 2555-EZ, or 4563.

Part 1

1. Number of qualifying children: _____ × $1,000. Enter the result. **1** _____

2. Enter the amount from Form 1040, line 38. **2** _____

3. Enter the amount shown below for your filing status.

    ● Married filing jointly — $110,000

    ● Single, head of household, or qualifying widow(er) — $75,000 } **3** _____

    ● Married filing separately — $55,000

4. Is the amount on line 2 more than the amount on line 3?

    ☐ **No.** Leave line 4 blank. Enter -0- on line 5, and go to line 6. **4** _____

    ☐ **Yes.** Subtract line 3 from line 2.
    If the result isn't a multiple of $1,000, increase it to the next multiple of $1,000. For example, increase $425 to $1,000, increase $1,025 to $2,000, etc.

5. Multiply the amount on line 4 by 5% (0.05). Enter the result. **5** _____

6. Is the amount on line 1 more than the amount on line 5?

    ☐ **No.** (STOP)
    You can't take the child tax credit on Form 1040, line 52. You also can't take the additional child tax credit on Form 1040, line 67. Complete the rest of your Form 1040.

    ☐ **Yes.** Subtract line 5 from line 1. Enter the result. **6** _____
    Go to Part 2.

2017 Child Tax Credit Worksheet—*Continued* *Keep for Your Records*

Before you begin Part 2: √ Figure the amount of any credits you are claiming on Form 5695, Part II*; Form 8910; Form 8936; or Schedule R.

Part 2		

7. Enter the amount from Form 1040, line 47.

7 [ ]

8. Add any amounts from:

Form 1040, line 48 _____

Form 1040, line 49 + _____

Form 1040, line 50 + _____

Form 1040, line 51 + _____

Form 5695, line 30*+ _____

Form 8910, line 15 + _____

Form 8936, line 23 + _____

Schedule R, line 22 + _____

Enter the total. **8** [ ]

9. Are the amounts on lines 7 and 8 the same?

☐ **Yes.** (STOP) You can't take this credit because there is no tax to reduce. However, you may be able to take the **additional child tax credit.** See the **TIP** below.

☐ **No.** Subtract line 8 from line 7.

9 [ ]

10. Is the amount on line 6 more than the amount on line 9?

☐ **Yes.** Enter the amount from line 9. Also, you may be able to take the **additional child tax credit.** See the **TIP** below.

☐ **No.** Enter the amount from line 6.

} **This is your child tax credit.**

10 [ ]

Enter this amount on Form 1040, line 52.

1040

TIP *You may be able to take the **additional child tax credit** on Form 1040, line 67, if you answered "Yes" on line 9 **or** line 10 above.*

- *First, complete your Form 1040 through lines 66a and 66b.*

- *Then, use Schedule 8812 to figure any additional child tax credit.*

* If applicable.

Need more information or forms? Visit IRS.gov.

Line 53

Residential Energy Credit

Residential energy efficient property credit. You may be able to take this credit by completing and attaching Form 5695 if you paid for any of the following during 2017.

- Qualified solar electric property for use in your home located in the United States.
- Qualified solar water heating property for use in your home located in the United States.

 At the time these instructions went to print, the nonbusiness energy property credit had expired. You can't claim it for any property placed in service after 2016. To find out if legislation extended this credit so you can claim it on your 2017 return, go to IRS.gov/Extenders or IRS.gov/Form1040.

Condos and co-ops. If you are a member of a condominium management association for a condominium you own or a tenant-stockholder in a cooperative housing corporation, you are treated as having paid your proportionate share of any costs of such association or corporation for purposes of this credit.

More details. For details, see Form 5695.

Line 54

Other Credits

Enter the total of the following credits on line 54 and check the appropriate box(es). Check all boxes that apply. If box c is checked, also enter the applicable form number. To find out if you can take the credit, see the form or publication indicated.

- General business credit. This credit consists of a number of credits that usually apply only to individuals who are partners, shareholders in an S corporation, self-employed, or who have rental property. See Form 3800 or Pub. 334.
- Credit for prior year minimum tax. If you paid alternative minimum tax in a prior year, see Form 8801.
- Mortgage interest credit. If a state or local government gave you a mortgage credit certificate, see Form 8396.

- Credit for the elderly or the disabled. See Schedule R.
- Adoption credit. You may be able to take this credit if you paid expenses to adopt a child or you adopted a child with special needs and the adoption became final in 2017. See the Instructions for Form 8839.
- District of Columbia first-time homebuyer credit. You can't claim this credit for a home you bought after 2011. You can claim it only if you have a credit carryforward from 2016. See Form 8859.
- Qualified plug-in electric drive motor vehicle credit. See Form 8936.
- Qualified electric vehicle credit. You can't claim this credit for a vehicle placed in service after 2006. You can claim this credit only if you have an electric vehicle passive activity credit carried forward from a prior year. See Form 8834.
- Alternative motor vehicle credit. See Form 8910 if you placed a new fuel cell motor vehicle in service during 2017.
- Credit to holders of tax credit bonds. See Form 8912.

Other Taxes

Line 58

Unreported Social Security and Medicare Tax from Forms 4137 and 8919

Enter the total of any taxes from Form 4137 and Form 8919. Check the appropriate box(es).

Form 4137. If you received tips of $20 or more in any month and you didn't report the full amount to your employer, you must pay the social security and Medicare or railroad retirement (RRTA) tax on the unreported tips.

Don't include the value of any non-cash tips, such as tickets or passes. You don't pay social security and Medicare taxes or RRTA tax on these noncash tips.

To figure the social security and Medicare tax, use Form 4137. If you owe RRTA tax, contact your employer. Your employer will figure and collect the RRTA tax.

 You may be charged a penalty equal to 50% of the social security and Medicare or RRTA tax due on tips you received but didn't report to your employer.

Form 8919. If you are an employee who received wages from an employer who didn't withhold social security and Medicare tax from your wages, use Form 8919 to figure your share of the unreported tax. Include on line 58 the amount from line 13 of Form 8919. Include the amount from line 6 of Form 8919 on Form 1040, line 7.

Line 59

Additional Tax on IRAs, Other Qualified Retirement Plans, etc.

If any of the following apply, see Form 5329 and its instructions to find out if you owe this tax and if you must file Form 5329. Also see Form 5329 and its instructions for definitions of the terms used here.

1. You received an early distribution from (a) an IRA or other qualified retirement plan, (b) an annuity, or (c) a modified endowment contract entered into after June 20, 1988, and the total distribution wasn't rolled over.

2. Excess contributions were made to your IRA, Coverdell education savings account (ESA), Archer MSA, health savings account (HSA), or ABLE account.

3. You received a taxable distribution from a Coverdell ESA, qualified tuition program, or ABLE account.

4. You were born before July 1, 1946, and didn't take the minimum required distribution from your IRA or other qualified retirement plan.

Exception. If only item (1) applies and distribution code 1 is correctly shown in box 7 of all your Forms 1099-R, you don't have to file Form 5329. Instead, multiply the taxable amount of the distribution by 10% (0.10) and enter the result on line 59. The taxable amount of the distribution is the part of the distribution you reported on Form 1040, line 15b or 16b, or on Form 4972. Also, enter "No" under the heading *Other Taxes* to the left of line 59 to indicate that you don't have to file Form 5329.

But you must file Form 5329 if distribution code 1 is incorrectly shown in box 7 of Form 1099-R or you qualify for an exception, such as the exceptions for qualified medical expenses, qualified higher education expenses, qualified first-time homebuyer distributions, or a qualified reservist distribution.

Line 60a

Household Employment Taxes

Enter the household employment taxes you owe for having a household employee. If any of the following apply, see Schedule H and its instructions to find out if you owe these taxes.

1. You paid any one household employee (defined below) cash wages of $2,000 or more in 2017. Cash wages include wages paid by check, money order, etc. But don't count amounts paid to an employee who was under age 18 at any time in 2017 and was a student.

2. You withheld federal income tax during 2017 at the request of any household employee.

3. You paid total cash wages of $1,000 or more in any calendar quarter of 2016 or 2017 to household employees.

Any person who does household work is a household employee if you can control what will be done and how it will be done. Household work includes work done in or around your home by babysitters, nannies, health aides, housekeepers, yard workers, and similar domestic workers.

Line 60b

First-Time Homebuyer Credit Repayment

Enter the first-time homebuyer credit you have to repay if you bought the home in 2008.

If you bought the home in 2008 and owned and used it as your main home for all of 2017, you can enter your 2017 repayment on this line without attaching Form 5405.

See the Form 5405 instructions for details and for exceptions to the repayment rule.

Line 61

Health Care: Individual Responsibility

For each month of 2017, you must either:

• Have qualifying health care coverage for yourself, your spouse (if filing jointly), and anyone you can or do claim as a dependent (you are treated as having coverage for any month in which you have coverage for at least 1 day of the month),

• Qualify for an exemption from the requirement to have health care coverage, or

• Make a shared responsibility payment with your return and enter the amount on this line.

If you had qualifying health care coverage (called minimum essential coverage) for every month of 2017 for yourself, your spouse (if filing jointly), and anyone you can or do claim as a dependent, check the box on this line and leave the entry space blank.

You can check the box even if:

• A dependent child who was born or adopted during the year wasn't covered by your insurance during the month of or months before birth or adoption (but the child must have had minimum essential coverage every month of 2017 following the birth or adoption), or

• A spouse or dependent who died during the year wasn't covered by your insurance during the month of death and months after death (but he or she must have had minimum essential coverage every month of 2017 before death).

If you can't check the box on this line, you must generally either claim a coverage exemption on Form 8965 or report a shared responsibility payment on line 61 for each month that you, your spouse (if filing jointly), or someone you can or do claim as a dependent didn't have coverage. See the Instructions for Form 8965 for information on coverage exemptions and figuring the shared responsibility payment. However, if you can be claimed as a dependent, you don't need to check the box, claim a coverage exemption or report a payment. Leave the entry space blank. You don't need to attach Form 8965 or see its instructions.

If you or someone in your household had minimum essential coverage in 2017, the provider of that coverage is required to send you and the IRS a Form 1095-A, 1095-B, or 1095-C (with Part III completed) that lists individuals in your family who were enrolled in the coverage and shows their months of coverage.

• Individuals enrolled in health insurance coverage through the Marketplace generally receive this information on Form 1095-A, Health Insurance Marketplace Statement.

• Individuals enrolled in health insurance coverage provided by their employer generally receive this information on either Form 1095-B, Health Coverage, or on Form 1095-C, Employer-Provided Health Insurance Offer and Coverage.

• Individuals enrolled in a government-sponsored health program or in other types of coverage generally receive this information on Form 1095-B, Health Coverage.

You should receive Form 1095-A by early February 2018 and Form 1095-B or Form 1095-C by early March 2018, if applicable. You don't need to wait to receive your Form 1095-B or 1095-C to file your return. You may rely on other information about your coverage to complete line 61. Don't include Form 1095-A, Form 1095-B, or Form 1095-C with your tax return.

Your health care coverage provider may have asked for your social security number. To understand why, go to *IRS.gov/ACASSN*.

Minimum essential coverage. Most health care coverage that people have is minimum essential coverage.

Minimum essential coverage includes:

• Most types of health care coverage provided by your employer;

• Many types of government-sponsored health care coverage including Medicare, most Medicaid coverage, and most health care coverage provided to veterans and active duty service members;

• Health care coverage you buy through the Marketplace; and

• Certain types of health care coverage you buy directly from an insurance company.

Need more information or forms? Visit IRS.gov.

See the Instructions for Form 8965 for more information on what qualifies as minimum essential coverage.

Reminder—Health care coverage. If you need health care coverage, go to *www.HealthCare.gov* to learn about health insurance options for you and your family, how to buy health insurance, and how you might qualify to get financial assistance to buy health insurance.

Premium tax credit. If you, your spouse, or a dependent enrolled in health insurance through the Marketplace, you may be able to claim the premium tax credit. See the instructions for line 69 and Form 8962.

Line 62

Other Taxes

Use line 62 to report any taxes not reported elsewhere on your return or other schedules. To find out if you owe the tax, see the form or publication indicated. Enter on line 62 the total of all the following taxes you owe.

Additional Medicare Tax. See Form 8959 and its instructions if the total of your 2017 wages and any self-employment income was more than:
- $125,000 if married filing separately;
- $250,000 if married filing jointly; or
- $200,000 if single, head of household, or qualifying widow(er).

Also see Form 8959 if you had railroad retirement (RRTA) compensation that was more than the amount just listed that applies to you.

If you are married filing jointly and either you or your spouse had wages or RRTA compensation of more than $200,000, your employer may have withheld Additional Medicare Tax even if you don't owe the tax. In that case, you may be able to get a refund of the tax withheld. See the Instructions for Form 8959 to find out how to report the withheld tax on Form 8959.

Check box a if you owe the tax.

Net Investment Income Tax. See Form 8960 and its instructions if the amount on Form 1040, line 38, is more than:

- $125,000 if married filing separately,
- $250,000 if married filing jointly or qualifying widow(er), or
- $200,000 if single or head of household.

If you file Form 2555 or 2555-EZ, see Form 8960 and its instructions if the amount on Form 1040, line 38, is more than:
- $22,900 if married filing separately,
- $147,900 if married filing jointly or qualifying widow(er), or
- $97,900 if single or head of household.

Check box b if you owe the tax.

Other taxes. For the following taxes, check box c and, in the space next to that box, enter the amount of the tax and the code that identifies it. If you need more room, attach a statement listing the amount of each tax and the code.

1. Additional tax on health savings account (HSA) distributions (see Form 8889, Part II). Identify as "HSA."

2. Additional tax on an HSA because you didn't remain an eligible individual during the testing period (see Form 8889, Part III). Identify as "HDHP."

3. Additional tax on Archer MSA distributions (see Form 8853). Identify as "MSA."

4. Additional tax on Medicare Advantage MSA distributions (see Form 8853). Identify as "Med MSA."

5. Recapture of the following credits.

   a. Investment credit (see Form 4255). Identify as "ICR."

   b. Low-income housing credit (see Form 8611). Identify as "LIHCR."

   c. Indian employment credit (see Form 8845). Identify as "IECR."

   d. New markets credit (see Form 8874). Identify as "NMCR."

   e. Credit for employer-provided child care facilities (see Form 8882). Identify as "ECCFR."

   f. Alternative motor vehicle credit (see Form 8910). Identify as "AMVCR."

   g. Alternative fuel vehicle refueling property credit (see Form 8911). Identify as "ARPCR."

   h. Qualified plug-in electric drive motor vehicle credit (see Form 8936). Identify as "8936R."

6. Recapture of federal mortgage subsidy. If you sold your home in 2017 and it was financed (in whole or in part) from the proceeds of any tax-exempt qualified mortgage bond or you claimed the mortgage interest credit, see Form 8828. Identify as "FMSR."

7. Section 72(m)(5) excess benefits tax (see Pub. 560). Identify as "Sec. 72(m)(5)."

8. Uncollected social security and Medicare or RRTA tax on tips or group-term life insurance. This tax should be shown in box 12 of Form W-2 with codes A and B or M and N. Identify as "UT."

9. Golden parachute payments. If you received an excess parachute payment (EPP), you must pay a 20% tax on it. This tax should be shown in box 12 of Form W-2 with code K. If you received a Form 1099-MISC, the tax is 20% of the EPP shown in box 13. Identify as "EPP."

10. Tax on accumulation distribution of trusts (see Form 4970). Identify as "ADT."

11. Excise tax on insider stock compensation from an expatriated corporation. See section 4985. Identify as "ISC."

12. Interest on the tax due on installment income from the sale of certain residential lots and timeshares. Identify as "453(l)(3)."

13. Interest on the deferred tax on gain from certain installment sales with a sales price over $150,000. Identify as "453A(c)."

14. Additional tax on recapture of a charitable contribution deduction relating to a fractional interest in tangible personal property. See Pub. 526. Identify as "FITPP."

15. Look-back interest under section 167(g) or 460(b). See Form 8697 or 8866. Identify as "8697" or "8866."

16. Additional tax on income you received from a nonqualified deferred compensation plan that fails to meet the requirements of section 409A. This income should be shown in box 12 of Form W-2 with code Z, or in box 15b of Form 1099-MISC. The tax is 20% of the

amount required to be included in income plus an interest amount determined under section 409A(a)(1)(B)(ii). See section 409A(a)(1)(B) for details. Identify as "NQDC."

17. Additional tax on compensation you received from a nonqualified deferred compensation plan described in section 457A if the compensation would have been includible in your income in an earlier year except that the amount wasn't determinable until 2017. The tax is 20% of the amount required to be included in income plus an interest amount determined under section 457A(c)(2). See section 457A for details. Identify as "457A."

18. Tax on noneffectively connected income for any part of the year you were a nonresident alien (see the Instructions for Form 1040NR). Identify as "1040NR."

19. Any interest amount from Form 8621, line 16f, relating to distributions from, and dispositions of, stock of a section 1291 fund. Identify as "1291INT."

20. Any interest amount from Form 8621, line 24. Identify as "1294INT."

Payments

Line 64

Federal Income Tax Withheld

Add the amounts shown as federal income tax withheld on your Forms W-2, W-2G, and 1099-R. Enter the total on line 64. The amount withheld should be shown in box 2 of Form W-2 and in box 4 of Form W-2G or 1099-R. Attach your Form(s) W-2 to the front of your return. Attach Forms W-2G and 1099-R to the front of your return if federal income tax was withheld.

If you received a 2017 Form 1099 showing federal income tax withheld on dividends, taxable or tax-exempt interest income, unemployment compensation, social security benefits, railroad retirement benefits, or other income you received, include the amount withheld in the total on line 64. This should be shown in box 4 of Form 1099, box 6 of Form SSA-1099, or box 10 of Form RRB-1099.

If you had Additional Medicare Tax withheld, include the amount shown on Form 8959, line 24, in the total on line 64. Attach Form 8959.

Include on line 64 any federal income tax withheld that is shown on a Schedule K-1.

Also include on line 64 any tax withheld that is shown on Form 1042-S, Form 8805, or Form 8288-A. You should attach the form to your return to claim a credit for the withholding.

Line 65

2017 Estimated Tax Payments

Enter any estimated federal income tax payments you made for 2017. Include any overpayment that you applied to your 2017 estimated tax from:

- Your 2016 return, or
- An amended return (Form 1040X).

If you and your spouse paid joint estimated tax but are now filing separate income tax returns, you can divide the amount paid in any way you choose as long as you both agree. If you can't agree, you must divide the payments in proportion to each spouse's individual tax as shown on your separate returns for 2017. For an example and more information, see Pub. 505. Be sure to show both social security numbers (SSNs) in the space provided on the separate returns. If you or your spouse paid separate estimated tax but you are now filing a joint return, add the amounts you each paid. Follow these instructions even if your spouse died in 2017 or in 2018 before filing a 2017 return.

Divorced taxpayers. If you got divorced in 2017 and you made joint estimated tax payments with your former spouse, enter your former spouse's SSN in the space provided on the front of Form 1040. If you were divorced and remarried in 2017, enter your present spouse's SSN in the space provided on the front of Form 1040. Also, under the heading *Payments* to the left of line 65, enter your former spouse's SSN, followed by "DIV."

Name change. If you changed your name and you made estimated tax payments using your former name, attach a statement to the front of Form 1040 that explains all the payments you and your spouse made in 2017 and the name(s) and SSN(s) under which you made them.

Need more information or forms? Visit IRS.gov.

Lines 66a and 66b—
Earned Income Credit (EIC)

What Is the EIC?

The EIC is a credit for certain people who work. The credit may give you a refund even if you don't owe any tax or didn't have any tax withheld.

 You may be able to elect to use your 2016 earned income to figure your EIC if (a) your 2016 earned income is more than your 2017 earned income, and (b) your main home was located in one of the Presidentially declared disaster areas eligible for this relief on the specified date. For details, see Pub. 976.

If you make the election to use your 2016 earned income to figure your EIC, enter "PYEI" and the amount of your 2016 earned income in the space next to line 66a.

To Take the EIC:

- Follow the steps below.
- Complete the worksheet that applies to you or let the IRS figure the credit for you.
- If you have a qualifying child, complete and attach Schedule EIC.

For help in determining if you are eligible for the EIC, go to *IRS.gov/EITC* and click on "EITC Assistant." This service is available in English and Spanish.

 If you take the EIC even though you aren't eligible and it is determined that your error is due to reckless or intentional disregard of the EIC rules, you won't be allowed to take the credit for 2 years even if you are otherwise eligible to do so. If you fraudulently take the EIC, you won't be allowed to take the credit for 10 years. See Form 8862, who must file, *later. You also may have to pay penalties.*

 Refunds for returns claiming the earned income credit can't be issued before mid-February 2018. This delay applies to the entire refund, not just the portion associated with the earned income credit.

Step 1 All Filers

1. If, in 2017:
   - 3 or more children lived with you, is the amount on Form 1040, line 38, less than $48,340 ($53,930 if married filing jointly)?
   - 2 children lived with you, is the amount on Form 1040, line 38, less than $45,007 ($50,597 if married filing jointly)?
   - 1 child lived with you, is the amount on Form 1040, line 38, less than $39,617 ($45,207 if married filing jointly)?
   - No children lived with you, is the amount on Form 1040, line 38, less than $15,010 ($20,600 if married filing jointly)?

   ☐ **Yes.** Continue ↘   ☐ **No.** (STOP)

   You can't take the credit.

2. Do you, and your spouse if filing a joint return, have a social security number that allows you to work and is valid for EIC purposes (explained later under *Definitions and Special Rules*)?

   ☐ **Yes.** Continue ↘   ☐ **No.** (STOP)

   You can't take the credit. Enter "No" on the dotted line next to line 66a.

3. Is your filing status married filing separately?

   ☐ **Yes.** (STOP)   ☐ **No.** Continue ↘

   You can't take the credit.

4. Are you filing Form 2555 or 2555-EZ (relating to foreign earned income)?

   ☐ **Yes.** (STOP)   ☐ **No.** Continue ↘

   You can't take the credit.

5. Were you or your spouse a nonresident alien for any part of 2017?

   ☐ **Yes.** See *Nonresident aliens,* later, under *Definitions and Special Rules.*   ☐ **No.** Go to Step 2.

Step 2 Investment Income

1. Add the amounts from Form 1040:

Line 8a		_____
Line 8b	+	_____
Line 9a	+	_____
Line 13*	+	_____

   Investment Income = [_____]

   *If line 13 is a loss, enter -0-.

2. Is your investment income more than $3,450?

   ☐ **Yes.** Continue ↘   ☐ **No.** Skip question 3; go to question 4.

3. Are you filing Form 4797 (relating to sales of business property)?

   ☐ **Yes.** See *Form 4797 filers,* later, under *Definitions and Special Rules.*   ☐ **No.** (STOP)

   You can't take the credit.

4. Do any of the following apply for 2017?
   - You are filing Schedule E.
   - You are reporting income from the rental of personal property not used in a trade or business.
   - You are filing Form 8814 (relating to election to report child's interest and dividends on your return).
   - You have income or loss from a passive activity.

   ☐ **Yes.** Use Worksheet 1 in Pub. 596 to see if you can take the credit. ☐ **No.** Go to Step 3.

Step 3 Qualifying Child

A qualifying child for the EIC is a child who is your...

Son, daughter, stepchild, foster child, brother, sister, stepbrother, stepsister, half brother, half sister, or a descendant of any of them (for example, your grandchild, niece, or nephew)

AND

was ...

Under age 19 at the end of 2017 and younger than you
(or your spouse, if filing jointly)

or

Under age 24 at the end of 2017, a student (defined later), and younger than you
(or your spouse, if filing jointly)

or

Any age and permanently and totally disabled (defined later)

AND

Who isn't filing a joint return for 2017
or is filing a joint return for 2017 only to claim a refund of withheld income tax or estimated tax paid (see Pub. 596 for examples)

AND

Who lived with you in the United States for more than half of 2017.

⚠️ **CAUTION** *You can't take the credit for a child who didn't live with you for more than half the year, even if you paid most of the child's living expenses. The IRS may ask you for documents to show you lived with each qualifying child. Documents you might want to keep for this purpose include school and child care records and other records that show your child's address.*

💡 **TIP** *If the child didn't live with you for more than half of 2017 because of a temporary absence, birth, death, or kidnapping, see* Exception to time lived with you, *later.*

⚠️ **CAUTION** *If the child meets the conditions to be a qualifying child of any other person (other than your spouse if filing a joint return) for 2017, see* Qualifying child of more than one person, *later. If the child was married, see* Married child, *later.*

---

1. Do you have at least one child who meets the conditions to be your qualifying child?

   ☐ **Yes.** The child must have a valid social security number (SSN) as defined later, unless the child was born and died in 2017. If at least one qualifying child has a valid SSN (or was born or died in 2017), go to question 2. Otherwise, you can't take the credit. ☐ **No.** Skip questions 2 and 3; go to Step 4.

2. Are you filing a joint return for 2017?

   ☐ **Yes.** Skip question 3 and Step 4; go to Step 5. ☐ **No.** Continue ↘

3. Could you be a qualifying child of another person for 2017? (Check "No" if the other person isn't required to file, and isn't filing, a 2017 tax return or is filing a 2017 return only to claim a refund of withheld income tax or estimated tax paid (see Pub. 596 for examples).)

   ☐ **Yes.** (STOP) You can't take the credit. Enter "No" on the dotted line next to line 66a. ☐ **No.** Skip Step 4; go to Step 5.

Step 4 Filers Without a Qualifying Child

1. Is the amount on Form 1040, line 38, less than $15,010 ($20,600 if married filing jointly)?

   ☐ **Yes.** Continue ↘ ☐ **No.** (STOP) You can't take the credit.

2. Were you, or your spouse if filing a joint return, at least age 25 but under age 65 at the end of 2017? (Check "Yes" if you, or your spouse if filing a joint return, were born after December 31, 1952, and before January 2, 1993.) If your spouse died in 2017 or if you are preparing a return for someone who died in 2017, see Pub. 596 before you answer.

   ☐ **Yes.** Continue ↘ ☐ **No.** (STOP) You can't take the credit.

3. Was your main home, and your spouse's if filing a joint return, in the United States for more than half of 2017? Members of the military stationed outside the United States, see *Members of the military,* later, before you answer.

   ☐ **Yes.** Continue ↘ ☐ **No.** (STOP) You can't take the credit. Enter "No" on the dotted line next to line 66a.

4. Are you filing a joint return for 2017?

    ☐ **Yes.** Skip questions 5   ☐ **No.** Continue ↘
and 6; go to Step 5.

5. Could you be a qualifying child of another person for 2017? (Check "No" if the other person isn't required to file, and isn't filing, a 2017 tax return or is filing a 2017 return only to claim a refund of withheld income tax or estimated tax paid (see Pub. 596 for examples).)

    ☐ **Yes.** (STOP)   ☐ **No.** Continue ↘

    You can't take the
credit. Enter "No" on
the dotted line next to
line 66a.

6. Can you be claimed as a dependent on someone else's 2017 tax return?

    ☐ **Yes.** (STOP)   ☐ **No.** Go to Step 5.

    You can't take the
credit.

Step 5   Earned Income

1. Are you filing Schedule SE because you were a member of the clergy or you had church employee income of $108.28 or more?

    ☐ **Yes.** See *Clergy* or   ☐ **No.** Complete the
Church employees,   following worksheet.
whichever applies.

1. Enter the amount from Form 1040, line 7 . . .   1._____

2. Enter any amount included on Form 1040, line 7, that is a taxable scholarship or fellowship grant not reported on a Form W-2 . . . .   2._____

3. Enter any amount included on Form 1040, line 7, that you received for work performed while an inmate in a penal institution. (Enter "PRI" and the same amount on the dotted line next to Form 1040, line 7) . . . .   3._____

4. Enter any amount included on Form 1040, line 7, that you received as a pension or annuity from a nonqualified deferred compensation plan or a nongovernmental section 457 plan. (Enter "DFC" and the same amount on the dotted line next to Form 1040, line 7.) This amount may be shown in box 11 of Form W-2. If you received such an amount but box 11 is blank, contact your employer for the amount received . . . . . .   4._____

5. Enter any amount included on Form 1040, line 7, that is a Medicaid waiver payment you exclude from income. (See the instructions for line 21) . . . .   5._____

6. Add lines 2, 3, 4, and 5 . . . .   6._____

7. Subtract line 6 from line 1 . . . .   7._____

8. Enter all of your nontaxable combat pay if you elect to include it in earned income. Also enter this amount on Form 1040, line 66b. See *Combat pay, nontaxable,* later . . . .   8._____

⚠ CAUTION   *Electing to include nontaxable combat pay may increase or decrease your EIC. Figure the credit with and without your nontaxable combat pay before making the election.*

9. Add lines 7 and 8. **This is your earned income*** . . . .   9._____

* You may be able to elect to use your 2016 earned income to figure your EIC if (a) your 2016 earned income was more than your 2017 earned income, and (b) your main home was in the one of the Presidentially declared disaster areas eligible for this relief on the specified date. For details, see Pub. 976. If you make this election, skip question 2 and go to question 3.

⚠ CAUTION   *Electing to use your 2016 earned income may increase or decrease your EIC. Figure the credit using your 2017 earned income. Then figure the credit using your 2016 earned income. Compare the amounts before making the election.*

⚠ CAUTION   *If you are using your 2016 earned income to figure your 2017 EIC and you elected to include nontaxable combat pay, be sure to use 2016 nontaxable combat pay and enter that amount on line 66b.*

2. Were you self-employed at any time in 2017, or are you filing Schedule SE because you were a member of the clergy or you had church employee income, or are you filing Schedule C or C-EZ as a statutory employee?

    ☐ **Yes.** Skip question 3   ☐ **No.** Continue ↘
and Step 6; go to
Worksheet B.

3. If you have:
   - 3 or more qualifying children, is your earned income less than $48,340 ($53,930 if married filing jointly)?
   - 2 qualifying children, is your earned income less than $45,007 ($50,597 if married filing jointly)?
   - 1 qualifying child, is your earned income less than $39,617 ($45,207 if married filing jointly)?
   - No qualifying children, is your earned income less than $15,010 ($20,600 if married filing jointly)?

    ☐ **Yes.** Go to Step 6.   ☐ **No.** (STOP)

                                    You can't take the credit.

Step 6   How To Figure the Credit

1. Do you want the IRS to figure the credit for you?

    ☐ **Yes.** See *Credit*   ☐ **No.** Go to Worksheet A.
figured by the IRS, later.

Definitions and Special Rules

Adopted child. An adopted child is always treated as your own child. An adopted child includes a child lawfully placed with you for legal adoption.

Church employees. Determine how much of the amount on Form 1040, line 7, also was reported on Schedule SE, Section B, line 5a. Subtract that amount from the amount on Form 1040, line 7, and enter the result on line 1 of the worksheet in Step 5 (instead of entering the actual amount from Form 1040, line 7). Be sure to answer "Yes" to question 2 in Step 5.

Clergy. The following instructions apply to ministers, members of religious orders who have not taken a vow of poverty, and Christian Science practitioners. If you are filing Schedule SE and the amount on line 2 of that schedule includes an amount that also was reported on Form 1040, line 7:

1. Enter "Clergy" on the dotted line next to Form 1040, line 66a.

2. Determine how much of the amount on Form 1040, line 7, also was reported on Schedule SE, Section A, line 2, or Section B, line 2.

3. Subtract that amount from the amount on Form 1040, line 7. Enter the result on line 1 of the worksheet in Step 5 (instead of entering the actual amount from Form 1040, line 7).

4. Be sure to answer "Yes" to question 2 in Step 5.

Combat pay, nontaxable. If you were a member of the U.S. Armed Forces who served in a combat zone, certain pay is excluded from your income. See *Combat Zone Exclusion* in Pub. 3. You can elect to include this pay in your earned income when figuring the EIC. The amount of your nontaxable combat pay should be shown in box 12 of Form(s) W-2 with code Q. If you are filing a joint return and both you and your spouse received nontaxable combat pay, you can each make your own election. In other words, if one of you makes the election, the other one also can make it but doesn't have to.

 If you are using your 2016 earned income to figure your 2017 EIC and you elected to include nontaxable combat pay, be sure to use 2016 nontaxable combat pay and enter that amount on line 66b.

Credit figured by the IRS. To have the IRS figure your EIC:

1. Enter "EIC" on the dotted line next to Form 1040, line 66a.

2. Be sure you enter the nontaxable combat pay you elect to include in earned income on Form 1040, line 66b. See *Combat pay, nontaxable*, earlier.

3. If you have a qualifying child, complete and attach Schedule EIC. If your EIC for a year after 1996 was reduced or disallowed, see *Form 8862, who must file*, later.

Exception to time lived with you. Temporary absences by you or the child for special circumstances, such as school, vacation, business, medical care, military service, or detention in a juvenile facility, count as time the child lived with you. Also see *Kidnapped child* in the instructions for line 6c and *Members of the military*, later. A child is considered to have lived with you for more than half of 2017 if the child was born or died in 2017 and your home was this child's home for more than half the time he or she was alive in 2017.

Form 4797 filers. If the amount on Form 1040, line 13, includes an amount from Form 4797, you must use Worksheet 1 in Pub. 596 to see if you can take the EIC. Otherwise, stop; you can't take the EIC.

Form 8862, who must file. You must file Form 8862 if your EIC for a year after 1996 was reduced or disallowed for any reason other than a math or clerical error. But don't file Form 8862 if either of the following applies.

• You filed Form 8862 for another year, the EIC was allowed for that year, and your EIC hasn't been reduced or disallowed again for any reason other than a math or clerical error.

• You are taking the EIC without a qualifying child and the only reason your EIC was reduced or disallowed in the other year was because it was determined that a child listed on Schedule EIC wasn't your qualifying child.

Also, don't file Form 8862 or take the credit for the:

• 2 years after the most recent tax year for which there was a final determination that your EIC claim was due to reckless or intentional disregard of the EIC rules, or

• 10 years after the most recent tax year for which there was a final determination that your EIC claim was due to fraud.

Foster child. A foster child is any child placed with you by an authorized placement agency or by judgment, decree, or other order of any court of competent jurisdiction. For more details on authorized placement agencies, see Pub. 596.

Married child. A child who was married at the end of 2017 is a qualifying child only if (a) you can claim him or her as your dependent on Form 1040, line 6c, or (b) you could have claimed him or her as your dependent except for the special rule for *Children of divorced or separated parents* in the instructions for line 6c.

Members of the military. If you were on extended active duty outside the United States, your main home is considered to be in the United States during that duty period. Extended active duty is military duty ordered for an indefinite period or for a period of more than 90 days. Once you begin serving extended active duty, you are considered to be on extended active duty even if you don't serve more than 90 days.

Nonresident aliens. If your filing status is married filing jointly, go to Step 2. Otherwise, stop; you can't take the EIC. Enter "No" on the dotted line next to line 66a.

Permanently and totally disabled. A person is permanently and totally disabled if, at any time in 2017, the person couldn't engage in any substantial gainful activity because of a physical or mental condition and a doctor has determined that this condition (a) has lasted or can be expected to last continuously for at least a year, or (b) can be expected to lead to death.

Qualifying child of more than one person. Even if a child meets the conditions to be the qualifying child of more than one person, only one person can claim the child as a qualifying child for all of the following tax benefits, unless the special rule for *Children of divorced or separated parents* in the instructions for line 6c applies.

1. Dependency exemption (line 6c).

2. Child tax credits (lines 52 and 67).

3. Head of household filing status (line 4).

Need more information or forms? Visit IRS.gov.

4. Credit for child and dependent care expenses (line 49).

5. Exclusion for dependent care benefits (Form 2441, Part III).

6. Earned income credit (lines 66a and 66b).

No other person can take any of the six tax benefits just listed based on the qualifying child. If you and any other person can claim the child as a qualifying child, the following rules apply.

• If only one of the persons is the child's parent, the child is treated as the qualifying child of the parent.

• If the parents file a joint return together and can claim the child as a qualifying child, the child is treated as the qualifying child of the parents.

• If the parents don't file a joint return together but both parents claim the child as a qualifying child, the IRS will treat the child as the qualifying child of the parent with whom the child lived for the longer period of time in 2017. If the child lived with each parent for the same amount of time, the IRS will treat the child as the qualifying child of the parent who had the higher adjusted gross income (AGI) for 2017.

• If no parent can claim the child as a qualifying child, the child is treated as the qualifying child of the person who had the highest AGI for 2017.

• If a parent can claim the child as a qualifying child but no parent does so claim the child, the child is treated as the qualifying child of the person who had the highest AGI for 2017, but only if that person's AGI is higher than the highest AGI of any parent of the child who can claim the child.

 If, under these rules, you can't claim a child as a qualifying child for the EIC, you may be able to claim the EIC under the rules for a taxpayer without a qualifying child. For more information, see Pub. 596.

Example. Your daughter meets the conditions to be a qualifying child for both you and your mother. Your daughter doesn't meet the conditions to be a qualifying child of any other person, including her other parent. Under the rules just described, you can claim your daughter as a qualifying child for all of the six tax benefits listed here for which you otherwise qualify. Your mother can't claim any of the six tax benefits listed here based on your daughter. However, if your mother's AGI is higher than yours and you don't claim your daughter as a qualifying child, your daughter is the qualifying child of your mother.

For more details and examples, see Pub. 596.

If you won't be taking the EIC with a qualifying child, enter "No" on the dotted line next to line 66a. Otherwise, go to Step 3, question 1.

Social security number (SSN). For the EIC, a valid SSN is a number issued by the Social Security Administration unless "Not Valid for Employment" is printed on the social security card and the number was issued solely to allow the recipient of the SSN to apply for or receive a federally funded benefit. However, if "Valid for Work Only With DHS Authorization" is printed on your social security card, your SSN is valid for EIC purposes only as long as the DHS authorization is still valid.

To find out how to get an SSN, see *Social Security Number (SSN)* near the beginning of these instructions. If you won't have an SSN by the date your return is due, see *What if You Can't File on Time?*

If you didn't have an SSN by the due date of your 2017 return (including extensions), you can't claim the EIC on either your original or an amended 2017 return, even if you later get an SSN. Also, if a child didn't have an SSN by the due date of your return (including extensions), you can't count that child as a qualifying child in figuring the EIC on either your original or an amended 2017 return, even if that child later gets an SSN.

Student. A student is a child who during any part of 5 calendar months of 2017 was enrolled as a full-time student at a school, or took a full-time, on-farm training course given by a school or a state, county, or local government agency. A school includes a technical, trade, or mechanical school. It doesn't include an on-the-job training course, correspondence school, or school offering courses only through the Internet.

Welfare benefits, effect of credit on. Any refund you receive as a result of taking the EIC can't be counted as income when determining if you or anyone else is eligible for benefits or assistance, or how much you or anyone else can receive, under any federal program or under any state or local program financed in whole or in part with federal funds. These programs include Temporary Assistance for Needy Families (TANF), Medicaid, Supplemental Security Income (SSI), and Supplemental Nutrition Assistance Program (food stamps). In addition, when determining eligibility, the refund can't be counted as a resource for at least 12 months after you receive it. Check with your local benefit coordinator to find out if your refund will affect your benefits.

Worksheet A—2017 EIC—Lines 66a and 66b

Keep for Your Records

Before you begin: ✓ Be sure you are using the correct worksheet. Use this worksheet only if you answered "No" to Step 5, question 2. Otherwise, use Worksheet B.

Part 1

All Filers Using Worksheet A

1. Enter your earned income from Step 5.

   1 ☐

2. Look up the amount on line 1 above in the EIC Table (right after Worksheet B) to find the credit. Be sure you use the correct column for your filing status and the number of children you have. Enter the credit here.

   If line 2 is zero, (STOP) You can't take the credit.
   Enter "No" on the dotted line next to line 66a.

   2 ☐

3. Enter the amount from Form 1040, line 38.

   3 ☐

4. Are the amounts on lines 3 and 1 the same?

   ☐ **Yes.** Skip line 5; enter the amount from line 2 on line 6.

   ☐ **No.** Go to line 5.

Part 2

Filers Who Answered "No" on Line 4

5. If you have:
   - No qualifying children, is the amount on line 3 less than $8,350 ($13,950 if married filing jointly)?
   - 1 or more qualifying children, is the amount on line 3 less than $18,350 ($23,950 if married filing jointly)?

   ☐ **Yes.** Leave line 5 blank; enter the amount from line 2 on line 6.

   ☐ **No.** Look up the amount on line 3 in the EIC Table to find the credit. Be sure you use the correct column for your filing status and the number of children you have. Enter the credit here.
   Look at the amounts on lines 5 and 2.
   Then, enter the **smaller** amount on line 6.

   5 ☐

Part 3

Your Earned Income Credit

6. **This is your earned income credit.**

   6 ☐

   Enter this amount on
   Form 1040, line 66a.

   Reminder—

   ✓ If you have a qualifying child, complete and attach Schedule EIC.

   ⚠ **CAUTION** *If your EIC for a year after 1996 was reduced or disallowed, see Form 8862, who must file, earlier, to find out if you must file Form 8862 to take the credit for 2017.*

Need more information or forms? Visit IRS.gov.

Worksheet B—2017 EIC—Lines 66a and 66b

Keep for Your Records

Use this worksheet if you answered "Yes" to Step 5, question 2.

✓ Complete the parts below (Parts 1 through 3) that apply to you. Then, continue to Part 4.

✓ If you are married filing a joint return, include your spouse's amounts, if any, with yours to figure the amounts to enter in Parts 1 through 3.

Part 1

Self-Employed, Members of the Clergy, and People With Church Employee Income Filing Schedule SE

1a. Enter the amount from Schedule SE, Section A, line 3, or Section B, line 3, whichever applies. | **1a** |

b. Enter any amount from Schedule SE, Section B, line 4b, and line 5a. | + | **1b** |

c. Combine lines 1a and 1b. | = | **1c** |

d. Enter the amount from Schedule SE, Section A, line 6, or Section B, line 13, whichever applies. | − | **1d** |

e. Subtract line 1d from 1c. | = | **1e** |

Part 2

Self-Employed NOT Required To File Schedule SE

For example, your net earnings from self-employment were less than $400.

2. Don't include on these lines any statutory employee income, any net profit from services performed as a notary public, any amount exempt from self-employment tax as the result of the filing and approval of Form 4029 or Form 4361, or any other amounts exempt from self-employment tax.

a. Enter any net farm profit or (loss) from Schedule F, line 34, and from farm partnerships, Schedule K-1 (Form 1065), box 14, code A*. | **2a** |

b. Enter any net profit or (loss) from Schedule C, line 31; Schedule C-EZ, line 3; Schedule K-1 (Form 1065), box 14, code A (other than farming); and Schedule K-1 (Form 1065-B), box 9, code J1*. | + | **2b** |

c. Combine lines 2a and 2b. | = | **2c** |

*If you have any Schedule K-1 amounts, complete the appropriate line(s) of Schedule SE, Section A. Reduce the Schedule K-1 amounts as described in the Partner's Instructions for Schedule K-1. Enter your name and social security number on Schedule SE and attach it to your return.

Part 3

Statutory Employees Filing Schedule C or C-EZ

3. Enter the amount from Schedule C, line 1, or Schedule C-EZ, line 1, that you are filing as a statutory employee. | **3** |

Part 4

All Filers Using Worksheet B

Note. If line 4b includes income on which you should have paid self-employment tax but didn't, we may reduce your credit by the amount of self-employment tax not paid.

4a. Enter your earned income from Step 5. | **4a** |

b. Combine lines 1e, 2c, 3, and 4a. **This is your total earned income.** | **4b** |

If line 4b is zero or less, (STOP) You can't take the credit. Enter "No" on the dotted line next to line 66a.

5. If you have:
- 3 or more qualifying children, is line 4b less than $48,340 ($53,930 if married filing jointly)?
- 2 qualifying children, is line 4b less than $45,007 ($50,597 if married filing jointly)?
- 1 qualifying child, is line 4b less than $39,617 ($45,207 if married filing jointly)?
- No qualifying children, is line 4b less than $15,010 ($20,600 if married filing jointly)?

☐ **Yes.** If you want the IRS to figure your credit, see *Credit figured by the IRS*, earlier. If you want to figure the credit yourself, enter the amount from line 4b on line 6 of this worksheet.

☐ **No.** (STOP) You can't take the credit. Enter "No" on the dotted line next to line 66a.

Worksheet B—2017 EIC—Lines 66a and 66b—*Continued*   *Keep for Your Records*

Part 5
 	
All Filers Using Worksheet B
	6. Enter your total earned income from Part 4, line 4b. **6** ☐
	
	7. Look up the amount on line 6 above in the EIC Table to find the credit. Be sure you use the correct column for your filing status and the number of children you have. Enter the credit here. **7** ☐
	
	   If line 7 is zero, (STOP) You can't take the credit. Enter "No" on the dotted line next to line 66a.
	
	8. Enter the amount from Form 1040, line 38. **8** ☐
	
	9. Are the amounts on lines 8 and 6 the same?
	
	   ☐ **Yes.** Skip line 10; enter the amount from line 7 on line 11.
	
	   ☐ **No.** Go to line 10.

Part 6
 	
Filers Who Answered "No" on Line 9
	10. If you have:
	  • No qualifying children, is the amount on line 8 less than $8,350 ($13,950 if married filing jointly)?
	  • 1 or more qualifying children, is the amount on line 8 less than $18,350 ($23,950 if married filing jointly)?
	
	   ☐ **Yes.** Leave line 10 blank; enter the amount from line 7 on line 11.
	
	   ☐ **No.** Look up the amount on line 8 in the EIC Table to find the credit. Be sure you use the correct column for your filing status and the number of children you have. Enter the credit here.
	     Look at the amounts on lines 10 and 7.
	     Then, enter the **smaller** amount on line 11. **10** ☐

Part 7 **Your Earned Income Credit**	**11.** **This is your earned income credit.** **11** ☐ Enter this amount on Form 1040, line 66a. **Reminder—** ✓ If you have a qualifying child, complete and attach Schedule EIC. 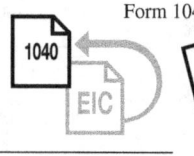  ⚠ **CAUTION** *If your EIC for a year after 1996 was reduced or disallowed, see Form 8862, who must file, earlier, to find out if you must file Form 8862 to take the credit for 2017.*

   Need more information or forms? Visit IRS.gov.

2017 Earned Income Credit (EIC) Table
Caution. This is **not** a tax table.

1. To find your credit, read down the "At least - But less than" columns and find the line that includes the amount you were told to look up from your EIC Worksheet.

2. Then, go to the column that includes your filing status and the number of qualifying children you have. Enter the credit from that column on your EIC Worksheet.

Example. If your filing status is single, you have one qualifying child, and the amount you are looking up from your EIC Worksheet is $2,455, you would enter $842.

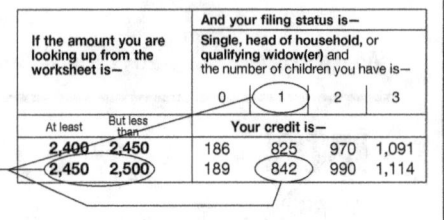

If the amount you are looking up from the worksheet is—		And your filing status is—			
		Single, head of household, or qualifying widow(er) and the number of children you have is—			
At least	But less than	0	1	2	3
		Your credit is—			
2,400	2,450	186	825	970	1,091
2,450	2,500	189	842	990	1,114

If the amount you are looking up from the worksheet is–		And your filing status is–								If the amount you are looking up from the worksheet is–		And your filing status is–							
		Single, head of household, or **qualifying widow(er)** and the number of children you have is–				Married filing jointly and the number of children you have is–						Single, head of household, or **qualifying widow(er)** and the number of children you have is–				Married filing jointly and the number of children you have is–			
		0	1	2	3	0	1	2	3			0	1	2	3	0	1	2	3
At least	But less than	Your credit is–				Your credit is–				At least	But less than	Your credit is–				Your credit is–			
$1	$50	$2	$9	$10	$11	$2	$9	$10	$11	2,800	2,850	216	961	1,130	1,271	216	961	1,130	1,271
50	100	6	26	30	34	6	26	30	34	2,850	2,900	220	978	1,150	1,294	220	978	1,150	1,294
100	150	10	43	50	56	10	43	50	56	2,900	2,950	224	995	1,170	1,316	224	995	1,170	1,316
150	200	13	60	70	79	13	60	70	79	2,950	3,000	228	1,012	1,190	1,339	228	1,012	1,190	1,339
200	250	17	77	90	101	17	77	90	101	3,000	3,050	231	1,029	1,210	1,361	231	1,029	1,210	1,361
250	300	21	94	110	124	21	94	110	124	3,050	3,100	235	1,046	1,230	1,384	235	1,046	1,230	1,384
300	350	25	111	130	146	25	111	130	146	3,100	3,150	239	1,063	1,250	1,406	239	1,063	1,250	1,406
350	400	29	128	150	169	29	128	150	169	3,150	3,200	243	1,080	1,270	1,429	243	1,080	1,270	1,429
400	450	33	145	170	191	33	145	170	191	3,200	3,250	247	1,097	1,290	1,451	247	1,097	1,290	1,451
450	500	36	162	190	214	36	162	190	214	3,250	3,300	251	1,114	1,310	1,474	251	1,114	1,310	1,474
500	550	40	179	210	236	40	179	210	236	3,300	3,350	254	1,131	1,330	1,496	254	1,131	1,330	1,496
550	600	44	196	230	259	44	196	230	259	3,350	3,400	258	1,148	1,350	1,519	258	1,148	1,350	1,519
600	650	48	213	250	281	48	213	250	281	3,400	3,450	262	1,165	1,370	1,541	262	1,165	1,370	1,541
650	700	52	230	270	304	52	230	270	304	3,450	3,500	266	1,182	1,390	1,564	266	1,182	1,390	1,564
700	750	55	247	290	326	55	247	290	326	3,500	3,550	270	1,199	1,410	1,586	270	1,199	1,410	1,586
750	800	59	264	310	349	59	264	310	349	3,550	3,600	273	1,216	1,430	1,609	273	1,216	1,430	1,609
800	850	63	281	330	371	63	281	330	371	3,600	3,650	277	1,233	1,450	1,631	277	1,233	1,450	1,631
850	900	67	298	350	394	67	298	350	394	3,650	3,700	281	1,250	1,470	1,654	281	1,250	1,470	1,654
900	950	71	315	370	416	71	315	370	416	3,700	3,750	285	1,267	1,490	1,676	285	1,267	1,490	1,676
950	1,000	75	332	390	439	75	332	390	439	3,750	3,800	289	1,284	1,510	1,699	289	1,284	1,510	1,699
1,000	1,050	78	349	410	461	78	349	410	461	3,800	3,850	293	1,301	1,530	1,721	293	1,301	1,530	1,721
1,050	1,100	82	366	430	484	82	366	430	484	3,850	3,900	296	1,318	1,550	1,744	296	1,318	1,550	1,744
1,100	1,150	86	383	450	506	86	383	450	506	3,900	3,950	300	1,335	1,570	1,766	300	1,335	1,570	1,766
1,150	1,200	90	400	470	529	90	400	470	529	3,950	4,000	304	1,352	1,590	1,789	304	1,352	1,590	1,789
1,200	1,250	94	417	490	551	94	417	490	551	4,000	4,050	308	1,369	1,610	1,811	308	1,369	1,610	1,811
1,250	1,300	98	434	510	574	98	434	510	574	4,050	4,100	312	1,386	1,630	1,834	312	1,386	1,630	1,834
1,300	1,350	101	451	530	596	101	451	530	596	4,100	4,150	316	1,403	1,650	1,856	316	1,403	1,650	1,856
1,350	1,400	105	468	550	619	105	468	550	619	4,150	4,200	319	1,420	1,670	1,879	319	1,420	1,670	1,879
1,400	1,450	109	485	570	641	109	485	570	641	4,200	4,250	323	1,437	1,690	1,901	323	1,437	1,690	1,901
1,450	1,500	113	502	590	664	113	502	590	664	4,250	4,300	327	1,454	1,710	1,924	327	1,454	1,710	1,924
1,500	1,550	117	519	610	686	117	519	610	686	4,300	4,350	331	1,471	1,730	1,946	331	1,471	1,730	1,946
1,550	1,600	120	536	630	709	120	536	630	709	4,350	4,400	335	1,488	1,750	1,969	335	1,488	1,750	1,969
1,600	1,650	124	553	650	731	124	553	650	731	4,400	4,450	339	1,505	1,770	1,991	339	1,505	1,770	1,991
1,650	1,700	128	570	670	754	128	570	670	754	4,450	4,500	342	1,522	1,790	2,014	342	1,522	1,790	2,014
1,700	1,750	132	587	690	776	132	587	690	776	4,500	4,550	346	1,539	1,810	2,036	346	1,539	1,810	2,036
1,750	1,800	136	604	710	799	136	604	710	799	4,550	4,600	350	1,556	1,830	2,059	350	1,556	1,830	2,059
1,800	1,850	140	621	730	821	140	621	730	821	4,600	4,650	354	1,573	1,850	2,081	354	1,573	1,850	2,081
1,850	1,900	143	638	750	844	143	638	750	844	4,650	4,700	358	1,590	1,870	2,104	358	1,590	1,870	2,104
1,900	1,950	147	655	770	866	147	655	770	866	4,700	4,750	361	1,607	1,890	2,126	361	1,607	1,890	2,126
1,950	2,000	151	672	790	889	151	672	790	889	4,750	4,800	365	1,624	1,910	2,149	365	1,624	1,910	2,149
2,000	2,050	155	689	810	911	155	689	810	911	4,800	4,850	369	1,641	1,930	2,171	369	1,641	1,930	2,171
2,050	2,100	159	706	830	934	159	706	830	934	4,850	4,900	373	1,658	1,950	2,194	373	1,658	1,950	2,194
2,100	2,150	163	723	850	956	163	723	850	956	4,900	4,950	377	1,675	1,970	2,216	377	1,675	1,970	2,216
2,150	2,200	166	740	870	979	166	740	870	979	4,950	5,000	381	1,692	1,990	2,239	381	1,692	1,990	2,239
2,200	2,250	170	757	890	1,001	170	757	890	1,001	5,000	5,050	384	1,709	2,010	2,261	384	1,709	2,010	2,261
2,250	2,300	174	774	910	1,024	174	774	910	1,024	5,050	5,100	388	1,726	2,030	2,284	388	1,726	2,030	2,284
2,300	2,350	178	791	930	1,046	178	791	930	1,046	5,100	5,150	392	1,743	2,050	2,306	392	1,743	2,050	2,306
2,350	2,400	182	808	950	1,069	182	808	950	1,069	5,150	5,200	396	1,760	2,070	2,329	396	1,760	2,070	2,329
2,400	2,450	186	825	970	1,091	186	825	970	1,091	5,200	5,250	400	1,777	2,090	2,351	400	1,777	2,090	2,351
2,450	2,500	189	842	990	1,114	189	842	990	1,114	5,250	5,300	404	1,794	2,110	2,374	404	1,794	2,110	2,374
2,500	2,550	193	859	1,010	1,136	193	859	1,010	1,136	5,300	5,350	407	1,811	2,130	2,396	407	1,811	2,130	2,396
2,550	2,600	197	876	1,030	1,159	197	876	1,030	1,159	5,350	5,400	411	1,828	2,150	2,419	411	1,828	2,150	2,419
2,600	2,650	201	893	1,050	1,181	201	893	1,050	1,181	5,400	5,450	415	1,845	2,170	2,441	415	1,845	2,170	2,441
2,650	2,700	205	910	1,070	1,204	205	910	1,070	1,204	5,450	5,500	419	1,862	2,190	2,464	419	1,862	2,190	2,464
2,700	2,750	208	927	1,090	1,226	208	927	1,090	1,226	5,500	5,550	423	1,879	2,210	2,486	423	1,879	2,210	2,486
2,750	2,800	212	944	1,110	1,249	212	944	1,110	1,249	5,550	5,600	426	1,896	2,230	2,509	426	1,896	2,230	2,509

(Continued)

Need more information or forms? Visit IRS.gov.

Earned Income Credit (EIC) Table - *Continued*

Left half

If the amount you are looking up from the worksheet is—		Single, head of household, or qualifying widow(er) and the number of children you have is—				Married filing jointly and the number of children you have is—			
At least	But less than	0	1	2	3	0	1	2	3
		Your credit is—				Your credit is—			
5,600	5,650	430	1,913	2,250	2,531	430	1,913	2,250	2,531
5,650	5,700	434	1,930	2,270	2,554	434	1,930	2,270	2,554
5,700	5,750	438	1,947	2,290	2,576	438	1,947	2,290	2,576
5,750	5,800	442	1,964	2,310	2,599	442	1,964	2,310	2,599
5,800	5,850	446	1,981	2,330	2,621	446	1,981	2,330	2,621
5,850	5,900	449	1,998	2,350	2,644	449	1,998	2,350	2,644
5,900	5,950	453	2,015	2,370	2,666	453	2,015	2,370	2,666
5,950	6,000	457	2,032	2,390	2,689	457	2,032	2,390	2,689
6,000	6,050	461	2,049	2,410	2,711	461	2,049	2,410	2,711
6,050	6,100	465	2,066	2,430	2,734	465	2,066	2,430	2,734
6,100	6,150	469	2,083	2,450	2,756	469	2,083	2,450	2,756
6,150	6,200	472	2,100	2,470	2,779	472	2,100	2,470	2,779
6,200	6,250	476	2,117	2,490	2,801	476	2,117	2,490	2,801
6,250	6,300	480	2,134	2,510	2,824	480	2,134	2,510	2,824
6,300	6,350	484	2,151	2,530	2,846	484	2,151	2,530	2,846
6,350	6,400	488	2,168	2,550	2,869	488	2,168	2,550	2,869
6,400	6,450	492	2,185	2,570	2,891	492	2,185	2,570	2,891
6,450	6,500	495	2,202	2,590	2,914	495	2,202	2,590	2,914
6,500	6,550	499	2,219	2,610	2,936	499	2,219	2,610	2,936
6,550	6,600	503	2,236	2,630	2,959	503	2,236	2,630	2,959
6,600	6,650	507	2,253	2,650	2,981	507	2,253	2,650	2,981
6,650	6,700	510	2,270	2,670	3,004	510	2,270	2,670	3,004
6,700	6,750	510	2,287	2,690	3,026	510	2,287	2,690	3,026
6,750	6,800	510	2,304	2,710	3,049	510	2,304	2,710	3,049
6,800	6,850	510	2,321	2,730	3,071	510	2,321	2,730	3,071
6,850	6,900	510	2,338	2,750	3,094	510	2,338	2,750	3,094
6,900	6,950	510	2,355	2,770	3,116	510	2,355	2,770	3,116
6,950	7,000	510	2,372	2,790	3,139	510	2,372	2,790	3,139
7,000	7,050	510	2,389	2,810	3,161	510	2,389	2,810	3,161
7,050	7,100	510	2,406	2,830	3,184	510	2,406	2,830	3,184
7,100	7,150	510	2,423	2,850	3,206	510	2,423	2,850	3,206
7,150	7,200	510	2,440	2,870	3,229	510	2,440	2,870	3,229
7,200	7,250	510	2,457	2,890	3,251	510	2,457	2,890	3,251
7,250	7,300	510	2,474	2,910	3,274	510	2,474	2,910	3,274
7,300	7,350	510	2,491	2,930	3,296	510	2,491	2,930	3,296
7,350	7,400	510	2,508	2,950	3,319	510	2,508	2,950	3,319
7,400	7,450	510	2,525	2,970	3,341	510	2,525	2,970	3,341
7,450	7,500	510	2,542	2,990	3,364	510	2,542	2,990	3,364
7,500	7,550	510	2,559	3,010	3,386	510	2,559	3,010	3,386
7,550	7,600	510	2,576	3,030	3,409	510	2,576	3,030	3,409
7,600	7,650	510	2,593	3,050	3,431	510	2,593	3,050	3,431
7,650	7,700	510	2,610	3,070	3,454	510	2,610	3,070	3,454
7,700	7,750	510	2,627	3,090	3,476	510	2,627	3,090	3,476
7,750	7,800	510	2,644	3,110	3,499	510	2,644	3,110	3,499
7,800	7,850	510	2,661	3,130	3,521	510	2,661	3,130	3,521
7,850	7,900	510	2,678	3,150	3,544	510	2,678	3,150	3,544
7,900	7,950	510	2,695	3,170	3,566	510	2,695	3,170	3,566
7,950	8,000	510	2,712	3,190	3,589	510	2,712	3,190	3,589
8,000	8,050	510	2,729	3,210	3,611	510	2,729	3,210	3,611
8,050	8,100	510	2,746	3,230	3,634	510	2,746	3,230	3,634
8,100	8,150	510	2,763	3,250	3,656	510	2,763	3,250	3,656
8,150	8,200	510	2,780	3,270	3,679	510	2,780	3,270	3,679
8,200	8,250	510	2,797	3,290	3,701	510	2,797	3,290	3,701
8,250	8,300	510	2,814	3,310	3,724	510	2,814	3,310	3,724
8,300	8,350	510	2,831	3,330	3,746	510	2,831	3,330	3,746
8,350	8,400	508	2,848	3,350	3,769	510	2,848	3,350	3,769
8,400	8,450	504	2,865	3,370	3,791	510	2,865	3,370	3,791
8,450	8,500	500	2,882	3,390	3,814	510	2,882	3,390	3,814
8,500	8,550	496	2,899	3,410	3,836	510	2,899	3,410	3,836
8,550	8,600	492	2,916	3,430	3,859	510	2,916	3,430	3,859
8,600	8,650	488	2,933	3,450	3,881	510	2,933	3,450	3,881
8,650	8,700	485	2,950	3,470	3,904	510	2,950	3,470	3,904
8,700	8,750	481	2,967	3,490	3,926	510	2,967	3,490	3,926
8,750	8,800	477	2,984	3,510	3,949	510	2,984	3,510	3,949

Right half

If the amount you are looking up from the worksheet is—		Single, head of household, or qualifying widow(er) and the number of children you have is—				Married filing jointly and the number of children you have is—			
At least	But less than	0	1	2	3	0	1	2	3
		Your credit is—				Your credit is—			
8,800	8,850	473	3,001	3,530	3,971	510	3,001	3,530	3,971
8,850	8,900	469	3,018	3,550	3,994	510	3,018	3,550	3,994
8,900	8,950	466	3,035	3,570	4,016	510	3,035	3,570	4,016
8,950	9,000	462	3,052	3,590	4,039	510	3,052	3,590	4,039
9,000	9,050	458	3,069	3,610	4,061	510	3,069	3,610	4,061
9,050	9,100	454	3,086	3,630	4,084	510	3,086	3,630	4,084
9,100	9,150	450	3,103	3,650	4,106	510	3,103	3,650	4,106
9,150	9,200	446	3,120	3,670	4,129	510	3,120	3,670	4,129
9,200	9,250	443	3,137	3,690	4,151	510	3,137	3,690	4,151
9,250	9,300	439	3,154	3,710	4,174	510	3,154	3,710	4,174
9,300	9,350	435	3,171	3,730	4,196	510	3,171	3,730	4,196
9,350	9,400	431	3,188	3,750	4,219	510	3,188	3,750	4,219
9,400	9,450	427	3,205	3,770	4,241	510	3,205	3,770	4,241
9,450	9,500	423	3,222	3,790	4,264	510	3,222	3,790	4,264
9,500	9,550	420	3,239	3,810	4,286	510	3,239	3,810	4,286
9,550	9,600	416	3,256	3,830	4,309	510	3,256	3,830	4,309
9,600	9,650	412	3,273	3,850	4,331	510	3,273	3,850	4,331
9,650	9,700	408	3,290	3,870	4,354	510	3,290	3,870	4,354
9,700	9,750	404	3,307	3,890	4,376	510	3,307	3,890	4,376
9,750	9,800	400	3,324	3,910	4,399	510	3,324	3,910	4,399
9,800	9,850	397	3,341	3,930	4,421	510	3,341	3,930	4,421
9,850	9,900	393	3,358	3,950	4,444	510	3,358	3,950	4,444
9,900	9,950	389	3,375	3,970	4,466	510	3,375	3,970	4,466
9,950	10,000	385	3,392	3,990	4,489	510	3,392	3,990	4,489
10,000	10,050	381	3,400	4,010	4,511	510	3,400	4,010	4,511
10,050	10,100	378	3,400	4,030	4,534	510	3,400	4,030	4,534
10,100	10,150	374	3,400	4,050	4,556	510	3,400	4,050	4,556
10,150	10,200	370	3,400	4,070	4,579	510	3,400	4,070	4,579
10,200	10,250	366	3,400	4,090	4,601	510	3,400	4,090	4,601
10,250	10,300	362	3,400	4,110	4,624	510	3,400	4,110	4,624
10,300	10,350	358	3,400	4,130	4,646	510	3,400	4,130	4,646
10,350	10,400	355	3,400	4,150	4,669	510	3,400	4,150	4,669
10,400	10,450	351	3,400	4,170	4,691	510	3,400	4,170	4,691
10,450	10,500	347	3,400	4,190	4,714	510	3,400	4,190	4,714
10,500	10,550	343	3,400	4,210	4,736	510	3,400	4,210	4,736
10,550	10,600	339	3,400	4,230	4,759	510	3,400	4,230	4,759
10,600	10,650	335	3,400	4,250	4,781	510	3,400	4,250	4,781
10,650	10,700	332	3,400	4,270	4,804	510	3,400	4,270	4,804
10,700	10,750	328	3,400	4,290	4,826	510	3,400	4,290	4,826
10,750	10,800	324	3,400	4,310	4,849	510	3,400	4,310	4,849
10,800	10,850	320	3,400	4,330	4,871	510	3,400	4,330	4,871
10,850	10,900	316	3,400	4,350	4,894	510	3,400	4,350	4,894
10,900	10,950	313	3,400	4,370	4,916	510	3,400	4,370	4,916
10,950	11,000	309	3,400	4,390	4,939	510	3,400	4,390	4,939
11,000	11,050	305	3,400	4,410	4,961	510	3,400	4,410	4,961
11,050	11,100	301	3,400	4,430	4,984	510	3,400	4,430	4,984
11,100	11,150	297	3,400	4,450	5,006	510	3,400	4,450	5,006
11,150	11,200	293	3,400	4,470	5,029	510	3,400	4,470	5,029
11,200	11,250	290	3,400	4,490	5,051	510	3,400	4,490	5,051
11,250	11,300	286	3,400	4,510	5,074	510	3,400	4,510	5,074
11,300	11,350	282	3,400	4,530	5,096	510	3,400	4,530	5,096
11,350	11,400	278	3,400	4,550	5,119	510	3,400	4,550	5,119
11,400	11,450	274	3,400	4,570	5,141	510	3,400	4,570	5,141
11,450	11,500	270	3,400	4,590	5,164	510	3,400	4,590	5,164
11,500	11,550	267	3,400	4,610	5,186	510	3,400	4,610	5,186
11,550	11,600	263	3,400	4,630	5,209	510	3,400	4,630	5,209
11,600	11,650	259	3,400	4,650	5,231	510	3,400	4,650	5,231
11,650	11,700	255	3,400	4,670	5,254	510	3,400	4,670	5,254
11,700	11,750	251	3,400	4,690	5,276	510	3,400	4,690	5,276
11,750	11,800	247	3,400	4,710	5,299	510	3,400	4,710	5,299
11,800	11,850	244	3,400	4,730	5,321	510	3,400	4,730	5,321
11,850	11,900	240	3,400	4,750	5,344	510	3,400	4,750	5,344
11,900	11,950	236	3,400	4,770	5,366	510	3,400	4,770	5,366
11,950	12,000	232	3,400	4,790	5,389	510	3,400	4,790	5,389

(Continued)

If the amount you are looking up from the worksheet is–		Single, head of household, or qualifying widow(er) and the number of children you have is–				Married filing jointly and the number of children you have is–			
At least	But less than	0	1	2	3	0	1	2	3
		Your credit is–				Your credit is–			
12,000	12,050	228	3,400	4,810	5,411	510	3,400	4,810	5,411
12,050	12,100	225	3,400	4,830	5,434	510	3,400	4,830	5,434
12,100	12,150	221	3,400	4,850	5,456	510	3,400	4,850	5,456
12,150	12,200	217	3,400	4,870	5,479	510	3,400	4,870	5,479
12,200	12,250	213	3,400	4,890	5,501	510	3,400	4,890	5,501
12,250	12,300	209	3,400	4,910	5,524	510	3,400	4,910	5,524
12,300	12,350	205	3,400	4,930	5,546	510	3,400	4,930	5,546
12,350	12,400	202	3,400	4,950	5,569	510	3,400	4,950	5,569
12,400	12,450	198	3,400	4,970	5,591	510	3,400	4,970	5,591
12,450	12,500	194	3,400	4,990	5,614	510	3,400	4,990	5,614
12,500	12,550	190	3,400	5,010	5,636	510	3,400	5,010	5,636
12,550	12,600	186	3,400	5,030	5,659	510	3,400	5,030	5,659
12,600	12,650	182	3,400	5,050	5,681	510	3,400	5,050	5,681
12,650	12,700	179	3,400	5,070	5,704	510	3,400	5,070	5,704
12,700	12,750	175	3,400	5,090	5,726	510	3,400	5,090	5,726
12,750	12,800	171	3,400	5,110	5,749	510	3,400	5,110	5,749
12,800	12,850	167	3,400	5,130	5,771	510	3,400	5,130	5,771
12,850	12,900	163	3,400	5,150	5,794	510	3,400	5,150	5,794
12,900	12,950	160	3,400	5,170	5,816	510	3,400	5,170	5,816
12,950	13,000	156	3,400	5,190	5,839	510	3,400	5,190	5,839
13,000	13,050	152	3,400	5,210	5,861	510	3,400	5,210	5,861
13,050	13,100	148	3,400	5,230	5,884	510	3,400	5,230	5,884
13,100	13,150	144	3,400	5,250	5,906	510	3,400	5,250	5,906
13,150	13,200	140	3,400	5,270	5,929	510	3,400	5,270	5,929
13,200	13,250	137	3,400	5,290	5,951	510	3,400	5,290	5,951
13,250	13,300	133	3,400	5,310	5,974	510	3,400	5,310	5,974
13,300	13,350	129	3,400	5,330	5,996	510	3,400	5,330	5,996
13,350	13,400	125	3,400	5,350	6,019	510	3,400	5,350	6,019
13,400	13,450	121	3,400	5,370	6,041	510	3,400	5,370	6,041
13,450	13,500	117	3,400	5,390	6,064	510	3,400	5,390	6,064
13,500	13,550	114	3,400	5,410	6,086	510	3,400	5,410	6,086
13,550	13,600	110	3,400	5,430	6,109	510	3,400	5,430	6,109
13,600	13,650	106	3,400	5,450	6,131	510	3,400	5,450	6,131
13,650	13,700	102	3,400	5,470	6,154	510	3,400	5,470	6,154
13,700	13,750	98	3,400	5,490	6,176	510	3,400	5,490	6,176
13,750	13,800	94	3,400	5,510	6,199	510	3,400	5,510	6,199
13,800	13,850	91	3,400	5,530	6,221	510	3,400	5,530	6,221
13,850	13,900	87	3,400	5,550	6,244	510	3,400	5,550	6,244
13,900	13,950	83	3,400	5,570	6,266	510	3,400	5,570	6,266
13,950	14,000	79	3,400	5,590	6,289	507	3,400	5,590	6,289
14,000	14,050	75	3,400	5,616	6,318	503	3,400	5,616	6,318
14,050	14,100	72	3,400	5,616	6,318	499	3,400	5,616	6,318
14,100	14,150	68	3,400	5,616	6,318	495	3,400	5,616	6,318
14,150	14,200	64	3,400	5,616	6,318	492	3,400	5,616	6,318
14,200	14,250	60	3,400	5,616	6,318	488	3,400	5,616	6,318
14,250	14,300	56	3,400	5,616	6,318	484	3,400	5,616	6,318
14,300	14,350	52	3,400	5,616	6,318	480	3,400	5,616	6,318
14,350	14,400	49	3,400	5,616	6,318	476	3,400	5,616	6,318
14,400	14,450	45	3,400	5,616	6,318	472	3,400	5,616	6,318
14,450	14,500	41	3,400	5,616	6,318	469	3,400	5,616	6,318
14,500	14,550	37	3,400	5,616	6,318	465	3,400	5,616	6,318
14,550	14,600	33	3,400	5,616	6,318	461	3,400	5,616	6,318
14,600	14,650	29	3,400	5,616	6,318	457	3,400	5,616	6,318
14,650	14,700	26	3,400	5,616	6,318	453	3,400	5,616	6,318
14,700	14,750	22	3,400	5,616	6,318	449	3,400	5,616	6,318
14,750	14,800	18	3,400	5,616	6,318	446	3,400	5,616	6,318
14,800	14,850	14	3,400	5,616	6,318	442	3,400	5,616	6,318
14,850	14,900	10	3,400	5,616	6,318	438	3,400	5,616	6,318
14,900	14,950	7	3,400	5,616	6,318	434	3,400	5,616	6,318
14,950	15,000	3	3,400	5,616	6,318	430	3,400	5,616	6,318
15,000	15,050	0	3,400	5,616	6,318	426	3,400	5,616	6,318
15,050	15,100	0	3,400	5,616	6,318	423	3,400	5,616	6,318
15,100	15,150	0	3,400	5,616	6,318	419	3,400	5,616	6,318
15,150	15,200	0	3,400	5,616	6,318	415	3,400	5,616	6,318
15,200	15,250	0	3,400	5,616	6,318	411	3,400	5,616	6,318
15,250	15,300	0	3,400	5,616	6,318	407	3,400	5,616	6,318
15,300	15,350	0	3,400	5,616	6,318	404	3,400	5,616	6,318
15,350	15,400	0	3,400	5,616	6,318	400	3,400	5,616	6,318
15,400	15,450	0	3,400	5,616	6,318	396	3,400	5,616	6,318
15,450	15,500	0	3,400	5,616	6,318	392	3,400	5,616	6,318
15,500	15,550	0	3,400	5,616	6,318	388	3,400	5,616	6,318
15,550	15,600	0	3,400	5,616	6,318	384	3,400	5,616	6,318
15,600	15,650	0	3,400	5,616	6,318	381	3,400	5,616	6,318
15,650	15,700	0	3,400	5,616	6,318	377	3,400	5,616	6,318
15,700	15,750	0	3,400	5,616	6,318	373	3,400	5,616	6,318
15,750	15,800	0	3,400	5,616	6,318	369	3,400	5,616	6,318
15,800	15,850	0	3,400	5,616	6,318	365	3,400	5,616	6,318
15,850	15,900	0	3,400	5,616	6,318	361	3,400	5,616	6,318
15,900	15,950	0	3,400	5,616	6,318	358	3,400	5,616	6,318
15,950	16,000	0	3,400	5,616	6,318	354	3,400	5,616	6,318
16,000	16,050	0	3,400	5,616	6,318	350	3,400	5,616	6,318
16,050	16,100	0	3,400	5,616	6,318	346	3,400	5,616	6,318
16,100	16,150	0	3,400	5,616	6,318	342	3,400	5,616	6,318
16,150	16,200	0	3,400	5,616	6,318	339	3,400	5,616	6,318
16,200	16,250	0	3,400	5,616	6,318	335	3,400	5,616	6,318
16,250	16,300	0	3,400	5,616	6,318	331	3,400	5,616	6,318
16,300	16,350	0	3,400	5,616	6,318	327	3,400	5,616	6,318
16,350	16,400	0	3,400	5,616	6,318	323	3,400	5,616	6,318
16,400	16,450	0	3,400	5,616	6,318	319	3,400	5,616	6,318
16,450	16,500	0	3,400	5,616	6,318	316	3,400	5,616	6,318
16,500	16,550	0	3,400	5,616	6,318	312	3,400	5,616	6,318
16,550	16,600	0	3,400	5,616	6,318	308	3,400	5,616	6,318
16,600	16,650	0	3,400	5,616	6,318	304	3,400	5,616	6,318
16,650	16,700	0	3,400	5,616	6,318	300	3,400	5,616	6,318
16,700	16,750	0	3,400	5,616	6,318	296	3,400	5,616	6,318
16,750	16,800	0	3,400	5,616	6,318	293	3,400	5,616	6,318
16,800	16,850	0	3,400	5,616	6,318	289	3,400	5,616	6,318
16,850	16,900	0	3,400	5,616	6,318	285	3,400	5,616	6,318
16,900	16,950	0	3,400	5,616	6,318	281	3,400	5,616	6,318
16,950	17,000	0	3,400	5,616	6,318	277	3,400	5,616	6,318
17,000	17,050	0	3,400	5,616	6,318	273	3,400	5,616	6,318
17,050	17,100	0	3,400	5,616	6,318	270	3,400	5,616	6,318
17,100	17,150	0	3,400	5,616	6,318	266	3,400	5,616	6,318
17,150	17,200	0	3,400	5,616	6,318	262	3,400	5,616	6,318
17,200	17,250	0	3,400	5,616	6,318	258	3,400	5,616	6,318
17,250	17,300	0	3,400	5,616	6,318	254	3,400	5,616	6,318
17,300	17,350	0	3,400	5,616	6,318	251	3,400	5,616	6,318
17,350	17,400	0	3,400	5,616	6,318	247	3,400	5,616	6,318
17,400	17,450	0	3,400	5,616	6,318	243	3,400	5,616	6,318
17,450	17,500	0	3,400	5,616	6,318	239	3,400	5,616	6,318
17,500	17,550	0	3,400	5,616	6,318	235	3,400	5,616	6,318
17,550	17,600	0	3,400	5,616	6,318	231	3,400	5,616	6,318
17,600	17,650	0	3,400	5,616	6,318	228	3,400	5,616	6,318
17,650	17,700	0	3,400	5,616	6,318	224	3,400	5,616	6,318
17,700	17,750	0	3,400	5,616	6,318	220	3,400	5,616	6,318
17,750	17,800	0	3,400	5,616	6,318	216	3,400	5,616	6,318
17,800	17,850	0	3,400	5,616	6,318	212	3,400	5,616	6,318
17,850	17,900	0	3,400	5,616	6,318	208	3,400	5,616	6,318
17,900	17,950	0	3,400	5,616	6,318	205	3,400	5,616	6,318
17,950	18,000	0	3,400	5,616	6,318	201	3,400	5,616	6,318
18,000	18,050	0	3,400	5,616	6,318	197	3,400	5,616	6,318
18,050	18,100	0	3,400	5,616	6,318	193	3,400	5,616	6,318
18,100	18,150	0	3,400	5,616	6,318	189	3,400	5,616	6,318
18,150	18,200	0	3,400	5,616	6,318	186	3,400	5,616	6,318
18,200	18,250	0	3,400	5,616	6,318	182	3,400	5,616	6,318
18,250	18,300	0	3,400	5,616	6,318	178	3,400	5,616	6,318
18,300	18,350	0	3,400	5,616	6,318	174	3,400	5,616	6,318
18,350	18,400	0	3,394	5,609	6,311	170	3,400	5,616	6,318

(Continued)

Need more information or forms? Visit IRS.gov.

Earned Income Credit (EIC) Table - *Continued*

(Caution. This is not a tax table.)

If the amount you are looking up from the worksheet is–		And your filing status is–							
		Single, head of household, or qualifying widow(er) and the number of children you have is–				Married filing jointly and the number of children you have is–			
At least	But less than	0	1	2	3	0	1	2	3
		Your credit is–				Your credit is–			
18,400	18,450	0	3,386	5,598	6,300	166	3,400	5,616	6,318
18,450	18,500	0	3,378	5,588	6,290	163	3,400	5,616	6,318
18,500	18,550	0	3,370	5,577	6,279	159	3,400	5,616	6,318
18,550	18,600	0	3,362	5,567	6,269	155	3,400	5,616	6,318
18,600	18,650	0	3,354	5,556	6,258	151	3,400	5,616	6,318
18,650	18,700	0	3,346	5,545	6,247	147	3,400	5,616	6,318
18,700	18,750	0	3,338	5,535	6,237	143	3,400	5,616	6,318
18,750	18,800	0	3,330	5,524	6,226	140	3,400	5,616	6,318
18,800	18,850	0	3,322	5,514	6,216	136	3,400	5,616	6,318
18,850	18,900	0	3,315	5,503	6,205	132	3,400	5,616	6,318
18,900	18,950	0	3,307	5,493	6,195	128	3,400	5,616	6,318
18,950	19,000	0	3,299	5,482	6,184	124	3,400	5,616	6,318
19,000	19,050	0	3,291	5,472	6,174	120	3,400	5,616	6,318
19,050	19,100	0	3,283	5,461	6,163	117	3,400	5,616	6,318
19,100	19,150	0	3,275	5,451	6,153	113	3,400	5,616	6,318
19,150	19,200	0	3,267	5,440	6,142	109	3,400	5,616	6,318
19,200	19,250	0	3,259	5,430	6,132	105	3,400	5,616	6,318
19,250	19,300	0	3,251	5,419	6,121	101	3,400	5,616	6,318
19,300	19,350	0	3,243	5,409	6,111	98	3,400	5,616	6,318
19,350	19,400	0	3,235	5,398	6,100	94	3,400	5,616	6,318
19,400	19,450	0	3,227	5,387	6,089	90	3,400	5,616	6,318
19,450	19,500	0	3,219	5,377	6,079	86	3,400	5,616	6,318
19,500	19,550	0	3,211	5,366	6,068	82	3,400	5,616	6,318
19,550	19,600	0	3,203	5,356	6,058	78	3,400	5,616	6,318
19,600	19,650	0	3,195	5,345	6,047	75	3,400	5,616	6,318
19,650	19,700	0	3,187	5,335	6,037	71	3,400	5,616	6,318
19,700	19,750	0	3,179	5,324	6,026	67	3,400	5,616	6,318
19,750	19,800	0	3,171	5,314	6,016	63	3,400	5,616	6,318
19,800	19,850	0	3,163	5,303	6,005	59	3,400	5,616	6,318
19,850	19,900	0	3,155	5,293	5,995	55	3,400	5,616	6,318
19,900	19,950	0	3,147	5,282	5,984	52	3,400	5,616	6,318
19,950	20,000	0	3,139	5,272	5,974	48	3,400	5,616	6,318
20,000	20,050	0	3,131	5,261	5,963	44	3,400	5,616	6,318
20,050	20,100	0	3,123	5,251	5,953	40	3,400	5,616	6,318
20,100	20,150	0	3,115	5,240	5,942	36	3,400	5,616	6,318
20,150	20,200	0	3,107	5,230	5,932	33	3,400	5,616	6,318
20,200	20,250	0	3,099	5,219	5,921	29	3,400	5,616	6,318
20,250	20,300	0	3,091	5,208	5,910	25	3,400	5,616	6,318
20,300	20,350	0	3,083	5,198	5,900	21	3,400	5,616	6,318
20,350	20,400	0	3,075	5,187	5,889	17	3,400	5,616	6,318
20,400	20,450	0	3,067	5,177	5,879	13	3,400	5,616	6,318
20,450	20,500	0	3,059	5,166	5,868	10	3,400	5,616	6,318
20,500	20,550	0	3,051	5,156	5,858	6	3,400	5,616	6,318
20,550	20,600	0	3,043	5,145	5,847	*	3,400	5,616	6,318
20,600	20,650	0	3,035	5,135	5,837	0	3,400	5,616	6,318
20,650	20,700	0	3,027	5,124	5,826	0	3,400	5,616	6,318
20,700	20,750	0	3,019	5,114	5,816	0	3,400	5,616	6,318
20,750	20,800	0	3,011	5,103	5,805	0	3,400	5,616	6,318
20,800	20,850	0	3,003	5,093	5,795	0	3,400	5,616	6,318
20,850	20,900	0	2,995	5,082	5,784	0	3,400	5,616	6,318
20,900	20,950	0	2,987	5,072	5,774	0	3,400	5,616	6,318
20,950	21,000	0	2,979	5,061	5,763	0	3,400	5,616	6,318
21,000	21,050	0	2,971	5,051	5,753	0	3,400	5,616	6,318
21,050	21,100	0	2,963	5,040	5,742	0	3,400	5,616	6,318
21,100	21,150	0	2,955	5,029	5,731	0	3,400	5,616	6,318
21,150	21,200	0	2,947	5,019	5,721	0	3,400	5,616	6,318
21,200	21,250	0	2,939	5,008	5,710	0	3,400	5,616	6,318
21,250	21,300	0	2,931	4,998	5,700	0	3,400	5,616	6,318
21,300	21,350	0	2,923	4,987	5,689	0	3,400	5,616	6,318
21,350	21,400	0	2,915	4,977	5,679	0	3,400	5,616	6,318
21,400	21,450	0	2,907	4,966	5,668	0	3,400	5,616	6,318
21,450	21,500	0	2,899	4,956	5,658	0	3,400	5,616	6,318
21,500	21,550	0	2,891	4,945	5,647	0	3,400	5,616	6,318
21,550	21,600	0	2,883	4,935	5,637	0	3,400	5,616	6,318

If the amount you are looking up from the worksheet is–		And your filing status is–							
		Single, head of household, or qualifying widow(er) and the number of children you have is–				Married filing jointly and the number of children you have is–			
At least	But less than	0	1	2	3	0	1	2	3
		Your credit is–				Your credit is–			
21,600	21,650	0	2,875	4,924	5,626	0	3,400	5,616	6,318
21,650	21,700	0	2,867	4,914	5,616	0	3,400	5,616	6,318
21,700	21,750	0	2,859	4,903	5,605	0	3,400	5,616	6,318
21,750	21,800	0	2,851	4,893	5,595	0	3,400	5,616	6,318
21,800	21,850	0	2,843	4,882	5,584	0	3,400	5,616	6,318
21,850	21,900	0	2,835	4,872	5,574	0	3,400	5,616	6,318
21,900	21,950	0	2,827	4,861	5,563	0	3,400	5,616	6,318
21,950	22,000	0	2,819	4,850	5,552	0	3,400	5,616	6,318
22,000	22,050	0	2,811	4,840	5,542	0	3,400	5,616	6,318
22,050	22,100	0	2,803	4,829	5,531	0	3,400	5,616	6,318
22,100	22,150	0	2,795	4,819	5,521	0	3,400	5,616	6,318
22,150	22,200	0	2,787	4,808	5,510	0	3,400	5,616	6,318
22,200	22,250	0	2,779	4,798	5,500	0	3,400	5,616	6,318
22,250	22,300	0	2,771	4,787	5,489	0	3,400	5,616	6,318
22,300	22,350	0	2,763	4,777	5,479	0	3,400	5,616	6,318
22,350	22,400	0	2,755	4,766	5,468	0	3,400	5,616	6,318
22,400	22,450	0	2,747	4,756	5,458	0	3,400	5,616	6,318
22,450	22,500	0	2,739	4,745	5,447	0	3,400	5,616	6,318
22,500	22,550	0	2,731	4,735	5,437	0	3,400	5,616	6,318
22,550	22,600	0	2,723	4,724	5,426	0	3,400	5,616	6,318
22,600	22,650	0	2,715	4,714	5,416	0	3,400	5,616	6,318
22,650	22,700	0	2,707	4,703	5,405	0	3,400	5,616	6,318
22,700	22,750	0	2,699	4,693	5,395	0	3,400	5,616	6,318
22,750	22,800	0	2,691	4,682	5,384	0	3,400	5,616	6,318
22,800	22,850	0	2,683	4,671	5,373	0	3,400	5,616	6,318
22,850	22,900	0	2,675	4,661	5,363	0	3,400	5,616	6,318
22,900	22,950	0	2,667	4,650	5,352	0	3,400	5,616	6,318
22,950	23,000	0	2,659	4,640	5,342	0	3,400	5,616	6,318
23,000	23,050	0	2,651	4,629	5,331	0	3,400	5,616	6,318
23,050	23,100	0	2,643	4,619	5,321	0	3,400	5,616	6,318
23,100	23,150	0	2,635	4,608	5,310	0	3,400	5,616	6,318
23,150	23,200	0	2,627	4,598	5,300	0	3,400	5,616	6,318
23,200	23,250	0	2,619	4,587	5,289	0	3,400	5,616	6,318
23,250	23,300	0	2,611	4,577	5,279	0	3,400	5,616	6,318
23,300	23,350	0	2,603	4,566	5,268	0	3,400	5,616	6,318
23,350	23,400	0	2,595	4,556	5,258	0	3,400	5,616	6,318
23,400	23,450	0	2,587	4,545	5,247	0	3,400	5,616	6,318
23,450	23,500	0	2,579	4,535	5,237	0	3,400	5,616	6,318
23,500	23,550	0	2,571	4,524	5,226	0	3,400	5,616	6,318
23,550	23,600	0	2,563	4,514	5,216	0	3,400	5,616	6,318
23,600	23,650	0	2,555	4,503	5,205	0	3,400	5,616	6,318
23,650	23,700	0	2,547	4,492	5,194	0	3,400	5,616	6,318
23,700	23,750	0	2,539	4,482	5,184	0	3,400	5,616	6,318
23,750	23,800	0	2,531	4,471	5,173	0	3,400	5,616	6,318
23,800	23,850	0	2,523	4,461	5,163	0	3,400	5,616	6,318
23,850	23,900	0	2,516	4,450	5,152	0	3,400	5,616	6,318
23,900	23,950	0	2,508	4,440	5,142	0	3,400	5,616	6,318
23,950	24,000	0	2,500	4,429	5,131	0	3,393	5,607	6,309
24,000	24,050	0	2,492	4,419	5,121	0	3,385	5,596	6,298
24,050	24,100	0	2,484	4,408	5,110	0	3,377	5,585	6,287
24,100	24,150	0	2,476	4,398	5,100	0	3,369	5,575	6,277
24,150	24,200	0	2,468	4,387	5,089	0	3,361	5,564	6,266
24,200	24,250	0	2,460	4,377	5,079	0	3,353	5,554	6,256
24,250	24,300	0	2,452	4,366	5,068	0	3,345	5,543	6,245
24,300	24,350	0	2,444	4,356	5,058	0	3,337	5,533	6,235
24,350	24,400	0	2,436	4,345	5,047	0	3,329	5,522	6,224
24,400	24,450	0	2,428	4,334	5,036	0	3,321	5,512	6,214
24,450	24,500	0	2,420	4,324	5,026	0	3,313	5,501	6,203
24,500	24,550	0	2,412	4,313	5,015	0	3,305	5,491	6,193
24,550	24,600	0	2,404	4,303	5,005	0	3,297	5,480	6,182
24,600	24,650	0	2,396	4,292	4,994	0	3,289	5,470	6,172
24,650	24,700	0	2,388	4,282	4,984	0	3,281	5,459	6,161
24,700	24,750	0	2,380	4,271	4,973	0	3,273	5,449	6,151
24,750	24,800	0	2,372	4,261	4,963	0	3,265	5,438	6,140

* If the amount you're looking up from the worksheet is at least $20,550 but less than $20,600, and you have no qualifying children, your credit is $2.
If the amount you're looking up from the worksheet is $20,600 or more, and you have no qualifying children, you can't take the credit.

(Continued)

If the amount you are looking up from the worksheet is–		And your filing status is–							
		Single, head of household, or qualifying widow(er) and the number of children you have is–				Married filing jointly and the number of children you have is–			
At least	But less than	0	1	2	3	0	1	2	3
		Your credit is–				Your credit is–			
24,800	24,850	0	2,364	4,250	4,952	0	3,257	5,428	6,130
24,850	24,900	0	2,356	4,240	4,942	0	3,249	5,417	6,119
24,900	24,950	0	2,348	4,229	4,931	0	3,241	5,406	6,108
24,950	25,000	0	2,340	4,219	4,921	0	3,233	5,396	6,098
25,000	25,050	0	2,332	4,208	4,910	0	3,225	5,385	6,087
25,050	25,100	0	2,324	4,198	4,900	0	3,217	5,375	6,077
25,100	25,150	0	2,316	4,187	4,889	0	3,209	5,364	6,066
25,150	25,200	0	2,308	4,177	4,879	0	3,201	5,354	6,056
25,200	25,250	0	2,300	4,166	4,868	0	3,193	5,343	6,045
25,250	25,300	0	2,292	4,155	4,857	0	3,185	5,333	6,035
25,300	25,350	0	2,284	4,145	4,847	0	3,177	5,322	6,024
25,350	25,400	0	2,276	4,134	4,836	0	3,169	5,312	6,014
25,400	25,450	0	2,268	4,124	4,826	0	3,161	5,301	6,003
25,450	25,500	0	2,260	4,113	4,815	0	3,153	5,291	5,993
25,500	25,550	0	2,252	4,103	4,805	0	3,145	5,280	5,982
25,550	25,600	0	2,244	4,092	4,794	0	3,137	5,270	5,972
25,600	25,650	0	2,236	4,082	4,784	0	3,129	5,259	5,961
25,650	25,700	0	2,228	4,071	4,773	0	3,121	5,249	5,951
25,700	25,750	0	2,220	4,061	4,763	0	3,113	5,238	5,940
25,750	25,800	0	2,212	4,050	4,752	0	3,105	5,227	5,929
25,800	25,850	0	2,204	4,040	4,742	0	3,097	5,217	5,919
25,850	25,900	0	2,196	4,029	4,731	0	3,089	5,206	5,908
25,900	25,950	0	2,188	4,019	4,721	0	3,081	5,196	5,898
25,950	26,000	0	2,180	4,008	4,710	0	3,073	5,185	5,887
26,000	26,050	0	2,172	3,998	4,700	0	3,065	5,175	5,877
26,050	26,100	0	2,164	3,987	4,689	0	3,057	5,164	5,866
26,100	26,150	0	2,156	3,976	4,678	0	3,049	5,154	5,856
26,150	26,200	0	2,148	3,966	4,668	0	3,041	5,143	5,845
26,200	26,250	0	2,140	3,955	4,657	0	3,033	5,133	5,835
26,250	26,300	0	2,132	3,945	4,647	0	3,025	5,122	5,824
26,300	26,350	0	2,124	3,934	4,636	0	3,017	5,112	5,814
26,350	26,400	0	2,116	3,924	4,626	0	3,009	5,101	5,803
26,400	26,450	0	2,108	3,913	4,615	0	3,001	5,091	5,793
26,450	26,500	0	2,100	3,903	4,605	0	2,993	5,080	5,782
26,500	26,550	0	2,092	3,892	4,594	0	2,985	5,069	5,771
26,550	26,600	0	2,084	3,882	4,584	0	2,977	5,059	5,761
26,600	26,650	0	2,076	3,871	4,573	0	2,969	5,048	5,750
26,650	26,700	0	2,068	3,861	4,563	0	2,961	5,038	5,740
26,700	26,750	0	2,060	3,850	4,552	0	2,953	5,027	5,729
26,750	26,800	0	2,052	3,840	4,542	0	2,945	5,017	5,719
26,800	26,850	0	2,044	3,829	4,531	0	2,937	5,006	5,708
26,850	26,900	0	2,036	3,819	4,521	0	2,929	4,996	5,698
26,900	26,950	0	2,028	3,808	4,510	0	2,921	4,985	5,687
26,950	27,000	0	2,020	3,797	4,499	0	2,913	4,975	5,677
27,000	27,050	0	2,012	3,787	4,489	0	2,905	4,964	5,666
27,050	27,100	0	2,004	3,776	4,478	0	2,897	4,954	5,656
27,100	27,150	0	1,996	3,766	4,468	0	2,889	4,943	5,645
27,150	27,200	0	1,988	3,755	4,457	0	2,881	4,933	5,635
27,200	27,250	0	1,980	3,745	4,447	0	2,873	4,922	5,624
27,250	27,300	0	1,972	3,734	4,436	0	2,865	4,912	5,614
27,300	27,350	0	1,964	3,724	4,426	0	2,857	4,901	5,603
27,350	27,400	0	1,956	3,713	4,415	0	2,849	4,890	5,592
27,400	27,450	0	1,948	3,703	4,405	0	2,841	4,880	5,582
27,450	27,500	0	1,940	3,692	4,394	0	2,834	4,869	5,571
27,500	27,550	0	1,932	3,682	4,384	0	2,826	4,859	5,561
27,550	27,600	0	1,924	3,671	4,373	0	2,818	4,848	5,550
27,600	27,650	0	1,916	3,661	4,363	0	2,810	4,838	5,540
27,650	27,700	0	1,908	3,650	4,352	0	2,802	4,827	5,529
27,700	27,750	0	1,900	3,640	4,342	0	2,794	4,817	5,519
27,750	27,800	0	1,892	3,629	4,331	0	2,786	4,806	5,508
27,800	27,850	0	1,884	3,618	4,320	0	2,778	4,796	5,498
27,850	27,900	0	1,876	3,608	4,310	0	2,770	4,785	5,487
27,900	27,950	0	1,868	3,597	4,299	0	2,762	4,775	5,477
27,950	28,000	0	1,860	3,587	4,289	0	2,754	4,764	5,466

If the amount you are looking up from the worksheet is–		And your filing status is–							
		Single, head of household, or qualifying widow(er) and the number of children you have is–				Married filing jointly and the number of children you have is–			
At least	But less than	0	1	2	3	0	1	2	3
		Your credit is–				Your credit is–			
28,000	28,050	0	1,852	3,576	4,278	0	2,746	4,754	5,456
28,050	28,100	0	1,844	3,566	4,268	0	2,738	4,743	5,445
28,100	28,150	0	1,836	3,555	4,257	0	2,730	4,733	5,435
28,150	28,200	0	1,828	3,545	4,247	0	2,722	4,722	5,424
28,200	28,250	0	1,820	3,534	4,236	0	2,714	4,711	5,413
28,250	28,300	0	1,812	3,524	4,226	0	2,706	4,701	5,403
28,300	28,350	0	1,804	3,513	4,215	0	2,698	4,690	5,392
28,350	28,400	0	1,796	3,503	4,205	0	2,690	4,680	5,382
28,400	28,450	0	1,788	3,492	4,194	0	2,682	4,669	5,371
28,450	28,500	0	1,780	3,482	4,184	0	2,674	4,659	5,361
28,500	28,550	0	1,772	3,471	4,173	0	2,666	4,648	5,350
28,550	28,600	0	1,764	3,461	4,163	0	2,658	4,638	5,340
28,600	28,650	0	1,756	3,450	4,152	0	2,650	4,627	5,329
28,650	28,700	0	1,748	3,439	4,141	0	2,642	4,617	5,319
28,700	28,750	0	1,740	3,429	4,131	0	2,634	4,606	5,308
28,750	28,800	0	1,732	3,418	4,120	0	2,626	4,596	5,298
28,800	28,850	0	1,724	3,408	4,110	0	2,618	4,585	5,287
28,850	28,900	0	1,717	3,397	4,099	0	2,610	4,575	5,277
28,900	28,950	0	1,709	3,387	4,089	0	2,602	4,564	5,266
28,950	29,000	0	1,701	3,376	4,078	0	2,594	4,554	5,256
29,000	29,050	0	1,693	3,366	4,068	0	2,586	4,543	5,245
29,050	29,100	0	1,685	3,355	4,057	0	2,578	4,532	5,234
29,100	29,150	0	1,677	3,345	4,047	0	2,570	4,522	5,224
29,150	29,200	0	1,669	3,334	4,036	0	2,562	4,511	5,213
29,200	29,250	0	1,661	3,324	4,026	0	2,554	4,501	5,203
29,250	29,300	0	1,653	3,313	4,015	0	2,546	4,490	5,192
29,300	29,350	0	1,645	3,303	4,005	0	2,538	4,480	5,182
29,350	29,400	0	1,637	3,292	3,994	0	2,530	4,469	5,171
29,400	29,450	0	1,629	3,281	3,983	0	2,522	4,459	5,161
29,450	29,500	0	1,621	3,271	3,973	0	2,514	4,448	5,150
29,500	29,550	0	1,613	3,260	3,962	0	2,506	4,438	5,140
29,550	29,600	0	1,605	3,250	3,952	0	2,498	4,427	5,129
29,600	29,650	0	1,597	3,239	3,941	0	2,490	4,417	5,119
29,650	29,700	0	1,589	3,229	3,931	0	2,482	4,406	5,108
29,700	29,750	0	1,581	3,218	3,920	0	2,474	4,396	5,098
29,750	29,800	0	1,573	3,208	3,910	0	2,466	4,385	5,087
29,800	29,850	0	1,565	3,197	3,899	0	2,458	4,375	5,077
29,850	29,900	0	1,557	3,187	3,889	0	2,450	4,364	5,066
29,900	29,950	0	1,549	3,176	3,878	0	2,442	4,353	5,055
29,950	30,000	0	1,541	3,166	3,868	0	2,434	4,343	5,045
30,000	30,050	0	1,533	3,155	3,857	0	2,426	4,332	5,034
30,050	30,100	0	1,525	3,145	3,847	0	2,418	4,322	5,024
30,100	30,150	0	1,517	3,134	3,836	0	2,410	4,311	5,013
30,150	30,200	0	1,509	3,124	3,826	0	2,402	4,301	5,003
30,200	30,250	0	1,501	3,113	3,815	0	2,394	4,290	4,992
30,250	30,300	0	1,493	3,102	3,804	0	2,386	4,280	4,982
30,300	30,350	0	1,485	3,092	3,794	0	2,378	4,269	4,971
30,350	30,400	0	1,477	3,081	3,783	0	2,370	4,259	4,961
30,400	30,450	0	1,469	3,071	3,773	0	2,362	4,248	4,950
30,450	30,500	0	1,461	3,060	3,762	0	2,354	4,238	4,940
30,500	30,550	0	1,453	3,050	3,752	0	2,346	4,227	4,929
30,550	30,600	0	1,445	3,039	3,741	0	2,338	4,217	4,919
30,600	30,650	0	1,437	3,029	3,731	0	2,330	4,206	4,908
30,650	30,700	0	1,429	3,018	3,720	0	2,322	4,196	4,898
30,700	30,750	0	1,421	3,008	3,710	0	2,314	4,185	4,887
30,750	30,800	0	1,413	2,997	3,699	0	2,306	4,174	4,876
30,800	30,850	0	1,405	2,987	3,689	0	2,298	4,164	4,866
30,850	30,900	0	1,397	2,976	3,678	0	2,290	4,153	4,855
30,900	30,950	0	1,389	2,966	3,668	0	2,282	4,143	4,845
30,950	31,000	0	1,381	2,955	3,657	0	2,274	4,132	4,834
31,000	31,050	0	1,373	2,945	3,647	0	2,266	4,122	4,824
31,050	31,100	0	1,365	2,934	3,636	0	2,258	4,111	4,813
31,100	31,150	0	1,357	2,923	3,625	0	2,250	4,101	4,803
31,150	31,200	0	1,349	2,913	3,615	0	2,242	4,090	4,792

(Continued)

Need more information or forms? Visit IRS.gov.

(**Caution.** This is **not** a tax table.)

If the amount you are looking up from the worksheet is–		Single, head of household, or qualifying widow(er) and the number of children you have is–				Married filing jointly and the number of children you have is–			
At least	But less than	0	1	2	3	0	1	2	3
		Your credit is–				Your credit is–			
31,200	31,250	0	1,341	2,902	3,604	0	2,234	4,080	4,782
31,250	31,300	0	1,333	2,892	3,594	0	2,226	4,069	4,771
31,300	31,350	0	1,325	2,881	3,583	0	2,218	4,059	4,761
31,350	31,400	0	1,317	2,871	3,573	0	2,210	4,048	4,750
31,400	31,450	0	1,309	2,860	3,562	0	2,202	4,038	4,740
31,450	31,500	0	1,301	2,850	3,552	0	2,194	4,027	4,729
31,500	31,550	0	1,293	2,839	3,541	0	2,186	4,016	4,718
31,550	31,600	0	1,285	2,829	3,531	0	2,178	4,006	4,708
31,600	31,650	0	1,277	2,818	3,520	0	2,170	3,995	4,697
31,650	31,700	0	1,269	2,808	3,510	0	2,162	3,985	4,687
31,700	31,750	0	1,261	2,797	3,499	0	2,154	3,974	4,676
31,750	31,800	0	1,253	2,787	3,489	0	2,146	3,964	4,666
31,800	31,850	0	1,245	2,776	3,478	0	2,138	3,953	4,655
31,850	31,900	0	1,237	2,766	3,468	0	2,130	3,943	4,645
31,900	31,950	0	1,229	2,755	3,457	0	2,122	3,932	4,634
31,950	32,000	0	1,221	2,744	3,446	0	2,114	3,922	4,624
32,000	32,050	0	1,213	2,734	3,436	0	2,106	3,911	4,613
32,050	32,100	0	1,205	2,723	3,425	0	2,098	3,901	4,603
32,100	32,150	0	1,197	2,713	3,415	0	2,090	3,890	4,592
32,150	32,200	0	1,189	2,702	3,404	0	2,082	3,880	4,582
32,200	32,250	0	1,181	2,692	3,394	0	2,074	3,869	4,571
32,250	32,300	0	1,173	2,681	3,383	0	2,066	3,859	4,561
32,300	32,350	0	1,165	2,671	3,373	0	2,058	3,848	4,550
32,350	32,400	0	1,157	2,660	3,362	0	2,050	3,837	4,539
32,400	32,450	0	1,149	2,650	3,352	0	2,042	3,827	4,529
32,450	32,500	0	1,141	2,639	3,341	0	2,035	3,816	4,518
32,500	32,550	0	1,133	2,629	3,331	0	2,027	3,806	4,508
32,550	32,600	0	1,125	2,618	3,320	0	2,019	3,795	4,497
32,600	32,650	0	1,117	2,608	3,310	0	2,011	3,785	4,487
32,650	32,700	0	1,109	2,597	3,299	0	2,003	3,774	4,476
32,700	32,750	0	1,101	2,587	3,289	0	1,995	3,764	4,466
32,750	32,800	0	1,093	2,576	3,278	0	1,987	3,753	4,455
32,800	32,850	0	1,085	2,565	3,267	0	1,979	3,743	4,445
32,850	32,900	0	1,077	2,555	3,257	0	1,971	3,732	4,434
32,900	32,950	0	1,069	2,544	3,246	0	1,963	3,722	4,424
32,950	33,000	0	1,061	2,534	3,236	0	1,955	3,711	4,413
33,000	33,050	0	1,053	2,523	3,225	0	1,947	3,701	4,403
33,050	33,100	0	1,045	2,513	3,215	0	1,939	3,690	4,392
33,100	33,150	0	1,037	2,502	3,204	0	1,931	3,680	4,382
33,150	33,200	0	1,029	2,492	3,194	0	1,923	3,669	4,371
33,200	33,250	0	1,021	2,481	3,183	0	1,915	3,658	4,360
33,250	33,300	0	1,013	2,471	3,173	0	1,907	3,648	4,350
33,300	33,350	0	1,005	2,460	3,162	0	1,899	3,637	4,339
33,350	33,400	0	997	2,450	3,152	0	1,891	3,627	4,329
33,400	33,450	0	989	2,439	3,141	0	1,883	3,616	4,318
33,450	33,500	0	981	2,429	3,131	0	1,875	3,606	4,308
33,500	33,550	0	973	2,418	3,120	0	1,867	3,595	4,297
33,550	33,600	0	965	2,408	3,110	0	1,859	3,585	4,287
33,600	33,650	0	957	2,397	3,099	0	1,851	3,574	4,276
33,650	33,700	0	949	2,386	3,088	0	1,843	3,564	4,266
33,700	33,750	0	941	2,376	3,078	0	1,835	3,553	4,255
33,750	33,800	0	933	2,365	3,067	0	1,827	3,543	4,245
33,800	33,850	0	925	2,355	3,057	0	1,819	3,532	4,234
33,850	33,900	0	918	2,344	3,046	0	1,811	3,522	4,224
33,900	33,950	0	910	2,334	3,036	0	1,803	3,511	4,213
33,950	34,000	0	902	2,323	3,025	0	1,795	3,501	4,203
34,000	34,050	0	894	2,313	3,015	0	1,787	3,490	4,192
34,050	34,100	0	886	2,302	3,004	0	1,779	3,479	4,181
34,100	34,150	0	878	2,292	2,994	0	1,771	3,469	4,171
34,150	34,200	0	870	2,281	2,983	0	1,763	3,458	4,160
34,200	34,250	0	862	2,271	2,973	0	1,755	3,448	4,150
34,250	34,300	0	854	2,260	2,962	0	1,747	3,437	4,139
34,300	34,350	0	846	2,250	2,952	0	1,739	3,427	4,129
34,350	34,400	0	838	2,239	2,941	0	1,731	3,416	4,118
34,400	34,450	0	830	2,228	2,930	0	1,723	3,406	4,108
34,450	34,500	0	822	2,218	2,920	0	1,715	3,395	4,097
34,500	34,550	0	814	2,207	2,909	0	1,707	3,385	4,087
34,550	34,600	0	806	2,197	2,899	0	1,699	3,374	4,076
34,600	34,650	0	798	2,186	2,888	0	1,691	3,364	4,066
34,650	34,700	0	790	2,176	2,878	0	1,683	3,353	4,055
34,700	34,750	0	782	2,165	2,867	0	1,675	3,343	4,045
34,750	34,800	0	774	2,155	2,857	0	1,667	3,332	4,034
34,800	34,850	0	766	2,144	2,846	0	1,659	3,322	4,024
34,850	34,900	0	758	2,134	2,836	0	1,651	3,311	4,013
34,900	34,950	0	750	2,123	2,825	0	1,643	3,300	4,002
34,950	35,000	0	742	2,113	2,815	0	1,635	3,290	3,992
35,000	35,050	0	734	2,102	2,804	0	1,627	3,279	3,981
35,050	35,100	0	726	2,092	2,794	0	1,619	3,269	3,971
35,100	35,150	0	718	2,081	2,783	0	1,611	3,258	3,960
35,150	35,200	0	710	2,071	2,773	0	1,603	3,248	3,950
35,200	35,250	0	702	2,060	2,762	0	1,595	3,237	3,939
35,250	35,300	0	694	2,049	2,751	0	1,587	3,227	3,929
35,300	35,350	0	686	2,039	2,741	0	1,579	3,216	3,918
35,350	35,400	0	678	2,028	2,730	0	1,571	3,206	3,908
35,400	35,450	0	670	2,018	2,720	0	1,563	3,195	3,897
35,450	35,500	0	662	2,007	2,709	0	1,555	3,185	3,887
35,500	35,550	0	654	1,997	2,699	0	1,547	3,174	3,876
35,550	35,600	0	646	1,986	2,688	0	1,539	3,164	3,866
35,600	35,650	0	638	1,976	2,678	0	1,531	3,153	3,855
35,650	35,700	0	630	1,965	2,667	0	1,523	3,143	3,845
35,700	35,750	0	622	1,955	2,657	0	1,515	3,132	3,834
35,750	35,800	0	614	1,944	2,646	0	1,507	3,121	3,823
35,800	35,850	0	606	1,934	2,636	0	1,499	3,111	3,813
35,850	35,900	0	598	1,923	2,625	0	1,491	3,100	3,802
35,900	35,950	0	590	1,913	2,615	0	1,483	3,090	3,792
35,950	36,000	0	582	1,902	2,604	0	1,475	3,079	3,781
36,000	36,050	0	574	1,892	2,594	0	1,467	3,069	3,771
36,050	36,100	0	566	1,881	2,583	0	1,459	3,058	3,760
36,100	36,150	0	558	1,870	2,572	0	1,451	3,048	3,750
36,150	36,200	0	550	1,860	2,562	0	1,443	3,037	3,739
36,200	36,250	0	542	1,849	2,551	0	1,435	3,027	3,729
36,250	36,300	0	534	1,839	2,541	0	1,427	3,016	3,718
36,300	36,350	0	526	1,828	2,530	0	1,419	3,006	3,708
36,350	36,400	0	518	1,818	2,520	0	1,411	2,995	3,697
36,400	36,450	0	510	1,807	2,509	0	1,403	2,985	3,687
36,450	36,500	0	502	1,797	2,499	0	1,395	2,974	3,676
36,500	36,550	0	494	1,786	2,488	0	1,387	2,963	3,665
36,550	36,600	0	486	1,776	2,478	0	1,379	2,953	3,655
36,600	36,650	0	478	1,765	2,467	0	1,371	2,942	3,644
36,650	36,700	0	470	1,755	2,457	0	1,363	2,932	3,634
36,700	36,750	0	462	1,744	2,446	0	1,355	2,921	3,623
36,750	36,800	0	454	1,734	2,436	0	1,347	2,911	3,613
36,800	36,850	0	446	1,723	2,425	0	1,339	2,900	3,602
36,850	36,900	0	438	1,713	2,415	0	1,331	2,890	3,592
36,900	36,950	0	430	1,702	2,404	0	1,323	2,879	3,581
36,950	37,000	0	422	1,691	2,393	0	1,315	2,869	3,571
37,000	37,050	0	414	1,681	2,383	0	1,307	2,858	3,560
37,050	37,100	0	406	1,670	2,372	0	1,299	2,848	3,550
37,100	37,150	0	398	1,660	2,362	0	1,291	2,837	3,539
37,150	37,200	0	390	1,649	2,351	0	1,283	2,827	3,529
37,200	37,250	0	382	1,639	2,341	0	1,275	2,816	3,518
37,250	37,300	0	374	1,629	2,330	0	1,267	2,806	3,508
37,300	37,350	0	366	1,618	2,320	0	1,259	2,795	3,497
37,350	37,400	0	358	1,607	2,309	0	1,251	2,784	3,486
37,400	37,450	0	350	1,597	2,299	0	1,243	2,774	3,476
37,450	37,500	0	342	1,586	2,288	0	1,236	2,763	3,465
37,500	37,550	0	334	1,576	2,278	0	1,228	2,753	3,455
37,550	37,600	0	326	1,565	2,267	0	1,220	2,742	3,444

(Continued)

Earned Income Credit (EIC) Table - *Continued*

(Caution. This is not a tax table.)

If the amount you are looking up from the worksheet is—		Single, head of household, or qualifying widow(er) and the number of children you have is—				Married filing jointly and the number of children you have is—			
At least	But less than	0	1	2	3	0	1	2	3
		Your credit is—				Your credit is—			
37,600	37,650	0	318	1,555	2,257	0	1,212	2,732	3,434
37,650	37,700	0	310	1,544	2,246	0	1,204	2,721	3,423
37,700	37,750	0	302	1,534	2,236	0	1,196	2,711	3,413
37,750	37,800	0	294	1,523	2,225	0	1,188	2,700	3,402
37,800	37,850	0	286	1,512	2,214	0	1,180	2,690	3,392
37,850	37,900	0	278	1,502	2,204	0	1,172	2,679	3,381
37,900	37,950	0	270	1,491	2,193	0	1,164	2,669	3,371
37,950	38,000	0	262	1,481	2,183	0	1,156	2,658	3,360
38,000	38,050	0	254	1,470	2,172	0	1,148	2,648	3,350
38,050	38,100	0	246	1,460	2,162	0	1,140	2,637	3,339
38,100	38,150	0	238	1,449	2,151	0	1,132	2,627	3,329
38,150	38,200	0	230	1,439	2,141	0	1,124	2,616	3,318
38,200	38,250	0	222	1,428	2,130	0	1,116	2,605	3,307
38,250	38,300	0	214	1,418	2,120	0	1,108	2,595	3,297
38,300	38,350	0	206	1,407	2,109	0	1,100	2,584	3,286
38,350	38,400	0	198	1,397	2,099	0	1,092	2,574	3,276
38,400	38,450	0	190	1,386	2,088	0	1,084	2,563	3,265
38,450	38,500	0	182	1,376	2,078	0	1,076	2,553	3,255
38,500	38,550	0	174	1,365	2,067	0	1,068	2,542	3,244
38,550	38,600	0	166	1,355	2,057	0	1,060	2,532	3,234
38,600	38,650	0	158	1,344	2,046	0	1,052	2,521	3,223
38,650	38,700	0	150	1,333	2,035	0	1,044	2,511	3,213
38,700	38,750	0	142	1,323	2,025	0	1,036	2,500	3,202
38,750	38,800	0	134	1,312	2,014	0	1,028	2,490	3,192
38,800	38,850	0	126	1,302	2,004	0	1,020	2,479	3,181
38,850	38,900	0	119	1,291	1,993	0	1,012	2,469	3,171
38,900	38,950	0	111	1,281	1,983	0	1,004	2,458	3,160
38,950	39,000	0	103	1,270	1,972	0	996	2,448	3,150
39,000	39,050	0	95	1,260	1,962	0	988	2,437	3,139
39,050	39,100	0	87	1,249	1,951	0	980	2,426	3,128
39,100	39,150	0	79	1,239	1,941	0	972	2,416	3,118
39,150	39,200	0	71	1,228	1,930	0	964	2,405	3,107
39,200	39,250	0	63	1,218	1,920	0	956	2,395	3,097
39,250	39,300	0	55	1,207	1,909	0	948	2,384	3,086
39,300	39,350	0	47	1,197	1,899	0	940	2,374	3,076
39,350	39,400	0	39	1,186	1,888	0	932	2,363	3,065
39,400	39,450	0	31	1,175	1,877	0	924	2,353	3,055
39,450	39,500	0	23	1,165	1,867	0	916	2,342	3,044
39,500	39,550	0	15	1,154	1,856	0	908	2,332	3,034
39,550	39,600	0	7	1,144	1,846	0	900	2,321	3,023
39,600	39,650	0	*	1,133	1,835	0	892	2,311	3,013
39,650	39,700	0	0	1,123	1,825	0	884	2,300	3,002
39,700	39,750	0	0	1,112	1,814	0	876	2,290	2,992
39,750	39,800	0	0	1,102	1,804	0	868	2,279	2,981
39,800	39,850	0	0	1,091	1,793	0	860	2,269	2,971
39,850	39,900	0	0	1,081	1,783	0	852	2,258	2,960
39,900	39,950	0	0	1,070	1,772	0	844	2,247	2,949
39,950	40,000	0	0	1,060	1,762	0	836	2,237	2,939
40,000	40,050	0	0	1,049	1,751	0	828	2,226	2,928
40,050	40,100	0	0	1,039	1,741	0	820	2,216	2,918
40,100	40,150	0	0	1,028	1,730	0	812	2,205	2,907
40,150	40,200	0	0	1,018	1,720	0	804	2,195	2,897
40,200	40,250	0	0	1,007	1,709	0	796	2,184	2,886
40,250	40,300	0	0	996	1,698	0	788	2,174	2,876
40,300	40,350	0	0	986	1,688	0	780	2,163	2,865
40,350	40,400	0	0	975	1,677	0	772	2,153	2,855
40,400	40,450	0	0	965	1,667	0	764	2,142	2,844
40,450	40,500	0	0	954	1,656	0	756	2,132	2,834
40,500	40,550	0	0	944	1,646	0	748	2,121	2,823
40,550	40,600	0	0	933	1,635	0	740	2,111	2,813
40,600	40,650	0	0	923	1,625	0	732	2,100	2,802
40,650	40,700	0	0	912	1,614	0	724	2,090	2,792
40,700	40,750	0	0	902	1,604	0	716	2,079	2,781
40,750	40,800	0	0	891	1,593	0	708	2,068	2,770

If the amount you are looking up from the worksheet is—		Single, head of household, or qualifying widow(er) and the number of children you have is—				Married filing jointly and the number of children you have is—			
At least	But less than	0	1	2	3	0	1	2	3
		Your credit is—				Your credit is—			
40,800	40,850	0	0	881	1,583	0	700	2,058	2,760
40,850	40,900	0	0	870	1,572	0	692	2,047	2,749
40,900	40,950	0	0	860	1,562	0	684	2,037	2,739
40,950	41,000	0	0	849	1,551	0	676	2,026	2,728
41,000	41,050	0	0	839	1,541	0	668	2,016	2,718
41,050	41,100	0	0	828	1,530	0	660	2,005	2,707
41,100	41,150	0	0	817	1,519	0	652	1,995	2,697
41,150	41,200	0	0	807	1,509	0	644	1,984	2,686
41,200	41,250	0	0	796	1,498	0	636	1,974	2,676
41,250	41,300	0	0	786	1,488	0	628	1,963	2,665
41,300	41,350	0	0	775	1,477	0	620	1,953	2,655
41,350	41,400	0	0	765	1,467	0	612	1,942	2,644
41,400	41,450	0	0	754	1,456	0	604	1,932	2,634
41,450	41,500	0	0	744	1,446	0	596	1,921	2,623
41,500	41,550	0	0	733	1,435	0	588	1,910	2,612
41,550	41,600	0	0	723	1,425	0	580	1,900	2,602
41,600	41,650	0	0	712	1,414	0	572	1,889	2,591
41,650	41,700	0	0	702	1,404	0	564	1,879	2,581
41,700	41,750	0	0	691	1,393	0	556	1,868	2,570
41,750	41,800	0	0	681	1,383	0	548	1,858	2,560
41,800	41,850	0	0	670	1,372	0	540	1,847	2,549
41,850	41,900	0	0	660	1,362	0	532	1,837	2,539
41,900	41,950	0	0	649	1,351	0	524	1,826	2,528
41,950	42,000	0	0	638	1,340	0	516	1,816	2,518
42,000	42,050	0	0	628	1,330	0	508	1,805	2,507
42,050	42,100	0	0	617	1,319	0	500	1,795	2,497
42,100	42,150	0	0	607	1,309	0	492	1,784	2,486
42,150	42,200	0	0	596	1,298	0	484	1,774	2,476
42,200	42,250	0	0	586	1,288	0	476	1,763	2,465
42,250	42,300	0	0	575	1,277	0	468	1,753	2,455
42,300	42,350	0	0	565	1,267	0	460	1,742	2,444
42,350	42,400	0	0	554	1,256	0	452	1,731	2,433
42,400	42,450	0	0	544	1,246	0	444	1,721	2,423
42,450	42,500	0	0	533	1,235	0	437	1,710	2,412
42,500	42,550	0	0	523	1,225	0	429	1,700	2,402
42,550	42,600	0	0	512	1,214	0	421	1,689	2,391
42,600	42,650	0	0	502	1,204	0	413	1,679	2,381
42,650	42,700	0	0	491	1,193	0	405	1,668	2,370
42,700	42,750	0	0	481	1,183	0	397	1,658	2,360
42,750	42,800	0	0	470	1,172	0	389	1,647	2,349
42,800	42,850	0	0	459	1,161	0	381	1,637	2,339
42,850	42,900	0	0	449	1,151	0	373	1,626	2,328
42,900	42,950	0	0	438	1,140	0	365	1,616	2,318
42,950	43,000	0	0	428	1,130	0	357	1,605	2,307
43,000	43,050	0	0	417	1,119	0	349	1,595	2,297
43,050	43,100	0	0	407	1,109	0	341	1,584	2,286
43,100	43,150	0	0	396	1,098	0	333	1,574	2,276
43,150	43,200	0	0	386	1,088	0	325	1,563	2,265
43,200	43,250	0	0	375	1,077	0	317	1,552	2,254
43,250	43,300	0	0	365	1,067	0	309	1,542	2,244
43,300	43,350	0	0	354	1,056	0	301	1,531	2,233
43,350	43,400	0	0	344	1,046	0	293	1,521	2,223
43,400	43,450	0	0	333	1,035	0	285	1,510	2,212
43,450	43,500	0	0	323	1,025	0	277	1,500	2,202
43,500	43,550	0	0	312	1,014	0	269	1,489	2,191
43,550	43,600	0	0	302	1,004	0	261	1,479	2,181
43,600	43,650	0	0	291	993	0	253	1,468	2,170
43,650	43,700	0	0	280	982	0	245	1,458	2,160
43,700	43,750	0	0	270	972	0	237	1,447	2,149
43,750	43,800	0	0	259	961	0	229	1,437	2,139
43,800	43,850	0	0	249	951	0	221	1,426	2,128
43,850	43,900	0	0	238	940	0	213	1,416	2,118
43,900	43,950	0	0	228	930	0	205	1,405	2,107
43,950	44,000	0	0	217	919	0	197	1,395	2,097

* If the amount you're looking up from the worksheet is at least $39,600 but less than $39,617, and you have one qualifying child, your credit is $1. If the amount you're looking up from the worksheet is $39,617 or more, and you have one qualifying child, you can't take the credit.

(Continued)

Need more information or forms? Visit IRS.gov.

Earned Income Credit (EIC) Table - *Continued*

(**Caution.** This is **not** a tax table.)

If the amount you are looking up from the worksheet is—		Single, head of household, or qualifying widow(er) and the number of children you have is—				Married filing jointly and the number of children you have is—			
At least	But less than	0	1	2	3	0	1	2	3
		Your credit is—				Your credit is—			
44,000	44,050	0	0	207	909	0	189	1,384	2,086
44,050	44,100	0	0	196	898	0	181	1,373	2,075
44,100	44,150	0	0	186	888	0	173	1,363	2,065
44,150	44,200	0	0	175	877	0	165	1,352	2,054
44,200	44,250	0	0	165	867	0	157	1,342	2,044
44,250	44,300	0	0	154	856	0	149	1,331	2,033
44,300	44,350	0	0	144	846	0	141	1,321	2,023
44,350	44,400	0	0	133	835	0	133	1,310	2,012
44,400	44,450	0	0	122	824	0	125	1,300	2,002
44,450	44,500	0	0	112	814	0	117	1,289	1,991
44,500	44,550	0	0	101	803	0	109	1,279	1,981
44,550	44,600	0	0	91	793	0	101	1,268	1,970
44,600	44,650	0	0	80	782	0	93	1,258	1,960
44,650	44,700	0	0	70	772	0	85	1,247	1,949
44,700	44,750	0	0	59	761	0	77	1,237	1,939
44,750	44,800	0	0	49	751	0	69	1,226	1,928
44,800	44,850	0	0	38	740	0	61	1,216	1,918
44,850	44,900	0	0	28	730	0	53	1,205	1,907
44,900	44,950	0	0	17	719	0	45	1,194	1,896
44,950	45,000	0	0	7	709	0	37	1,184	1,886
45,000	45,050	0	0	*	698	0	29	1,173	1,875
45,050	45,100	0	0	0	688	0	21	1,163	1,865
45,100	45,150	0	0	0	677	0	13	1,152	1,854
45,150	45,200	0	0	0	667	0	5	1,142	1,844
45,200	45,250	0	0	0	656	0	0	1,131	1,833
45,250	45,300	0	0	0	645	0	0	1,121	1,823
45,300	45,350	0	0	0	635	0	0	1,110	1,812
45,350	45,400	0	0	0	624	0	0	1,100	1,802
45,400	45,450	0	0	0	614	0	0	1,089	1,791
45,450	45,500	0	0	0	603	0	0	1,079	1,781
45,500	45,550	0	0	0	593	0	0	1,068	1,770
45,550	45,600	0	0	0	582	0	0	1,058	1,760
45,600	45,650	0	0	0	572	0	0	1,047	1,749
45,650	45,700	0	0	0	561	0	0	1,037	1,739
45,700	45,750	0	0	0	551	0	0	1,026	1,728
45,750	45,800	0	0	0	540	0	0	1,015	1,717
45,800	45,850	0	0	0	530	0	0	1,005	1,707
45,850	45,900	0	0	0	519	0	0	994	1,696
45,900	45,950	0	0	0	509	0	0	984	1,686
45,950	46,000	0	0	0	498	0	0	973	1,675
46,000	46,050	0	0	0	488	0	0	963	1,665
46,050	46,100	0	0	0	477	0	0	952	1,654
46,100	46,150	0	0	0	466	0	0	942	1,644
46,150	46,200	0	0	0	456	0	0	931	1,633
46,200	46,250	0	0	0	445	0	0	921	1,623
46,250	46,300	0	0	0	435	0	0	910	1,612
46,300	46,350	0	0	0	424	0	0	900	1,602
46,350	46,400	0	0	0	414	0	0	889	1,591
46,400	46,450	0	0	0	403	0	0	879	1,581
46,450	46,500	0	0	0	393	0	0	868	1,570
46,500	46,550	0	0	0	382	0	0	857	1,559
46,550	46,600	0	0	0	372	0	0	847	1,549
46,600	46,650	0	0	0	361	0	0	836	1,538
46,650	46,700	0	0	0	351	0	0	826	1,528
46,700	46,750	0	0	0	340	0	0	815	1,517
46,750	46,800	0	0	0	330	0	0	805	1,507
46,800	46,850	0	0	0	319	0	0	794	1,496
46,850	46,900	0	0	0	309	0	0	784	1,486
46,900	46,950	0	0	0	298	0	0	773	1,475
46,950	47,000	0	0	0	287	0	0	763	1,465
47,000	47,050	0	0	0	277	0	0	752	1,454
47,050	47,100	0	0	0	266	0	0	742	1,444
47,100	47,150	0	0	0	256	0	0	731	1,433
47,150	47,200	0	0	0	245	0	0	721	1,423
47,200	47,250	0	0	0	235	0	0	710	1,412
47,250	47,300	0	0	0	224	0	0	700	1,402
47,300	47,350	0	0	0	214	0	0	689	1,391
47,350	47,400	0	0	0	203	0	0	678	1,380
47,400	47,450	0	0	0	193	0	0	668	1,370
47,450	47,500	0	0	0	182	0	0	657	1,359
47,500	47,550	0	0	0	172	0	0	647	1,349
47,550	47,600	0	0	0	161	0	0	636	1,338
47,600	47,650	0	0	0	151	0	0	626	1,328
47,650	47,700	0	0	0	140	0	0	615	1,317
47,700	47,750	0	0	0	130	0	0	605	1,307
47,750	47,800	0	0	0	119	0	0	594	1,296
47,800	47,850	0	0	0	108	0	0	584	1,286
47,850	47,900	0	0	0	98	0	0	573	1,275
47,900	47,950	0	0	0	87	0	0	563	1,265
47,950	48,000	0	0	0	77	0	0	552	1,254
48,000	48,050	0	0	0	66	0	0	542	1,244
48,050	48,100	0	0	0	56	0	0	531	1,233
48,100	48,150	0	0	0	45	0	0	521	1,223
48,150	48,200	0	0	0	35	0	0	510	1,212
48,200	48,250	0	0	0	24	0	0	499	1,201
48,250	48,300	0	0	0	14	0	0	489	1,191
48,300	48,350	0	0	0	**	0	0	478	1,180
48,350	48,400	0	0	0	0	0	0	468	1,170
48,400	48,450	0	0	0	0	0	0	457	1,159
48,450	48,500	0	0	0	0	0	0	447	1,149
48,500	48,550	0	0	0	0	0	0	436	1,138
48,550	48,600	0	0	0	0	0	0	426	1,128
48,600	48,650	0	0	0	0	0	0	415	1,117
48,650	48,700	0	0	0	0	0	0	405	1,107
48,700	48,750	0	0	0	0	0	0	394	1,096
48,750	48,800	0	0	0	0	0	0	384	1,086
48,800	48,850	0	0	0	0	0	0	373	1,075
48,850	48,900	0	0	0	0	0	0	363	1,065
48,900	48,950	0	0	0	0	0	0	352	1,054
48,950	49,000	0	0	0	0	0	0	342	1,044
49,000	49,050	0	0	0	0	0	0	331	1,033
49,050	49,100	0	0	0	0	0	0	320	1,022
49,100	49,150	0	0	0	0	0	0	310	1,012
49,150	49,200	0	0	0	0	0	0	299	1,001
49,200	49,250	0	0	0	0	0	0	289	991
49,250	49,300	0	0	0	0	0	0	278	980
49,300	49,350	0	0	0	0	0	0	268	970
49,350	49,400	0	0	0	0	0	0	257	959
49,400	49,450	0	0	0	0	0	0	247	949
49,450	49,500	0	0	0	0	0	0	236	938
49,500	49,550	0	0	0	0	0	0	226	928
49,550	49,600	0	0	0	0	0	0	215	917

* If the amount you're looking up from the worksheet is at least $45,000 but less than $45,007, and you have two qualifying children, your credit is $1. If the amount you're looking up from the worksheet is $45,007 or more, and you have two qualifying children, you can't take the credit.

** If the amount you're looking up from the worksheet is at least $48,300 but less than $48,340, and you have three or more qualifying children, your credit is $4. If the amount you're looking up from the worksheet is $48,340 or more, and you have three or more qualifying children, you can't take the credit.

(Continued)

If the amount you are looking up from the worksheet is—		And your filing status is—							
		Single, head of household, or qualifying widow(er) and the number of children you have is—				Married filing jointly and the number of children you have is—			
At least	But less than	0	1	2	3	0	1	2	3
		Your credit is—				Your credit is—			
49,600	49,650	0	0	0	0	0	0	205	907
49,650	49,700	0	0	0	0	0	0	194	896
49,700	49,750	0	0	0	0	0	0	184	886
49,750	49,800	0	0	0	0	0	0	173	875
49,800	49,850	0	0	0	0	0	0	163	865
49,850	49,900	0	0	0	0	0	0	152	854
49,900	49,950	0	0	0	0	0	0	141	843
49,950	50,000	0	0	0	0	0	0	131	833
50,000	50,050	0	0	0	0	0	0	120	822
50,050	50,100	0	0	0	0	0	0	110	812
50,100	50,150	0	0	0	0	0	0	99	801
50,150	50,200	0	0	0	0	0	0	89	791
50,200	50,250	0	0	0	0	0	0	78	780
50,250	50,300	0	0	0	0	0	0	68	770
50,300	50,350	0	0	0	0	0	0	57	759
50,350	50,400	0	0	0	0	0	0	47	749
50,400	50,450	0	0	0	0	0	0	36	738
50,450	50,500	0	0	0	0	0	0	26	728
50,500	50,550	0	0	0	0	0	0	15	717
50,550	50,600	0	0	0	0	0	0	*	707
50,600	50,650	0	0	0	0	0	0	0	696
50,650	50,700	0	0	0	0	0	0	0	686
50,700	50,750	0	0	0	0	0	0	0	675
50,750	50,800	0	0	0	0	0	0	0	664
50,800	50,850	0	0	0	0	0	0	0	654
50,850	50,900	0	0	0	0	0	0	0	643
50,900	50,950	0	0	0	0	0	0	0	633
50,950	51,000	0	0	0	0	0	0	0	622
51,000	51,050	0	0	0	0	0	0	0	612
51,050	51,100	0	0	0	0	0	0	0	601
51,100	51,150	0	0	0	0	0	0	0	591
51,150	51,200	0	0	0	0	0	0	0	580
51,200	51,250	0	0	0	0	0	0	0	570
51,250	51,300	0	0	0	0	0	0	0	559
51,300	51,350	0	0	0	0	0	0	0	549
51,350	51,400	0	0	0	0	0	0	0	538
51,400	51,450	0	0	0	0	0	0	0	528
51,450	51,500	0	0	0	0	0	0	0	517
51,500	51,550	0	0	0	0	0	0	0	506
51,550	51,600	0	0	0	0	0	0	0	496
51,600	51,650	0	0	0	0	0	0	0	485
51,650	51,700	0	0	0	0	0	0	0	475
51,700	51,750	0	0	0	0	0	0	0	464
51,750	51,800	0	0	0	0	0	0	0	454
51,800	51,850	0	0	0	0	0	0	0	443
51,850	51,900	0	0	0	0	0	0	0	433
51,900	51,950	0	0	0	0	0	0	0	422
51,950	52,000	0	0	0	0	0	0	0	412

If the amount you are looking up from the worksheet is—		And your filing status is—							
		Single, head of household, or qualifying widow(er) and the number of children you have is—				Married filing jointly and the number of children you have is—			
At least	But less than	0	1	2	3	0	1	2	3
		Your credit is—				Your credit is—			
52,000	52,050	0	0	0	0	0	0	0	401
52,050	52,100	0	0	0	0	0	0	0	391
52,100	52,150	0	0	0	0	0	0	0	380
52,150	52,200	0	0	0	0	0	0	0	370
52,200	52,250	0	0	0	0	0	0	0	359
52,250	52,300	0	0	0	0	0	0	0	349
52,300	52,350	0	0	0	0	0	0	0	338
52,350	52,400	0	0	0	0	0	0	0	327
52,400	52,450	0	0	0	0	0	0	0	317
52,450	52,500	0	0	0	0	0	0	0	306
52,500	52,550	0	0	0	0	0	0	0	296
52,550	52,600	0	0	0	0	0	0	0	285
52,600	52,650	0	0	0	0	0	0	0	275
52,650	52,700	0	0	0	0	0	0	0	264
52,700	52,750	0	0	0	0	0	0	0	254
52,750	52,800	0	0	0	0	0	0	0	243
52,800	52,850	0	0	0	0	0	0	0	233
52,850	52,900	0	0	0	0	0	0	0	222
52,900	52,950	0	0	0	0	0	0	0	212
52,950	53,000	0	0	0	0	0	0	0	201
53,000	53,050	0	0	0	0	0	0	0	191
53,050	53,100	0	0	0	0	0	0	0	180
53,100	53,150	0	0	0	0	0	0	0	170
53,150	53,200	0	0	0	0	0	0	0	159
53,200	53,250	0	0	0	0	0	0	0	148
53,250	53,300	0	0	0	0	0	0	0	138
53,300	53,350	0	0	0	0	0	0	0	127
53,350	53,400	0	0	0	0	0	0	0	117
53,400	53,450	0	0	0	0	0	0	0	106
53,450	53,500	0	0	0	0	0	0	0	96
53,500	53,550	0	0	0	0	0	0	0	85
53,550	53,600	0	0	0	0	0	0	0	75
53,600	53,650	0	0	0	0	0	0	0	64
53,650	53,700	0	0	0	0	0	0	0	54
53,700	53,750	0	0	0	0	0	0	0	43
53,750	53,800	0	0	0	0	0	0	0	33
53,800	53,850	0	0	0	0	0	0	0	22
53,850	53,900	0	0	0	0	0	0	0	12
53,900	53,930	0	0	0	0	0	0	0	3

* If the amount you're looking up from the worksheet is at least $50,550 but less than $50,597, and you have two qualifying children, your credit is $5. If the amount you're looking up from the worksheet is $50,597 or more, and you have two qualifying children, you can't take the credit.

Need more information or forms? Visit IRS.gov.

Line 67

Additional Child Tax Credit

 You may be able to use your 2016 earned income to figure your additional child tax credit if (a) your 2016 earned income is more than your 2017 earned income, and (b) your main home was located in one of the Presidentially declared disaster areas eligible for this relief on the specified date. For details, see Pub. 976.

If you make the election to use your 2016 earned income to figure your additional child tax credit, enter "PYEI" and the amount of your 2016 earned income in the space next to line 67. If you are claiming both the EIC and the additional child tax credit, you only need to enter "PYEI" and the amount of your 2016 earned income next to line 66a. For more information, see the Instructions for Schedule 8812.

 If you elect to use your 2016 earned income to figure your EIC, you must also use your 2016 earned income to figure your additional child tax credit.

 If you elect to use your 2016 earned income to figure your additional child tax credit, you must enter the amount of your 2016 nontaxable combat pay on line 66b.

What Is the Additional Child Tax Credit?

This credit is for certain people who have at least one qualifying child for the child tax credit (as defined in Steps 1, 2, and 3 of the instructions for line 6c). The additional child tax credit may give you a refund even if you don't owe any tax or didn't have any tax withheld.

Two Steps To Take the Additional Child Tax Credit!

Step 1. Be sure you figured the amount, if any, of your child tax credit. See the instructions for line 52.

Step 2. Read the TIP at the end of your Child Tax Credit Worksheet. Use Schedule 8812 to see if you can take the additional child tax credit, but only if

you meet the condition given in that TIP.

Form 8862 required. If your 2016 additional child tax credit was denied or reduced for any reason other than a math or clerical error, you must attach a completed Form 8862 to your 2017 tax return to claim the credit in 2017. See Form 8862 and its instructions for details.

 If you take the additional child tax credit even though you aren't eligible and it is determined that your error is due to reckless or intentional disregard of the additional child tax credit rules, you won't be allowed to take the child tax credit or the additional child tax credit for 2 years even if you're otherwise eligible to do so. If you fraudulently take the additional child tax credit, you won't be allowed to take either credit for 10 years. You also may have to pay penalties.

 Refunds for returns claiming the additional child tax credit can't be issued before mid-February 2018. This delay applies to the entire refund, not just the portion associated with the additional child tax credit.

Line 68

American Opportunity Credit

If you meet the requirements to claim an education credit (see the instructions for line 50), enter on line 68 the amount, if any, from Form 8863, line 8. You may be able to increase an education credit and reduce your total tax or increase your tax refund if the student chooses to include all or part of a Pell grant or certain other scholarships or fellowships in income. See Pub. 970 and the Instructions for Form 8863 for more information.

Form 8862 required. If your 2016 American opportunity credit was denied or reduced for any reason other than a math or clerical error, you must attach a completed Form 8862 to your 2017 tax return to claim the credit in 2017. See Form 8862 and its instructions for details.

 If you take the American opportunity credit even though you aren't eligible and it is determined that your error is due to reckless or intentional disregard of the American opportunity credit rules, you won't be allowed to take the credit for 2 years even if you're otherwise eligible to do so. If you fraudulently take the American opportunity credit, you won't be allowed to take the credit for 10 years. You also may have to pay penalties.

Line 69

Net Premium Tax Credit

The premium tax credit helps pay for health insurance purchased through the Marketplace. You may be eligible to claim the premium tax credit if you, your spouse, or a dependent enrolled in health insurance through the Marketplace. Eligible individuals may have advance payments of the premium tax credit made on their behalf directly to the insurance company. You (or whoever enrolled you) should have received Form 1095-A from the Marketplace with information about your coverage and any advance credit payments. Complete Form 8962 to determine the amount of your premium tax credit, if any. If the premium tax credit you can claim exceeds your advance credit payments, your net premium tax credit will be shown on Form 8962, line 26. Enter that amount, if any, on Form 1040, line 69. For more information, see the Instructions for Form 8962.

Line 70

Amount Paid With Request for Extension To File

If you got an automatic extension of time to file Form 1040 by filing Form 4868 or by making a payment, enter the amount of the payment or any amount you paid with Form 4868. If you paid by debit or credit card, don't include on line 70 the convenience fee you were charged. Also, include any amounts paid with Form 2350.

 You may be able to deduct any credit or debit card convenience fees on your 2018 Schedule A.

Need more information or forms? Visit IRS.gov.

Line 71

Excess Social Security and Tier 1 RRTA Tax Withheld

If you, or your spouse if filing a joint return, had more than one employer for 2017 and total wages of more than $127,200, too much social security or tier 1 railroad retirement (RRTA) tax may have been withheld. You can take a credit on this line for the amount withheld in excess of $7,886. But if any one employer withheld more than $7,886, you can't claim the excess on your return. The employer should adjust the tax for you. If the employer doesn't adjust the overcollection, you can file a claim for refund using Form 843. Figure this amount separately for you and your spouse.

You can't claim a refund for excess tier 2 RRTA tax on Form 1040. Instead, use Form 843.

For more details, see Pub. 505.

Line 72

Credit for Federal Tax on Fuels

Enter any credit for federal excise taxes paid on fuels that are ultimately used for a nontaxable purpose (for example, an off-highway business use). Attach Form 4136.

Line 73

Check the box(es) on line 73 to report any credit from Form 2439 or 8885.

If you are claiming a credit for repayment of amounts you included in your income in an earlier year because it appeared you had a right to the income, include the credit on line 73. Check box d and enter "I.R.C. 1341" in the space next to that box. See Pub. 525 for details about this credit.

If you made a tax payment that doesn't belong on any other line, include the payment on line 73. Check box d and enter "Tax" in the space next to that box.

If you check more than one box, enter the total of the line 73 credits and payments.

Refund

Line 75

Amount Overpaid

If line 75 is under $1, we will send a refund only on written request.

Refund Offset

If you owe past-due federal tax, state income tax, state unemployment compensation debts, child support, spousal support, or certain federal nontax debts, such as student loans, all or part of the overpayment on line 75 may be used (offset) to pay the past-due amount. Offsets for federal taxes are made by the IRS. All other offsets are made by the Treasury Department's Bureau of the Fiscal Service. For federal tax offsets, you will receive a notice from the IRS. For all other offsets, you will receive a notice from the Fiscal Service. To find out if you may have an offset or if you have any questions about it, contact the agency to which you owe the debt.

Injured Spouse

If you file a joint return and your spouse hasn't paid past-due federal tax, state income tax, state unemployment compensation debts, child support, spousal support, or a federal nontax debt, such as a student loan, part or all of the overpayment on line 75 may be used (offset) to pay the past-due amount. But your part of the overpayment may be refunded to you if certain conditions apply and you complete Form 8379. For details, use *Tax Topic 203* or see Form 8379.

Lines 76a Through 76d

Amount Refunded to You

If you want to check the status of your refund, just use the IRS2Go app or go to *IRS.gov/Refunds*. See *Refund Information,* later. Information about your refund will generally be available within 24 hours after the IRS receives your *e-filed* return, or 4 weeks after you mail your paper return. If you filed Form 8379 with your return, wait 14 weeks (11 weeks if you filed electronically). Have your 2017 tax return handy so you can enter your social security number, your filing status, and the exact whole dollar amount of your refund.

Where's My Refund will provide an actual personalized refund date as soon as the IRS processes your tax return and approves your refund.

Effect of refund on benefits. Any refund you receive can't be counted as income when determining if you or anyone else is eligible for benefits or assistance, or how much you or anyone else can receive, under any federal program or under any state or local program financed in whole or in part with federal funds. These programs include Temporary Assistance for Needy Families (TANF), Medicaid, Supplemental Security Income (SSI), and Supplemental Nutrition Assistance Program (food stamps). In addition, when determining eligibility, the refund can't be counted as a resource for at least 12 months after you receive it. Check with your local benefit coordinator to find out if your refund will affect your benefits.

DIRECT ▸DEPOSIT
Simple. Safe. Secure.

Fast Refunds! Join the eight in 10 taxpayers who choose direct deposit—a fast, simple, safe, secure way to have your refund deposited automatically to your checking or savings account, including an individual retirement arrangement (IRA). See the information about IRAs later.

If you want us to directly deposit the amount shown on line 76a to your checking or savings account, including an IRA, at a bank or other financial institution (such as a mutual fund, brokerage firm, or credit union) in the United States:

- Complete lines 76b through 76d (if you want your refund deposited to only one account), or
- Check the box on line 76a and attach Form 8888 if you want to split the direct deposit of your refund into more than one account or use all or part of your refund to buy paper series I savings bonds.

If you don't want your refund directly deposited to your account, don't check the box on line 76a. Draw a line through the boxes on lines 76b and 76d. We will send you a check instead.

Account must be in your name. Don't request a deposit of your refund to an account that isn't in your name, such as your tax return preparer's account. Although you may owe your tax return preparer a fee for preparing your return, don't have any part of your refund deposited into the preparer's account to pay the fee.

The number of refunds that can be directly deposited to a single account or prepaid debit card is limited to three a year. After this limit is reached, paper checks will be sent instead. Learn more at *IRS.gov/DepositLimit*.

Why Use Direct Deposit?

• You get your refund faster by direct deposit than you do by check.

• Payment is more secure. There is no check that can get lost or stolen.

• It is more convenient. You don't have to make a trip to the bank to deposit your check.

• It saves tax dollars. It costs the government less to refund by direct deposit.

• It's proven itself. Nearly 98% of social security and veterans' benefits are sent electronically using direct deposit.

 If you file a joint return and check the box on line 76a and attach Form 8888 or fill in lines 76b through 76d, your spouse may get at least part of the refund.

IRA. You can have your refund (or part of it) directly deposited to a traditional IRA, Roth IRA, or SEP-IRA, but not a SIMPLE IRA. You must establish the IRA at a bank or other financial institution before you request direct deposit. Make sure your direct deposit will be accepted. You also must notify the trustee or custodian of your account of the year to which the deposit is to be applied (unless the trustee or custodian won't accept a deposit for 2017). If you don't, the trustee or custodian can assume the deposit is for the year during which you are filing the return. For example, if you file your 2017 return during 2018 and don't notify the trustee or custodian in advance, the trustee or custodian can assume the deposit to your IRA is for 2018. If you designate your deposit to be for 2017, you must verify that the deposit was actually made to the account by the due date of the return (not counting

extensions). If the deposit isn't made by that date, the deposit isn't an IRA contribution for 2017. In that case, you must file an amended 2017 return and reduce any IRA deduction and any retirement savings contributions credit you claimed.

 You and your spouse, if filing jointly, each may be able to contribute up to $5,500 ($6,500 if age 50 or older at the end of 2017) to a traditional IRA or Roth IRA, for 2017. You may owe a penalty if your contributions exceed these limits, and the limits may be lower depending on your compensation and income. For more information on IRA contributions, see Pub. 590-A.

For more information on IRAs, see Pub. 590-A and Pub. 590-B.

TreasuryDirect®. You can request a deposit of your refund (or part of it) to a TreasuryDirect® online account to buy U.S. Treasury marketable securities and savings bonds. For more information, go to *go.usa.gov/3KvcP*.

Form 8888. You can have your refund directly deposited into more than one account or use it to buy up to $5,000 in paper series I savings bonds. You don't need a TreasuryDirect® account to do this. For more information, see the Form 8888 instructions.

Line 76a

You can't file Form 8888 to split your refund into more than one account or buy paper series I savings bonds if Form 8379 is filed with your return.

Line 76b

The routing number must be nine digits. The first two digits must be 01 through 12 or 21 through 32. On the sample check shown here, the routing number is 250250025. Charles and Mary Ellen Keys would use that routing number unless their financial institution instructed them to use a different routing number for direct deposits.

Ask your financial institution for the correct routing number to enter on line 76b if:

• The routing number on a deposit slip is different from the routing number on your checks,

• Your deposit is to a savings account that doesn't allow you to write checks, or

• Your checks state they are payable through a financial institution different from the one at which you have your checking account.

Line 76c

Check the appropriate box for the type of account. Don't check more than one box. If the deposit is to an account such as an IRA, health savings account, brokerage account, or other similar account, ask your financial institution whether you should check the "Checking" or "Savings" box. You must check the correct box to ensure your deposit is accepted. If your deposit is to a TreasuryDirect® online account, check the "Savings" box.

Line 76d

The account number can be up to 17 characters (both numbers and letters). Include hyphens but omit spaces and special symbols. Enter the number from left to right and leave any unused boxes blank. On the sample check shown here, the account number is 20202086. Don't include the check number.

If the direct deposit to your account(s) is different from the amount you expected, you will receive an explanation in the mail about 2 weeks after your refund is deposited.

Reasons Your Direct Deposit Request Will Be Rejected

If any of the following apply, your direct deposit request will be rejected and a check will be sent instead.

• You are asking to have a joint refund deposited to an individual account, and your financial institution(s) won't allow this. The IRS isn't responsible if a financial institution rejects a direct deposit.

• The name on your account doesn't match the name on the refund, and your financial institution(s) won't allow a refund to be deposited unless the name on the refund matches the name on the account.

• Three direct deposits of tax refunds already have been made to the same account or prepaid debit card.

Need more information or forms? Visit IRS.gov.

• You haven't given a valid account number.

• You file your 2017 return after November 30, 2018.

• Any numbers or letters on lines 76b through 76d are crossed out or whited out.

 The IRS isn't responsible for a lost refund if you enter the wrong account information. Check with your financial institution to get the correct routing and account numbers and to make sure your direct deposit will be accepted.

Line 77

Applied to Your 2018 Estimated Tax

Enter on line 77 the amount, if any, of the overpayment on line 75 you want applied to your 2018 estimated tax. We will apply this amount to your account unless you include a statement requesting us to apply it to your spouse's account. Include your spouse's social security number in the statement.

 This election to apply part or all of the amount overpaid to your 2018 estimated tax can't be changed later.

Amount You Owe

 To avoid interest and penalties, pay your taxes in full by April 17, 2018. You don't have to pay if line 78 is under $1.

Include any estimated payments from line 79 in the amount you enter on line 78. Don't include any estimated payments for 2018 in this payment. Instead, make the estimated payment separately.

Bad check or payment. The penalty for writing a bad check to the IRS is $25 or 2% of the check, whichever is more. However, if the amount of the check is less than $25, the penalty equals the amount of the check. This also applies to other forms of payments if the IRS doesn't receive the funds. Use *Tax Topic 206*.

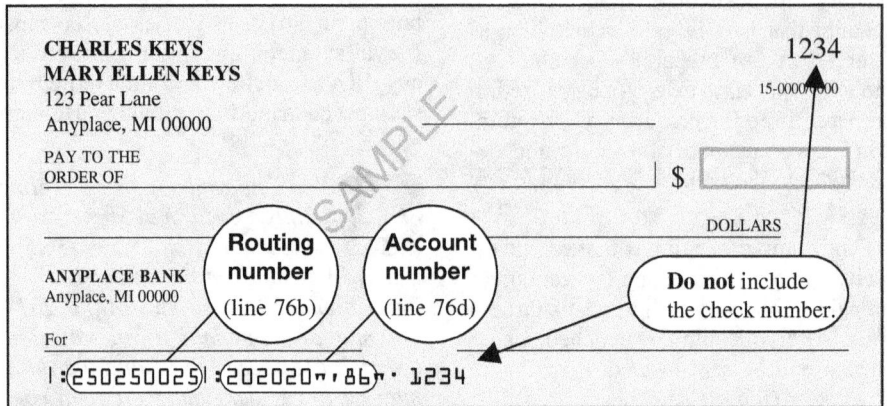

 The routing and account numbers may be in different places on your check.

Line 78

Amount You Owe

IRS offers several payment options. You can pay online, by phone, mobile device, cash (maximum $1,000 per day and per transaction), check or money order. Go to *IRS.gov/Payments* for payment options.

Pay Online

IRS offers an electronic payment option that is right for you. Paying online is convenient and secure and helps make sure we get your payments on time. To pay your taxes online or for more information, go to *IRS.gov/Payments*. You can pay using any of the following methods.

• **IRS Direct Pay** for online transfers directly from your checking or savings account at no cost to you, go to *IRS.gov/Payments*.

• **Pay by Card.** To pay by debit or credit card, go to *IRS.gov/Payments*. A convenience fee is charged by these service providers.

• **Electronic Fund Withdrawal** (EFW) is an integrated *e-file*/e-pay option offered when filing your federal taxes electronically using tax preparation software, through a tax professional, or the IRS at *IRS.gov/Payments*.

• **Online Payment Agreement.** If you can't pay in full by the due date of your tax return you can apply for an online monthly installment agreement at *IRS.gov/Payments*. Once you complete the online process, you will receive immediate notification of whether your

agreement has been approved. A user fee charge is charged.

• **IRS2Go** is the mobile application of the IRS; you can access Direct Pay or Pay By Card by downloading the application.

Pay by Phone

Paying by phone is another safe and secure method of paying electronically. Use one of the following methods **(1)** call one of the debit or credit card service providers or **(2)** use the Electronic Federal Tax Payment System (EFTPS).

Debit or credit card. Call one of our service providers. Each charges a fee that varies by provider, card type, and payment amount.

WorldPay US, Inc.
1-844-729-8298
(1-844-PAY-TAX-8™)
www.payUSAtax.com

Official Payments
1-888-UPAY-TAX™
(1-888-872-9829)
www.officialpayments.com

Link2Gov Corporation
1-888-PAY-1040™
(1-888-729-1040)
www.PAY1040.com

EFTPS. To use EFTPS, you must be enrolled either online or have an enrollment form mailed to you. To make a payment using EFTPS, call 1-800-555-4477 (English) or 1-800-244-4829 (Español). People who are deaf, hard of hearing, or have a speech disability and who have access to TTY/TDD equipment can call 1-800-733-4829. For more information about EFTPS, go to *IRS.gov/Payments* or *www.EFTPS.gov*.

Pay by Mobile Device

To pay through your mobile device, download the IRS2Go app.

Pay by Cash

Cash is an in-person payment option for individuals provided through retail partners with a maximum of $1,000 per day per transaction. To make a cash payment, you must first be registered online at *www.officialpayments.com/fed*, our Official Payment provider.

Pay by Check or Money Order

Before submitting a payment through the mail, please consider alternative methods. One of our safe, quick, and easy electronic payment options might be right for you. If you choose to mail a tax payment, make your check or money order payable to "United States Treasury" for the full amount due. Don't send cash. Don't attach the payment to your return. Write "2017 Form 1040" and your name, address, daytime phone number, and social security number (SSN) on your payment and attach Form 1040-V. For the most up-to-date information on Form 1040-V, go to *IRS.gov/Form1040V*. If you are filing a joint return, enter the SSN shown first on your tax return.

To help us process your payment, enter the amount on the right side of the check like this: $ XXX.XX. Don't use dashes or lines (for example, don't enter "$ XXX—" or "$ XXX^{xx}/100").

Mail your 2017 tax return, payment, and Form 1040-V to the address shown on the form that applies to you.

No checks of $100 million or more accepted. The IRS can't accept a single check (including a cashier's check) for amounts of $100,000,000 ($100 million) or more. If you are sending $100 million or more by check, you'll need to spread the payment over 2 or more checks with each check made out for an amount less than $100 million. This limit doesn't apply to other methods of payment (such as electronic payments). Please consider

a method of payment other than check if the amount of the payment is over $100 million.

What If You Can't Pay?

If you can't pay the full amount shown on line 78 when you file, you can ask for:

- An installment agreement, or
- An extension of time to pay.

Installment agreement. Under an installment agreement, you can pay all or part of the tax you owe in monthly installments. However, even if an installment agreement is granted, you will be charged interest and may be charged a late payment penalty on the tax not paid by April 17, 2018. You also must pay a fee. To limit the interest and penalty charges, pay as much of the tax as possible when you file. But before requesting an installment agreement, you should consider other less costly alternatives, such as a bank loan or credit card payment.

To ask for an installment agreement, you can apply online or use Form 9465. To apply online, go to IRS.gov and click on *Apply for an Online Payment Plan*.

Extension of time to pay. If paying the tax when it is due would cause you an undue hardship, you can ask for an extension of time to pay by filing Form 1127 by April 17, 2018. An extension generally won't be granted for more than 6 months. You will be charged interest on the tax not paid by April 15, 2018. You must pay the tax before the extension runs out. Penalties and interest will be imposed until taxes are paid in full. For the most up-to-date information on Form 1127, go to *IRS.gov/Form1127*.

Line 79

Estimated Tax Penalty

You may owe this penalty if:

- Line 78 is at least $1,000 and it is more than 10% of the tax shown on your return, or
- You didn't pay enough estimated tax by any of the due dates. This is true even if you are due a refund.

For most people, the "tax shown on your return" is the amount on your 2017 Form 1040, line 63, minus the total of any amounts shown on lines 61, 66a, 67, 68, 69, and 72 and Forms 8828, 4137,

5329 (Parts III through IX only), 8885, and 8919. Also subtract from line 63 any:

- Tax on an excess parachute payment,
- Excise tax on insider stock compensation of an expatriated corporation,
- Uncollected social security and Medicare or RRTA tax on tips or group-term life insurance, and
- Look-back interest due under section 167(g) or 460(b).

When figuring the amount on line 63, include household employment taxes only if line 64 is more than zero or you would owe the penalty even if you didn't include those taxes.

Exception. You won't owe the penalty if your 2016 tax return was for a tax year of 12 full months and either of the following applies.

1. You had no tax shown on your 2016 return and you were a U.S. citizen or resident for all of 2016.

2. The total of lines 64, 65, and 71 on your 2017 return is at least 100% of the tax shown on your 2016 return (110% of that amount if you aren't a farmer or fisherman, and your adjusted gross income (AGI) shown on your 2016 return was more than $150,000 (more than $75,000 if married filing separately for 2017)). Your estimated tax payments for 2017 must have been made on time and for the required amount.

For most people, the "tax shown on your 2016 return" is the amount on your 2016 Form 1040, line 63, minus the total of any amounts shown on lines 61, 66a, 67, 68, 69, and 72 and Forms 8828, 4137, 5329 (Parts III through IX only), 8885, and 8919. Also subtract from line 63 any:

- Tax on an excess parachute payment,
- Excise tax on insider stock compensation of an expatriated corporation,
- Uncollected social security and Medicare or RRTA tax on tips or group-term life insurance, and
- Look-back interest due under section 167(g) or 460(b).

When figuring the amount on line 63, include household employment taxes only if line 64 is more than zero or you would have owed the estimated tax penalty for 2016 even if you didn't include those taxes.

Need more information or forms? Visit IRS.gov.

Figuring the Penalty

If the *Exception* just described doesn't apply and you choose to figure the penalty yourself, use Form 2210 (or 2210-F for farmers and fishermen).

Enter any penalty on line 79. Add the penalty to any tax due and enter the total on line 78.

However, if you have an overpayment on line 75, subtract the penalty from the amount you would otherwise enter on line 76a or line 77. Lines 76a, 77, and 79 must equal line 75.

If the penalty is more than the overpayment on line 75, enter -0- on lines 76a and 77. Then subtract line 75 from line 79 and enter the result on line 78.

Don't file Form 2210 with your return unless Form 2210 indicates that you must do so. Instead, keep it for your records.

 Because Form 2210 is complicated, you can leave line 79 blank and the IRS will figure the penalty and send you a bill. We won't charge you interest on the penalty if you pay by the date specified on the bill. If your income varied during the year, the annualized income installment method may reduce the amount of your penalty. But you must file Form 2210 because the IRS can't figure your penalty under this method. See the Instructions for Form 2210 for other situations in which you may be able to lower your penalty by filing Form 2210.

Third Party Designee

If you want to allow your preparer, a friend, a family member, or any other person you choose to discuss your 2017 tax return with the IRS, check the "Yes" box in the "Third Party Designee" area of your return. Also, enter the designee's name, phone number, and any five digits the designee chooses as his or her personal identification number (PIN).

If you check the "Yes" box, you, and your spouse if filing a joint return, are authorizing the IRS to call the designee to answer any questions that may arise during the processing of your return. You also are authorizing the designee to:

• Give the IRS any information that is missing from your return,

• Call the IRS for information about the processing of your return or the status of your refund or payment(s),

• Receive copies of notices or transcripts related to your return, upon request, and

• Respond to certain IRS notices about math errors, offsets, and return preparation.

You aren't authorizing the designee to receive any refund check, bind you to anything (including any additional tax liability), or otherwise represent you before the IRS. If you want to expand the designee's authorization, see Pub. 947.

The authorization will automatically end no later than the due date (not counting extensions) for filing your 2018 tax return. This is April 15, 2019, for most people.

Sign Your Return

Form 1040 isn't considered a valid return unless you sign it. If you are filing a joint return, your spouse also must sign. If your spouse can't sign the return, see Pub. 501. Be sure to date your return and enter your occupation(s). If you have someone prepare your return, you are still responsible for the correctness of the return. If your return is signed by a representative for you, you must have a power of attorney attached that specifically authorizes the representative to sign your return. To do this, you can use Form 2848. If you are filing a joint return as a surviving spouse, see *Death of a Taxpayer,* later.

Court-Appointed Conservator, Guardian, or Other Fiduciary

If you are a court-appointed conservator, guardian, or other fiduciary for a mentally or physically incompetent individual who has to file Form 1040, sign your name for the individual and file Form 56.

Child's Return

If your child can't sign his or her return, either parent can sign the child's name in the space provided. Then, enter "By (your signature), parent for minor child."

Daytime Phone Number

Providing your daytime phone number may help speed the processing of your return. We may have questions about items on your return, such as the earned income credit or the credit for child and dependent care expenses. If you answer our questions over the phone, we may be able to continue processing your return without mailing you a letter. If you are filing a joint return, you can enter either your or your spouse's daytime phone number.

Electronic Return Signatures

To file your return electronically, you must sign the return electronically using a personal identification number (PIN). If you are filing online using software, you must use a Self-Select PIN. If you are filing electronically using a tax practitioner, you can use a Self-Select PIN or a Practitioner PIN.

Self-Select PIN. The Self-Select PIN method allows you to create your own PIN. If you are married filing jointly, you and your spouse will each need to create a PIN and enter these PINs as your electronic signatures.

A PIN is any combination of five digits you choose except five zeros. If you use a PIN, there is nothing to sign and nothing to mail—not even your Forms W-2.

To verify your identity, you will be prompted to enter your adjusted gross income (AGI) from your originally filed 2016 federal income tax return, if applicable. Don't use your AGI from an amended return (Form 1040X) or a math error correction made by the IRS. AGI is the amount shown on your 2016 Form 1040, line 38; Form 1040A, line 22; or Form 1040EZ, line 4. If you don't have your 2016 income tax return, call the IRS at 1-800-908-9946 to get a free transcript of your return or visit *IRS.gov/ Transcript*. (If you filed electronically last year, you may use your prior year PIN to verify your identity instead of your prior year AGI. The prior year PIN is the five-digit PIN you used to electronically sign your 2016 return.) You also will be prompted to enter your date of birth (DOB).

You can't use the Self-Select PIN method if you are a first-time filer under age 16 at the end of 2017.

Practitioner PIN. The Practitioner PIN method allows you to authorize your tax practitioner to enter or generate your PIN. The practitioner can provide you with details.

Form 8453. You must send in a paper Form 8453 if you have to attach certain forms or other documents that can't be electronically filed. See Form 8453.

Identity Protection PIN

For 2017, if you received an Identity Protection Personal Identification Number (IP PIN) from the IRS, enter it in the IP PIN spaces provided below your daytime phone number. You must correctly enter all six numbers of your IP PIN. If you didn't receive an IP PIN, leave these spaces blank.

 New IP PINs are issued every year. Enter the latest IP PIN you received. IP PINs for 2017 tax returns generally were sent in December 2017.

If you are filing a joint return and both taxpayers receive an IP PIN, only the taxpayer whose social security number (SSN) appears first on the tax return should enter his or her IP PIN. However, if you are filing electronically, both taxpayers must enter their IP PINs.

If you need more information, go to *IRS.gov/CP01A*. If you received an IP PIN but misplaced it, call 1-800-908-4490.

Paid Preparer Must Sign Your Return

Generally, anyone you pay to prepare your return must sign it and include their Preparer Tax Identification Number (PTIN) in the space provided. The pre-parer must give you a copy of the return for your records. Someone who prepares your return but doesn't charge you shouldn't sign your return.

Assemble Your Return

Assemble any schedules and forms behind Form 1040 in order of the "Attachment Sequence No." shown in the upper right corner of the schedule or form. If you have supporting statements, arrange them in the same order as the schedules or forms they support and attach them last. Don't attach correspondence or other items unless required to do so. Attach Forms W-2 and 2439 to the front of Form 1040. If you received a Form W-2c (a corrected Form W-2), attach your original Forms W-2 and any Forms W-2c. Attach Forms W-2G and 1099-R to the front of Form 1040 if tax was withheld.

2017 Tax Table

 CAUTION

See the instructions for line 44 to see if you must use the Tax Table below to figure your tax.

Example. Mr. and Mrs. Brown are filing a joint return. Their taxable income on Form 1040, line 43, is $25,300. First, they find the $25,300-25,350 taxable income line. Next, they find the column for married filing jointly and read down the column. The amount shown where the taxable income line and filing status column meet is $2,866. This is the tax amount they should enter on Form 1040, line 44.

Sample Table

At Least	But Less Than	Single	Married filing jointly*	Married filing separately	Head of a household
			Your tax is—		
25,200	25,250	3,318	2,851	3,318	3,116
25,250	25,300	3,325	2,859	3,325	3,124
25,300	25,350	3,333	(2,866)	3,333	3,131
25,350	25,400	3,340	2,874	3,340	3,139

This illustration displays the tax table amounts for 25,300–25,350, the line the Browns would use to find their tax.

If line 43 (taxable income) is— At least	But less than	Single	Married filing jointly *	Married filing sepa-rately	Head of a house-hold
			Your tax is—		
0	5	0	0	0	0
5	15	1	1	1	1
15	25	2	2	2	2
25	50	4	4	4	4
50	75	6	6	6	6
75	100	9	9	9	9
100	125	11	11	11	11
125	150	14	14	14	14
150	175	16	16	16	16
175	200	19	19	19	19
200	225	21	21	21	21
225	250	24	24	24	24
250	275	26	26	26	26
275	300	29	29	29	29
300	325	31	31	31	31
325	350	34	34	34	34
350	375	36	36	36	36
375	400	39	39	39	39
400	425	41	41	41	41
425	450	44	44	44	44
450	475	46	46	46	46
475	500	49	49	49	49
500	525	51	51	51	51
525	550	54	54	54	54
550	575	56	56	56	56
575	600	59	59	59	59
600	625	61	61	61	61
625	650	64	64	64	64
650	675	66	66	66	66
675	700	69	69	69	69
700	725	71	71	71	71
725	750	74	74	74	74
750	775	76	76	76	76
775	800	79	79	79	79
800	825	81	81	81	81
825	850	84	84	84	84
850	875	86	86	86	86
875	900	89	89	89	89
900	925	91	91	91	91
925	950	94	94	94	94
950	975	96	96	96	96
975	1,000	99	99	99	99

1,000

At least	But less than	Single	Married filing jointly *	Married filing sepa-rately	Head of a house-hold
			Your tax is—		
1,000	1,025	101	101	101	101
1,025	1,050	104	104	104	104
1,050	1,075	106	106	106	106
1,075	1,100	109	109	109	109
1,100	1,125	111	111	111	111
1,125	1,150	114	114	114	114
1,150	1,175	116	116	116	116
1,175	1,200	119	119	119	119
1,200	1,225	121	121	121	121
1,225	1,250	124	124	124	124
1,250	1,275	126	126	126	126
1,275	1,300	129	129	129	129
1,300	1,325	131	131	131	131
1,325	1,350	134	134	134	134
1,350	1,375	136	136	136	136
1,375	1,400	139	139	139	139
1,400	1,425	141	141	141	141
1,425	1,450	144	144	144	144
1,450	1,475	146	146	146	146
1,475	1,500	149	149	149	149
1,500	1,525	151	151	151	151
1,525	1,550	154	154	154	154
1,550	1,575	156	156	156	156
1,575	1,600	159	159	159	159
1,600	1,625	161	161	161	161
1,625	1,650	164	164	164	164
1,650	1,675	166	166	166	166
1,675	1,700	169	169	169	169
1,700	1,725	171	171	171	171
1,725	1,750	174	174	174	174
1,750	1,775	176	176	176	176
1,775	1,800	179	179	179	179
1,800	1,825	181	181	181	181
1,825	1,850	184	184	184	184
1,850	1,875	186	186	186	186
1,875	1,900	189	189	189	189
1,900	1,925	191	191	191	191
1,925	1,950	194	194	194	194
1,950	1,975	196	196	196	196
1,975	2,000	199	199	199	199

2,000

At least	But less than	Single	Married filing jointly *	Married filing sepa-rately	Head of a house-hold
			Your tax is—		
2,000	2,025	201	201	201	201
2,025	2,050	204	204	204	204
2,050	2,075	206	206	206	206
2,075	2,100	209	209	209	209
2,100	2,125	211	211	211	211
2,125	2,150	214	214	214	214
2,150	2,175	216	216	216	216
2,175	2,200	219	219	219	219
2,200	2,225	221	221	221	221
2,225	2,250	224	224	224	224
2,250	2,275	226	226	226	226
2,275	2,300	229	229	229	229
2,300	2,325	231	231	231	231
2,325	2,350	234	234	234	234
2,350	2,375	236	236	236	236
2,375	2,400	239	239	239	239
2,400	2,425	241	241	241	241
2,425	2,450	244	244	244	244
2,450	2,475	246	246	246	246
2,475	2,500	249	249	249	249
2,500	2,525	251	251	251	251
2,525	2,550	254	254	254	254
2,550	2,575	256	256	256	256
2,575	2,600	259	259	259	259
2,600	2,625	261	261	261	261
2,625	2,650	264	264	264	264
2,650	2,675	266	266	266	266
2,675	2,700	269	269	269	269
2,700	2,725	271	271	271	271
2,725	2,750	274	274	274	274
2,750	2,775	276	276	276	276
2,775	2,800	279	279	279	279
2,800	2,825	281	281	281	281
2,825	2,850	284	284	284	284
2,850	2,875	286	286	286	286
2,875	2,900	289	289	289	289
2,900	2,925	291	291	291	291
2,925	2,950	294	294	294	294
2,950	2,975	296	296	296	296
2,975	3,000	299	299	299	299

(Continued)

* This column must also be used by a qualifying widow(er).

3,000

If line 43 (taxable income) is—		And you are—			
At least	But less than	Single	Married filing jointly *	Married filing separately	Head of a house-hold
		Your tax is—			
3,000	3,050	303	303	303	303
3,050	3,100	308	308	308	308
3,100	3,150	313	313	313	313
3,150	3,200	318	318	318	318
3,200	3,250	323	323	323	323
3,250	3,300	328	328	328	328
3,300	3,350	333	333	333	333
3,350	3,400	338	338	338	338
3,400	3,450	343	343	343	343
3,450	3,500	348	348	348	348
3,500	3,550	353	353	353	353
3,550	3,600	358	358	358	358
3,600	3,650	363	363	363	363
3,650	3,700	368	368	368	368
3,700	3,750	373	373	373	373
3,750	3,800	378	378	378	378
3,800	3,850	383	383	383	383
3,850	3,900	388	388	388	388
3,900	3,950	393	393	393	393
3,950	4,000	398	398	398	398

4,000

At least	But less than	Single	Married filing jointly *	Married filing separately	Head of a house-hold
4,000	4,050	403	403	403	403
4,050	4,100	408	408	408	408
4,100	4,150	413	413	413	413
4,150	4,200	418	418	418	418
4,200	4,250	423	423	423	423
4,250	4,300	428	428	428	428
4,300	4,350	433	433	433	433
4,350	4,400	438	438	438	438
4,400	4,450	443	443	443	443
4,450	4,500	448	448	448	448
4,500	4,550	453	453	453	453
4,550	4,600	458	458	458	458
4,600	4,650	463	463	463	463
4,650	4,700	468	468	468	468
4,700	4,750	473	473	473	473
4,750	4,800	478	478	478	478
4,800	4,850	483	483	483	483
4,850	4,900	488	488	488	488
4,900	4,950	493	493	493	493
4,950	5,000	498	498	498	498

5,000

At least	But less than	Single	Married filing jointly *	Married filing separately	Head of a house-hold
5,000	5,050	503	503	503	503
5,050	5,100	508	508	508	508
5,100	5,150	513	513	513	513
5,150	5,200	518	518	518	518
5,200	5,250	523	523	523	523
5,250	5,300	528	528	528	528
5,300	5,350	533	533	533	533
5,350	5,400	538	538	538	538
5,400	5,450	543	543	543	543
5,450	5,500	548	548	548	548
5,500	5,550	553	553	553	553
5,550	5,600	558	558	558	558
5,600	5,650	563	563	563	563
5,650	5,700	568	568	568	568
5,700	5,750	573	573	573	573
5,750	5,800	578	578	578	578
5,800	5,850	583	583	583	583
5,850	5,900	588	588	588	588
5,900	5,950	593	593	593	593
5,950	6,000	598	598	598	598

6,000

At least	But less than	Single	Married filing jointly *	Married filing separately	Head of a house-hold
6,000	6,050	603	603	603	603
6,050	6,100	608	608	608	608
6,100	6,150	613	613	613	613
6,150	6,200	618	618	618	618
6,200	6,250	623	623	623	623
6,250	6,300	628	628	628	628
6,300	6,350	633	633	633	633
6,350	6,400	638	638	638	638
6,400	6,450	643	643	643	643
6,450	6,500	648	648	648	648
6,500	6,550	653	653	653	653
6,550	6,600	658	658	658	658
6,600	6,650	663	663	663	663
6,650	6,700	668	668	668	668
6,700	6,750	673	673	673	673
6,750	6,800	678	678	678	678
6,800	6,850	683	683	683	683
6,850	6,900	688	688	688	688
6,900	6,950	693	693	693	693
6,950	7,000	698	698	698	698

7,000

At least	But less than	Single	Married filing jointly *	Married filing separately	Head of a house-hold
7,000	7,050	703	703	703	703
7,050	7,100	708	708	708	708
7,100	7,150	713	713	713	713
7,150	7,200	718	718	718	718
7,200	7,250	723	723	723	723
7,250	7,300	728	728	728	728
7,300	7,350	733	733	733	733
7,350	7,400	738	738	738	738
7,400	7,450	743	743	743	743
7,450	7,500	748	748	748	748
7,500	7,550	753	753	753	753
7,550	7,600	758	758	758	758
7,600	7,650	763	763	763	763
7,650	7,700	768	768	768	768
7,700	7,750	773	773	773	773
7,750	7,800	778	778	778	778
7,800	7,850	783	783	783	783
7,850	7,900	788	788	788	788
7,900	7,950	793	793	793	793
7,950	8,000	798	798	798	798

8,000

At least	But less than	Single	Married filing jointly *	Married filing separately	Head of a house-hold
8,000	8,050	803	803	803	803
8,050	8,100	808	808	808	808
8,100	8,150	813	813	813	813
8,150	8,200	818	818	818	818
8,200	8,250	823	823	823	823
8,250	8,300	828	828	828	828
8,300	8,350	833	833	833	833
8,350	8,400	838	838	838	838
8,400	8,450	843	843	843	843
8,450	8,500	848	848	848	848
8,500	8,550	853	853	853	853
8,550	8,600	858	858	858	858
8,600	8,650	863	863	863	863
8,650	8,700	868	868	868	868
8,700	8,750	873	873	873	873
8,750	8,800	878	878	878	878
8,800	8,850	883	883	883	883
8,850	8,900	888	888	888	888
8,900	8,950	893	893	893	893
8,950	9,000	898	898	898	898

9,000

At least	But less than	Single	Married filing jointly *	Married filing separately	Head of a house-hold
9,000	9,050	903	903	903	903
9,050	9,100	908	908	908	908
9,100	9,150	913	913	913	913
9,150	9,200	918	918	918	918
9,200	9,250	923	923	923	923
9,250	9,300	928	928	928	928
9,300	9,350	933	933	933	933
9,350	9,400	940	938	940	938
9,400	9,450	948	943	948	943
9,450	9,500	955	948	955	948
9,500	9,550	963	953	963	953
9,550	9,600	970	958	970	958
9,600	9,650	978	963	978	963
9,650	9,700	985	968	985	968
9,700	9,750	993	973	993	973
9,750	9,800	1,000	978	1,000	978
9,800	9,850	1,008	983	1,008	983
9,850	9,900	1,015	988	1,015	988
9,900	9,950	1,023	993	1,023	993
9,950	10,000	1,030	998	1,030	998

10,000

At least	But less than	Single	Married filing jointly *	Married filing separately	Head of a house-hold
10,000	10,050	1,038	1,003	1,038	1,003
10,050	10,100	1,045	1,008	1,045	1,008
10,100	10,150	1,053	1,013	1,053	1,013
10,150	10,200	1,060	1,018	1,060	1,018
10,200	10,250	1,068	1,023	1,068	1,023
10,250	10,300	1,075	1,028	1,075	1,028
10,300	10,350	1,083	1,033	1,083	1,033
10,350	10,400	1,090	1,038	1,090	1,038
10,400	10,450	1,098	1,043	1,098	1,043
10,450	10,500	1,105	1,048	1,105	1,048
10,500	10,550	1,113	1,053	1,113	1,053
10,550	10,600	1,120	1,058	1,120	1,058
10,600	10,650	1,128	1,063	1,128	1,063
10,650	10,700	1,135	1,068	1,135	1,068
10,700	10,750	1,143	1,073	1,143	1,073
10,750	10,800	1,150	1,078	1,150	1,078
10,800	10,850	1,158	1,083	1,158	1,083
10,850	10,900	1,165	1,088	1,165	1,088
10,900	10,950	1,173	1,093	1,173	1,093
10,950	11,000	1,180	1,098	1,180	1,098

11,000

At least	But less than	Single	Married filing jointly *	Married filing separately	Head of a house-hold
11,000	11,050	1,188	1,103	1,188	1,103
11,050	11,100	1,195	1,108	1,195	1,108
11,100	11,150	1,203	1,113	1,203	1,113
11,150	11,200	1,210	1,118	1,210	1,118
11,200	11,250	1,218	1,123	1,218	1,123
11,250	11,300	1,225	1,128	1,225	1,128
11,300	11,350	1,233	1,133	1,233	1,133
11,350	11,400	1,240	1,138	1,240	1,138
11,400	11,450	1,248	1,143	1,248	1,143
11,450	11,500	1,255	1,148	1,255	1,148
11,500	11,550	1,263	1,153	1,263	1,153
11,550	11,600	1,270	1,158	1,270	1,158
11,600	11,650	1,278	1,163	1,278	1,163
11,650	11,700	1,285	1,168	1,285	1,168
11,700	11,750	1,293	1,173	1,293	1,173
11,750	11,800	1,300	1,178	1,300	1,178
11,800	11,850	1,308	1,183	1,308	1,183
11,850	11,900	1,315	1,188	1,315	1,188
11,900	11,950	1,323	1,193	1,323	1,193
11,950	12,000	1,330	1,198	1,330	1,198

* This column must also be used by a qualifying widow(er).

(Continued)

Need more information or forms? Visit IRS.gov.

12,000

At least	But less than	Single	Married filing jointly *	Married filing separately	Head of a household
12,000	12,050	1,338	1,203	1,338	1,203
12,050	12,100	1,345	1,208	1,345	1,208
12,100	12,150	1,353	1,213	1,353	1,213
12,150	12,200	1,360	1,218	1,360	1,218
12,200	12,250	1,368	1,223	1,368	1,223
12,250	12,300	1,375	1,228	1,375	1,228
12,300	12,350	1,383	1,233	1,383	1,233
12,350	12,400	1,390	1,238	1,390	1,238
12,400	12,450	1,398	1,243	1,398	1,243
12,450	12,500	1,405	1,248	1,405	1,248
12,500	12,550	1,413	1,253	1,413	1,253
12,550	12,600	1,420	1,258	1,420	1,258
12,600	12,650	1,428	1,263	1,428	1,263
12,650	12,700	1,435	1,268	1,435	1,268
12,700	12,750	1,443	1,273	1,443	1,273
12,750	12,800	1,450	1,278	1,450	1,278
12,800	12,850	1,458	1,283	1,458	1,283
12,850	12,900	1,465	1,288	1,465	1,288
12,900	12,950	1,473	1,293	1,473	1,293
12,950	13,000	1,480	1,298	1,480	1,298

13,000

At least	But less than	Single	Married filing jointly *	Married filing separately	Head of a household
13,000	13,050	1,488	1,303	1,488	1,303
13,050	13,100	1,495	1,308	1,495	1,308
13,100	13,150	1,503	1,313	1,503	1,313
13,150	13,200	1,510	1,318	1,510	1,318
13,200	13,250	1,518	1,323	1,518	1,323
13,250	13,300	1,525	1,328	1,525	1,328
13,300	13,350	1,533	1,333	1,533	1,333
13,350	13,400	1,540	1,338	1,540	1,339
13,400	13,450	1,548	1,343	1,548	1,346
13,450	13,500	1,555	1,348	1,555	1,354
13,500	13,550	1,563	1,353	1,563	1,361
13,550	13,600	1,570	1,358	1,570	1,369
13,600	13,650	1,578	1,363	1,578	1,376
13,650	13,700	1,585	1,368	1,585	1,384
13,700	13,750	1,593	1,373	1,593	1,391
13,750	13,800	1,600	1,378	1,600	1,399
13,800	13,850	1,608	1,383	1,608	1,406
13,850	13,900	1,615	1,388	1,615	1,414
13,900	13,950	1,623	1,393	1,623	1,421
13,950	14,000	1,630	1,398	1,630	1,429

14,000

At least	But less than	Single	Married filing jointly *	Married filing separately	Head of a household
14,000	14,050	1,638	1,403	1,638	1,436
14,050	14,100	1,645	1,408	1,645	1,444
14,100	14,150	1,653	1,413	1,653	1,451
14,150	14,200	1,660	1,418	1,660	1,459
14,200	14,250	1,668	1,423	1,668	1,466
14,250	14,300	1,675	1,428	1,675	1,474
14,300	14,350	1,683	1,433	1,683	1,481
14,350	14,400	1,690	1,438	1,690	1,489
14,400	14,450	1,698	1,443	1,698	1,496
14,450	14,500	1,705	1,448	1,705	1,504
14,500	14,550	1,713	1,453	1,713	1,511
14,550	14,600	1,720	1,458	1,720	1,519
14,600	14,650	1,728	1,463	1,728	1,526
14,650	14,700	1,735	1,468	1,735	1,534
14,700	14,750	1,743	1,473	1,743	1,541
14,750	14,800	1,750	1,478	1,750	1,549
14,800	14,850	1,758	1,483	1,758	1,556
14,850	14,900	1,765	1,488	1,765	1,564
14,900	14,950	1,773	1,493	1,773	1,571
14,950	15,000	1,780	1,498	1,780	1,579

15,000

At least	But less than	Single	Married filing jointly *	Married filing separately	Head of a household
15,000	15,050	1,788	1,503	1,788	1,586
15,050	15,100	1,795	1,508	1,795	1,594
15,100	15,150	1,803	1,513	1,803	1,601
15,150	15,200	1,810	1,518	1,810	1,609
15,200	15,250	1,818	1,523	1,818	1,616
15,250	15,300	1,825	1,528	1,825	1,624
15,300	15,350	1,833	1,533	1,833	1,631
15,350	15,400	1,840	1,538	1,840	1,639
15,400	15,450	1,848	1,543	1,848	1,646
15,450	15,500	1,855	1,548	1,855	1,654
15,500	15,550	1,863	1,553	1,863	1,661
15,550	15,600	1,870	1,558	1,870	1,669
15,600	15,650	1,878	1,563	1,878	1,676
15,650	15,700	1,885	1,568	1,885	1,684
15,700	15,750	1,893	1,573	1,893	1,691
15,750	15,800	1,900	1,578	1,900	1,699
15,800	15,850	1,908	1,583	1,908	1,706
15,850	15,900	1,915	1,588	1,915	1,714
15,900	15,950	1,923	1,593	1,923	1,721
15,950	16,000	1,930	1,598	1,930	1,729

16,000

At least	But less than	Single	Married filing jointly *	Married filing separately	Head of a household
16,000	16,050	1,938	1,603	1,938	1,736
16,050	16,100	1,945	1,608	1,945	1,744
16,100	16,150	1,953	1,613	1,953	1,751
16,150	16,200	1,960	1,618	1,960	1,759
16,200	16,250	1,968	1,623	1,968	1,766
16,250	16,300	1,975	1,628	1,975	1,774
16,300	16,350	1,983	1,633	1,983	1,781
16,350	16,400	1,990	1,638	1,990	1,789
16,400	16,450	1,998	1,643	1,998	1,796
16,450	16,500	2,005	1,648	2,005	1,804
16,500	16,550	2,013	1,653	2,013	1,811
16,550	16,600	2,020	1,658	2,020	1,819
16,600	16,650	2,028	1,663	2,028	1,826
16,650	16,700	2,035	1,668	2,035	1,834
16,700	16,750	2,043	1,673	2,043	1,841
16,750	16,800	2,050	1,678	2,050	1,849
16,800	16,850	2,058	1,683	2,058	1,856
16,850	16,900	2,065	1,688	2,065	1,864
16,900	16,950	2,073	1,693	2,073	1,871
16,950	17,000	2,080	1,698	2,080	1,879

17,000

At least	But less than	Single	Married filing jointly *	Married filing separately	Head of a household
17,000	17,050	2,088	1,703	2,088	1,886
17,050	17,100	2,095	1,708	2,095	1,894
17,100	17,150	2,103	1,713	2,103	1,901
17,150	17,200	2,110	1,718	2,110	1,909
17,200	17,250	2,118	1,723	2,118	1,916
17,250	17,300	2,125	1,728	2,125	1,924
17,300	17,350	2,133	1,733	2,133	1,931
17,350	17,400	2,140	1,738	2,140	1,939
17,400	17,450	2,148	1,743	2,148	1,946
17,450	17,500	2,155	1,748	2,155	1,954
17,500	17,550	2,163	1,753	2,163	1,961
17,550	17,600	2,170	1,758	2,170	1,969
17,600	17,650	2,178	1,763	2,178	1,976
17,650	17,700	2,185	1,768	2,185	1,984
17,700	17,750	2,193	1,773	2,193	1,991
17,750	17,800	2,200	1,778	2,200	1,999
17,800	17,850	2,208	1,783	2,208	2,006
17,850	17,900	2,215	1,788	2,215	2,014
17,900	17,950	2,223	1,793	2,223	2,021
17,950	18,000	2,230	1,798	2,230	2,029

18,000

At least	But less than	Single	Married filing jointly *	Married filing separately	Head of a household
18,000	18,050	2,238	1,803	2,238	2,036
18,050	18,100	2,245	1,808	2,245	2,044
18,100	18,150	2,253	1,813	2,253	2,051
18,150	18,200	2,260	1,818	2,260	2,059
18,200	18,250	2,268	1,823	2,268	2,066
18,250	18,300	2,275	1,828	2,275	2,074
18,300	18,350	2,283	1,833	2,283	2,081
18,350	18,400	2,290	1,838	2,290	2,089
18,400	18,450	2,298	1,843	2,298	2,096
18,450	18,500	2,305	1,848	2,305	2,104
18,500	18,550	2,313	1,853	2,313	2,111
18,550	18,600	2,320	1,858	2,320	2,119
18,600	18,650	2,328	1,863	2,328	2,126
18,650	18,700	2,335	1,869	2,335	2,134
18,700	18,750	2,343	1,876	2,343	2,141
18,750	18,800	2,350	1,884	2,350	2,149
18,800	18,850	2,358	1,891	2,358	2,156
18,850	18,900	2,365	1,899	2,365	2,164
18,900	18,950	2,373	1,906	2,373	2,171
18,950	19,000	2,380	1,914	2,380	2,179

19,000

At least	But less than	Single	Married filing jointly *	Married filing separately	Head of a household
19,000	19,050	2,388	1,921	2,388	2,186
19,050	19,100	2,395	1,929	2,395	2,194
19,100	19,150	2,403	1,936	2,403	2,201
19,150	19,200	2,410	1,944	2,410	2,209
19,200	19,250	2,418	1,951	2,418	2,216
19,250	19,300	2,425	1,959	2,425	2,224
19,300	19,350	2,433	1,966	2,433	2,231
19,350	19,400	2,440	1,974	2,440	2,239
19,400	19,450	2,448	1,981	2,448	2,246
19,450	19,500	2,455	1,989	2,455	2,254
19,500	19,550	2,463	1,996	2,463	2,261
19,550	19,600	2,470	2,004	2,470	2,269
19,600	19,650	2,478	2,011	2,478	2,276
19,650	19,700	2,485	2,019	2,485	2,284
19,700	19,750	2,493	2,026	2,493	2,291
19,750	19,800	2,500	2,034	2,500	2,299
19,800	19,850	2,508	2,041	2,508	2,306
19,850	19,900	2,515	2,049	2,515	2,314
19,900	19,950	2,523	2,056	2,523	2,321
19,950	20,000	2,530	2,064	2,530	2,329

20,000

At least	But less than	Single	Married filing jointly *	Married filing separately	Head of a household
20,000	20,050	2,538	2,071	2,538	2,336
20,050	20,100	2,545	2,079	2,545	2,344
20,100	20,150	2,553	2,086	2,553	2,351
20,150	20,200	2,560	2,094	2,560	2,359
20,200	20,250	2,568	2,101	2,568	2,366
20,250	20,300	2,575	2,109	2,575	2,374
20,300	20,350	2,583	2,116	2,583	2,381
20,350	20,400	2,590	2,124	2,590	2,389
20,400	20,450	2,598	2,131	2,598	2,396
20,450	20,500	2,605	2,139	2,605	2,404
20,500	20,550	2,613	2,146	2,613	2,411
20,550	20,600	2,620	2,154	2,620	2,419
20,600	20,650	2,628	2,161	2,628	2,426
20,650	20,700	2,635	2,169	2,635	2,434
20,700	20,750	2,643	2,176	2,643	2,441
20,750	20,800	2,650	2,184	2,650	2,449
20,800	20,850	2,658	2,191	2,658	2,456
20,850	20,900	2,665	2,199	2,665	2,464
20,900	20,950	2,673	2,206	2,673	2,471
20,950	21,000	2,680	2,214	2,680	2,479

(Continued)

* This column must also be used by a qualifying widow(er).

If line 43 (taxable income) is—		And you are—			
At least	But less than	Single	Married filing jointly *	Married filing separately	Head of a house-hold
		Your tax is—			

21,000

At least	But less than	Single	Married filing jointly *	Married filing separately	Head of a household
21,000	21,050	2,688	2,221	2,688	2,486
21,050	21,100	2,695	2,229	2,695	2,494
21,100	21,150	2,703	2,236	2,703	2,501
21,150	21,200	2,710	2,244	2,710	2,509
21,200	21,250	2,718	2,251	2,718	2,516
21,250	21,300	2,725	2,259	2,725	2,524
21,300	21,350	2,733	2,266	2,733	2,531
21,350	21,400	2,740	2,274	2,740	2,539
21,400	21,450	2,748	2,281	2,748	2,546
21,450	21,500	2,755	2,289	2,755	2,554
21,500	21,550	2,763	2,296	2,763	2,561
21,550	21,600	2,770	2,304	2,770	2,569
21,600	21,650	2,778	2,311	2,778	2,576
21,650	21,700	2,785	2,319	2,785	2,584
21,700	21,750	2,793	2,326	2,793	2,591
21,750	21,800	2,800	2,334	2,800	2,599
21,800	21,850	2,808	2,341	2,808	2,606
21,850	21,900	2,815	2,349	2,815	2,614
21,900	21,950	2,823	2,356	2,823	2,621
21,950	22,000	2,830	2,364	2,830	2,629

22,000

At least	But less than	Single	Married filing jointly *	Married filing separately	Head of a household
22,000	22,050	2,838	2,371	2,838	2,636
22,050	22,100	2,845	2,379	2,845	2,644
22,100	22,150	2,853	2,386	2,853	2,651
22,150	22,200	2,860	2,394	2,860	2,659
22,200	22,250	2,868	2,401	2,868	2,666
22,250	22,300	2,875	2,409	2,875	2,674
22,300	22,350	2,883	2,416	2,883	2,681
22,350	22,400	2,890	2,424	2,890	2,689
22,400	22,450	2,898	2,431	2,898	2,696
22,450	22,500	2,905	2,439	2,905	2,704
22,500	22,550	2,913	2,446	2,913	2,711
22,550	22,600	2,920	2,454	2,920	2,719
22,600	22,650	2,928	2,461	2,928	2,726
22,650	22,700	2,935	2,469	2,935	2,734
22,700	22,750	2,943	2,476	2,943	2,741
22,750	22,800	2,950	2,484	2,950	2,749
22,800	22,850	2,958	2,491	2,958	2,756
22,850	22,900	2,965	2,499	2,965	2,764
22,900	22,950	2,973	2,506	2,973	2,771
22,950	23,000	2,980	2,514	2,980	2,779

23,000

At least	But less than	Single	Married filing jointly *	Married filing separately	Head of a household
23,000	23,050	2,988	2,521	2,988	2,786
23,050	23,100	2,995	2,529	2,995	2,794
23,100	23,150	3,003	2,536	3,003	2,801
23,150	23,200	3,010	2,544	3,010	2,809
23,200	23,250	3,018	2,551	3,018	2,816
23,250	23,300	3,025	2,559	3,025	2,824
23,300	23,350	3,033	2,566	3,033	2,831
23,350	23,400	3,040	2,574	3,040	2,839
23,400	23,450	3,048	2,581	3,048	2,846
23,450	23,500	3,055	2,589	3,055	2,854
23,500	23,550	3,063	2,596	3,063	2,861
23,550	23,600	3,070	2,604	3,070	2,869
23,600	23,650	3,078	2,611	3,078	2,876
23,650	23,700	3,085	2,619	3,085	2,884
23,700	23,750	3,093	2,626	3,093	2,891
23,750	23,800	3,100	2,634	3,100	2,899
23,800	23,850	3,108	2,641	3,108	2,906
23,850	23,900	3,115	2,649	3,115	2,914
23,900	23,950	3,123	2,656	3,123	2,921
23,950	24,000	3,130	2,664	3,130	2,929

24,000

At least	But less than	Single	Married filing jointly *	Married filing separately	Head of a household
24,000	24,050	3,138	2,671	3,138	2,936
24,050	24,100	3,145	2,679	3,145	2,944
24,100	24,150	3,153	2,686	3,153	2,951
24,150	24,200	3,160	2,694	3,160	2,959
24,200	24,250	3,168	2,701	3,168	2,966
24,250	24,300	3,175	2,709	3,175	2,974
24,300	24,350	3,183	2,716	3,183	2,981
24,350	24,400	3,190	2,724	3,190	2,989
24,400	24,450	3,198	2,731	3,198	2,996
24,450	24,500	3,205	2,739	3,205	3,004
24,500	24,550	3,213	2,746	3,213	3,011
24,550	24,600	3,220	2,754	3,220	3,019
24,600	24,650	3,228	2,761	3,228	3,026
24,650	24,700	3,235	2,769	3,235	3,034
24,700	24,750	3,243	2,776	3,243	3,041
24,750	24,800	3,250	2,784	3,250	3,049
24,800	24,850	3,258	2,791	3,258	3,056
24,850	24,900	3,265	2,799	3,265	3,064
24,900	24,950	3,273	2,806	3,273	3,071
24,950	25,000	3,280	2,814	3,280	3,079

25,000

At least	But less than	Single	Married filing jointly *	Married filing separately	Head of a household
25,000	25,050	3,288	2,821	3,288	3,086
25,050	25,100	3,295	2,829	3,295	3,094
25,100	25,150	3,303	2,836	3,303	3,101
25,150	25,200	3,310	2,844	3,310	3,109
25,200	25,250	3,318	2,851	3,318	3,116
25,250	25,300	3,325	2,859	3,325	3,124
25,300	25,350	3,333	2,866	3,333	3,131
25,350	25,400	3,340	2,874	3,340	3,139
25,400	25,450	3,348	2,881	3,348	3,146
25,450	25,500	3,355	2,889	3,355	3,154
25,500	25,550	3,363	2,896	3,363	3,161
25,550	25,600	3,370	2,904	3,370	3,169
25,600	25,650	3,378	2,911	3,378	3,176
25,650	25,700	3,385	2,919	3,385	3,184
25,700	25,750	3,393	2,926	3,393	3,191
25,750	25,800	3,400	2,934	3,400	3,199
25,800	25,850	3,408	2,941	3,408	3,206
25,850	25,900	3,415	2,949	3,415	3,214
25,900	25,950	3,423	2,956	3,423	3,221
25,950	26,000	3,430	2,964	3,430	3,229

26,000

At least	But less than	Single	Married filing jointly *	Married filing separately	Head of a household
26,000	26,050	3,438	2,971	3,438	3,236
26,050	26,100	3,445	2,979	3,445	3,244
26,100	26,150	3,453	2,986	3,453	3,251
26,150	26,200	3,460	2,994	3,460	3,259
26,200	26,250	3,468	3,001	3,468	3,266
26,250	26,300	3,475	3,009	3,475	3,274
26,300	26,350	3,483	3,016	3,483	3,281
26,350	26,400	3,490	3,024	3,490	3,289
26,400	26,450	3,498	3,031	3,498	3,296
26,450	26,500	3,505	3,039	3,505	3,304
26,500	26,550	3,513	3,046	3,513	3,311
26,550	26,600	3,520	3,054	3,520	3,319
26,600	26,650	3,528	3,061	3,528	3,326
26,650	26,700	3,535	3,069	3,535	3,334
26,700	26,750	3,543	3,076	3,543	3,341
26,750	26,800	3,550	3,084	3,550	3,349
26,800	26,850	3,558	3,091	3,558	3,356
26,850	26,900	3,565	3,099	3,565	3,364
26,900	26,950	3,573	3,106	3,573	3,371
26,950	27,000	3,580	3,114	3,580	3,379

27,000

At least	But less than	Single	Married filing jointly *	Married filing separately	Head of a household
27,000	27,050	3,588	3,121	3,588	3,386
27,050	27,100	3,595	3,129	3,595	3,394
27,100	27,150	3,603	3,136	3,603	3,401
27,150	27,200	3,610	3,144	3,610	3,409
27,200	27,250	3,618	3,151	3,618	3,416
27,250	27,300	3,625	3,159	3,625	3,424
27,300	27,350	3,633	3,166	3,633	3,431
27,350	27,400	3,640	3,174	3,640	3,439
27,400	27,450	3,648	3,181	3,648	3,446
27,450	27,500	3,655	3,189	3,655	3,454
27,500	27,550	3,663	3,196	3,663	3,461
27,550	27,600	3,670	3,204	3,670	3,469
27,600	27,650	3,678	3,211	3,678	3,476
27,650	27,700	3,685	3,219	3,685	3,484
27,700	27,750	3,693	3,226	3,693	3,491
27,750	27,800	3,700	3,234	3,700	3,499
27,800	27,850	3,708	3,241	3,708	3,506
27,850	27,900	3,715	3,249	3,715	3,514
27,900	27,950	3,723	3,256	3,723	3,521
27,950	28,000	3,730	3,264	3,730	3,529

28,000

At least	But less than	Single	Married filing jointly *	Married filing separately	Head of a household
28,000	28,050	3,738	3,271	3,738	3,536
28,050	28,100	3,745	3,279	3,745	3,544
28,100	28,150	3,753	3,286	3,753	3,551
28,150	28,200	3,760	3,294	3,760	3,559
28,200	28,250	3,768	3,301	3,768	3,566
28,250	28,300	3,775	3,309	3,775	3,574
28,300	28,350	3,783	3,316	3,783	3,581
28,350	28,400	3,790	3,324	3,790	3,589
28,400	28,450	3,798	3,331	3,798	3,596
28,450	28,500	3,805	3,339	3,805	3,604
28,500	28,550	3,813	3,346	3,813	3,611
28,550	28,600	3,820	3,354	3,820	3,619
28,600	28,650	3,828	3,361	3,828	3,626
28,650	28,700	3,835	3,369	3,835	3,634
28,700	28,750	3,843	3,376	3,843	3,641
28,750	28,800	3,850	3,384	3,850	3,649
28,800	28,850	3,858	3,391	3,858	3,656
28,850	28,900	3,865	3,399	3,865	3,664
28,900	28,950	3,873	3,406	3,873	3,671
28,950	29,000	3,880	3,414	3,880	3,679

29,000

At least	But less than	Single	Married filing jointly *	Married filing separately	Head of a household
29,000	29,050	3,888	3,421	3,888	3,686
29,050	29,100	3,895	3,429	3,895	3,694
29,100	29,150	3,903	3,436	3,903	3,701
29,150	29,200	3,910	3,444	3,910	3,709
29,200	29,250	3,918	3,451	3,918	3,716
29,250	29,300	3,925	3,459	3,925	3,724
29,300	29,350	3,933	3,466	3,933	3,731
29,350	29,400	3,940	3,474	3,940	3,739
29,400	29,450	3,948	3,481	3,948	3,746
29,450	29,500	3,955	3,489	3,955	3,754
29,500	29,550	3,963	3,496	3,963	3,761
29,550	29,600	3,970	3,504	3,970	3,769
29,600	29,650	3,978	3,511	3,978	3,776
29,650	29,700	3,985	3,519	3,985	3,784
29,700	29,750	3,993	3,526	3,993	3,791
29,750	29,800	4,000	3,534	4,000	3,799
29,800	29,850	4,008	3,541	4,008	3,806
29,850	29,900	4,015	3,549	4,015	3,814
29,900	29,950	4,023	3,556	4,023	3,821
29,950	30,000	4,030	3,564	4,030	3,829

* This column must also be used by a qualifying widow(er).

(Continued)

Need more information or forms? Visit IRS.gov.

If line 43 (taxable income) is—		And you are—			
At least	But less than	Single	Married filing jointly *	Married filing separately	Head of a household
		Your tax is—			

30,000

At least	But less than	Single	MFJ *	MFS	HoH
30,000	30,050	4,038	3,571	4,038	3,836
30,050	30,100	4,045	3,579	4,045	3,844
30,100	30,150	4,053	3,586	4,053	3,851
30,150	30,200	4,060	3,594	4,060	3,859
30,200	30,250	4,068	3,601	4,068	3,866
30,250	30,300	4,075	3,609	4,075	3,874
30,300	30,350	4,083	3,616	4,083	3,881
30,350	30,400	4,090	3,624	4,090	3,889
30,400	30,450	4,098	3,631	4,098	3,896
30,450	30,500	4,105	3,639	4,105	3,904
30,500	30,550	4,113	3,646	4,113	3,911
30,550	30,600	4,120	3,654	4,120	3,919
30,600	30,650	4,128	3,661	4,128	3,926
30,650	30,700	4,135	3,669	4,135	3,934
30,700	30,750	4,143	3,676	4,143	3,941
30,750	30,800	4,150	3,684	4,150	3,949
30,800	30,850	4,158	3,691	4,158	3,956
30,850	30,900	4,165	3,699	4,165	3,964
30,900	30,950	4,173	3,706	4,173	3,971
30,950	31,000	4,180	3,714	4,180	3,979

31,000

At least	But less than	Single	MFJ *	MFS	HoH
31,000	31,050	4,188	3,721	4,188	3,986
31,050	31,100	4,195	3,729	4,195	3,994
31,100	31,150	4,203	3,736	4,203	4,001
31,150	31,200	4,210	3,744	4,210	4,009
31,200	31,250	4,218	3,751	4,218	4,016
31,250	31,300	4,225	3,759	4,225	4,024
31,300	31,350	4,233	3,766	4,233	4,031
31,350	31,400	4,240	3,774	4,240	4,039
31,400	31,450	4,248	3,781	4,248	4,046
31,450	31,500	4,255	3,789	4,255	4,054
31,500	31,550	4,263	3,796	4,263	4,061
31,550	31,600	4,270	3,804	4,270	4,069
31,600	31,650	4,278	3,811	4,278	4,076
31,650	31,700	4,285	3,819	4,285	4,084
31,700	31,750	4,293	3,826	4,293	4,091
31,750	31,800	4,300	3,834	4,300	4,099
31,800	31,850	4,308	3,841	4,308	4,106
31,850	31,900	4,315	3,849	4,315	4,114
31,900	31,950	4,323	3,856	4,323	4,121
31,950	32,000	4,330	3,864	4,330	4,129

32,000

At least	But less than	Single	MFJ *	MFS	HoH
32,000	32,050	4,338	3,871	4,338	4,136
32,050	32,100	4,345	3,879	4,345	4,144
32,100	32,150	4,353	3,886	4,353	4,151
32,150	32,200	4,360	3,894	4,360	4,159
32,200	32,250	4,368	3,901	4,368	4,166
32,250	32,300	4,375	3,909	4,375	4,174
32,300	32,350	4,383	3,916	4,383	4,181
32,350	32,400	4,390	3,924	4,390	4,189
32,400	32,450	4,398	3,931	4,398	4,196
32,450	32,500	4,405	3,939	4,405	4,204
32,500	32,550	4,413	3,946	4,413	4,211
32,550	32,600	4,420	3,954	4,420	4,219
32,600	32,650	4,428	3,961	4,428	4,226
32,650	32,700	4,435	3,969	4,435	4,234
32,700	32,750	4,443	3,976	4,443	4,241
32,750	32,800	4,450	3,984	4,450	4,249
32,800	32,850	4,458	3,991	4,458	4,256
32,850	32,900	4,465	3,999	4,465	4,264
32,900	32,950	4,473	4,006	4,473	4,271
32,950	33,000	4,480	4,014	4,480	4,279

33,000

At least	But less than	Single	MFJ *	MFS	HoH
33,000	33,050	4,488	4,021	4,488	4,286
33,050	33,100	4,495	4,029	4,495	4,294
33,100	33,150	4,503	4,036	4,503	4,301
33,150	33,200	4,510	4,044	4,510	4,309
33,200	33,250	4,518	4,051	4,518	4,316
33,250	33,300	4,525	4,059	4,525	4,324
33,300	33,350	4,533	4,066	4,533	4,331
33,350	33,400	4,540	4,074	4,540	4,339
33,400	33,450	4,548	4,081	4,548	4,346
33,450	33,500	4,555	4,089	4,555	4,354
33,500	33,550	4,563	4,096	4,563	4,361
33,550	33,600	4,570	4,104	4,570	4,369
33,600	33,650	4,578	4,111	4,578	4,376
33,650	33,700	4,585	4,119	4,585	4,384
33,700	33,750	4,593	4,126	4,593	4,391
33,750	33,800	4,600	4,134	4,600	4,399
33,800	33,850	4,608	4,141	4,608	4,406
33,850	33,900	4,615	4,149	4,615	4,414
33,900	33,950	4,623	4,156	4,623	4,421
33,950	34,000	4,630	4,164	4,630	4,429

34,000

At least	But less than	Single	MFJ *	MFS	HoH
34,000	34,050	4,638	4,171	4,638	4,436
34,050	34,100	4,645	4,179	4,645	4,444
34,100	34,150	4,653	4,186	4,653	4,451
34,150	34,200	4,660	4,194	4,660	4,459
34,200	34,250	4,668	4,201	4,668	4,466
34,250	34,300	4,675	4,209	4,675	4,474
34,300	34,350	4,683	4,216	4,683	4,481
34,350	34,400	4,690	4,224	4,690	4,489
34,400	34,450	4,698	4,231	4,698	4,496
34,450	34,500	4,705	4,239	4,705	4,504
34,500	34,550	4,713	4,246	4,713	4,511
34,550	34,600	4,720	4,254	4,720	4,519
34,600	34,650	4,728	4,261	4,728	4,526
34,650	34,700	4,735	4,269	4,735	4,534
34,700	34,750	4,743	4,276	4,743	4,541
34,750	34,800	4,750	4,284	4,750	4,549
34,800	34,850	4,758	4,291	4,758	4,556
34,850	34,900	4,765	4,299	4,765	4,564
34,900	34,950	4,773	4,306	4,773	4,571
34,950	35,000	4,780	4,314	4,780	4,579

35,000

At least	But less than	Single	MFJ *	MFS	HoH
35,000	35,050	4,788	4,321	4,788	4,586
35,050	35,100	4,795	4,329	4,795	4,594
35,100	35,150	4,803	4,336	4,803	4,601
35,150	35,200	4,810	4,344	4,810	4,609
35,200	35,250	4,818	4,351	4,818	4,616
35,250	35,300	4,825	4,359	4,825	4,624
35,300	35,350	4,833	4,366	4,833	4,631
35,350	35,400	4,840	4,374	4,840	4,639
35,400	35,450	4,848	4,381	4,848	4,646
35,450	35,500	4,855	4,389	4,855	4,654
35,500	35,550	4,863	4,396	4,863	4,661
35,550	35,600	4,870	4,404	4,870	4,669
35,600	35,650	4,878	4,411	4,878	4,676
35,650	35,700	4,885	4,419	4,885	4,684
35,700	35,750	4,893	4,426	4,893	4,691
35,750	35,800	4,900	4,434	4,900	4,699
35,800	35,850	4,908	4,441	4,908	4,706
35,850	35,900	4,915	4,449	4,915	4,714
35,900	35,950	4,923	4,456	4,923	4,721
35,950	36,000	4,930	4,464	4,930	4,729

36,000

At least	But less than	Single	MFJ *	MFS	HoH
36,000	36,050	4,938	4,471	4,938	4,736
36,050	36,100	4,945	4,479	4,945	4,744
36,100	36,150	4,953	4,486	4,953	4,751
36,150	36,200	4,960	4,494	4,960	4,759
36,200	36,250	4,968	4,501	4,968	4,766
36,250	36,300	4,975	4,509	4,975	4,774
36,300	36,350	4,983	4,516	4,983	4,781
36,350	36,400	4,990	4,524	4,990	4,789
36,400	36,450	4,998	4,531	4,998	4,796
36,450	36,500	5,005	4,539	5,005	4,804
36,500	36,550	5,013	4,546	5,013	4,811
36,550	36,600	5,020	4,554	5,020	4,819
36,600	36,650	5,028	4,561	5,028	4,826
36,650	36,700	5,035	4,569	5,035	4,834
36,700	36,750	5,043	4,576	5,043	4,841
36,750	36,800	5,050	4,584	5,050	4,849
36,800	36,850	5,058	4,591	5,058	4,856
36,850	36,900	5,065	4,599	5,065	4,864
36,900	36,950	5,073	4,606	5,073	4,871
36,950	37,000	5,080	4,614	5,080	4,879

37,000

At least	But less than	Single	MFJ *	MFS	HoH
37,000	37,050	5,088	4,621	5,088	4,886
37,050	37,100	5,095	4,629	5,095	4,894
37,100	37,150	5,103	4,636	5,103	4,901
37,150	37,200	5,110	4,644	5,110	4,909
37,200	37,250	5,118	4,651	5,118	4,916
37,250	37,300	5,125	4,659	5,125	4,924
37,300	37,350	5,133	4,666	5,133	4,931
37,350	37,400	5,140	4,674	5,140	4,939
37,400	37,450	5,148	4,681	5,148	4,946
37,450	37,500	5,155	4,689	5,155	4,954
37,500	37,550	5,163	4,696	5,163	4,961
37,550	37,600	5,170	4,704	5,170	4,969
37,600	37,650	5,178	4,711	5,178	4,976
37,650	37,700	5,185	4,719	5,185	4,984
37,700	37,750	5,193	4,726	5,193	4,991
37,750	37,800	5,200	4,734	5,200	4,999
37,800	37,850	5,208	4,741	5,208	5,006
37,850	37,900	5,215	4,749	5,215	5,014
37,900	37,950	5,223	4,756	5,223	5,021
37,950	38,000	5,233	4,764	5,233	5,029

38,000

At least	But less than	Single	MFJ *	MFS	HoH
38,000	38,050	5,245	4,771	5,245	5,036
38,050	38,100	5,258	4,779	5,258	5,044
38,100	38,150	5,270	4,786	5,270	5,051
38,150	38,200	5,283	4,794	5,283	5,059
38,200	38,250	5,295	4,801	5,295	5,066
38,250	38,300	5,308	4,809	5,308	5,074
38,300	38,350	5,320	4,816	5,320	5,081
38,350	38,400	5,333	4,824	5,333	5,089
38,400	38,450	5,345	4,831	5,345	5,096
38,450	38,500	5,358	4,839	5,358	5,104
38,500	38,550	5,370	4,846	5,370	5,111
38,550	38,600	5,383	4,854	5,383	5,119
38,600	38,650	5,395	4,861	5,395	5,126
38,650	38,700	5,408	4,869	5,408	5,134
38,700	38,750	5,420	4,876	5,420	5,141
38,750	38,800	5,433	4,884	5,433	5,149
38,800	38,850	5,445	4,891	5,445	5,156
38,850	38,900	5,458	4,899	5,458	5,164
38,900	38,950	5,470	4,906	5,470	5,171
38,950	39,000	5,483	4,914	5,483	5,179

(Continued)

* This column must also be used by a qualifying widow(er).

39,000 – 41,000

At least	But less than	Single	Married filing jointly *	Married filing separately	Head of a household
		Your tax is—			
39,000					
39,000	39,050	5,495	4,921	5,495	5,186
39,050	39,100	5,508	4,929	5,508	5,194
39,100	39,150	5,520	4,936	5,520	5,201
39,150	39,200	5,533	4,944	5,533	5,209
39,200	39,250	5,545	4,951	5,545	5,216
39,250	39,300	5,558	4,959	5,558	5,224
39,300	39,350	5,570	4,966	5,570	5,231
39,350	39,400	5,583	4,974	5,583	5,239
39,400	39,450	5,595	4,981	5,595	5,246
39,450	39,500	5,608	4,989	5,608	5,254
39,500	39,550	5,620	4,996	5,620	5,261
39,550	39,600	5,633	5,004	5,633	5,269
39,600	39,650	5,645	5,011	5,645	5,276
39,650	39,700	5,658	5,019	5,658	5,284
39,700	39,750	5,670	5,026	5,670	5,291
39,750	39,800	5,683	5,034	5,683	5,299
39,800	39,850	5,695	5,041	5,695	5,306
39,850	39,900	5,708	5,049	5,708	5,314
39,900	39,950	5,720	5,056	5,720	5,321
39,950	40,000	5,733	5,064	5,733	5,329
40,000					
40,000	40,050	5,745	5,071	5,745	5,336
40,050	40,100	5,758	5,079	5,758	5,344
40,100	40,150	5,770	5,086	5,770	5,351
40,150	40,200	5,783	5,094	5,783	5,359
40,200	40,250	5,795	5,101	5,795	5,366
40,250	40,300	5,808	5,109	5,808	5,374
40,300	40,350	5,820	5,116	5,820	5,381
40,350	40,400	5,833	5,124	5,833	5,389
40,400	40,450	5,845	5,131	5,845	5,396
40,450	40,500	5,858	5,139	5,858	5,404
40,500	40,550	5,870	5,146	5,870	5,411
40,550	40,600	5,883	5,154	5,883	5,419
40,600	40,650	5,895	5,161	5,895	5,426
40,650	40,700	5,908	5,169	5,908	5,434
40,700	40,750	5,920	5,176	5,920	5,441
40,750	40,800	5,933	5,184	5,933	5,449
40,800	40,850	5,945	5,191	5,945	5,456
40,850	40,900	5,958	5,199	5,958	5,464
40,900	40,950	5,970	5,206	5,970	5,471
40,950	41,000	5,983	5,214	5,983	5,479
41,000					
41,000	41,050	5,995	5,221	5,995	5,486
41,050	41,100	6,008	5,229	6,008	5,494
41,100	41,150	6,020	5,236	6,020	5,501
41,150	41,200	6,033	5,244	6,033	5,509
41,200	41,250	6,045	5,251	6,045	5,516
41,250	41,300	6,058	5,259	6,058	5,524
41,300	41,350	6,070	5,266	6,070	5,531
41,350	41,400	6,083	5,274	6,083	5,539
41,400	41,450	6,095	5,281	6,095	5,546
41,450	41,500	6,108	5,289	6,108	5,554
41,500	41,550	6,120	5,296	6,120	5,561
41,550	41,600	6,133	5,304	6,133	5,569
41,600	41,650	6,145	5,311	6,145	5,576
41,650	41,700	6,158	5,319	6,158	5,584
41,700	41,750	6,170	5,326	6,170	5,591
41,750	41,800	6,183	5,334	6,183	5,599
41,800	41,850	6,195	5,341	6,195	5,606
41,850	41,900	6,208	5,349	6,208	5,614
41,900	41,950	6,220	5,356	6,220	5,621
41,950	42,000	6,233	5,364	6,233	5,629

42,000 – 44,000

At least	But less than	Single	Married filing jointly *	Married filing separately	Head of a household
		Your tax is—			
42,000					
42,000	42,050	6,245	5,371	6,245	5,636
42,050	42,100	6,258	5,379	6,258	5,644
42,100	42,150	6,270	5,386	6,270	5,651
42,150	42,200	6,283	5,394	6,283	5,659
42,200	42,250	6,295	5,401	6,295	5,666
42,250	42,300	6,308	5,409	6,308	5,674
42,300	42,350	6,320	5,416	6,320	5,681
42,350	42,400	6,333	5,424	6,333	5,689
42,400	42,450	6,345	5,431	6,345	5,696
42,450	42,500	6,358	5,439	6,358	5,704
42,500	42,550	6,370	5,446	6,370	5,711
42,550	42,600	6,383	5,454	6,383	5,719
42,600	42,650	6,395	5,461	6,395	5,726
42,650	42,700	6,408	5,469	6,408	5,734
42,700	42,750	6,420	5,476	6,420	5,741
42,750	42,800	6,433	5,484	6,433	5,749
42,800	42,850	6,445	5,491	6,445	5,756
42,850	42,900	6,458	5,499	6,458	5,764
42,900	42,950	6,470	5,506	6,470	5,771
42,950	43,000	6,483	5,514	6,483	5,779
43,000					
43,000	43,050	6,495	5,521	6,495	5,786
43,050	43,100	6,508	5,529	6,508	5,794
43,100	43,150	6,520	5,536	6,520	5,801
43,150	43,200	6,533	5,544	6,533	5,809
43,200	43,250	6,545	5,551	6,545	5,816
43,250	43,300	6,558	5,559	6,558	5,824
43,300	43,350	6,570	5,566	6,570	5,831
43,350	43,400	6,583	5,574	6,583	5,839
43,400	43,450	6,595	5,581	6,595	5,846
43,450	43,500	6,608	5,589	6,608	5,854
43,500	43,550	6,620	5,596	6,620	5,861
43,550	43,600	6,633	5,604	6,633	5,869
43,600	43,650	6,645	5,611	6,645	5,876
43,650	43,700	6,658	5,619	6,658	5,884
43,700	43,750	6,670	5,626	6,670	5,891
43,750	43,800	6,683	5,634	6,683	5,899
43,800	43,850	6,695	5,641	6,695	5,906
43,850	43,900	6,708	5,649	6,708	5,914
43,900	43,950	6,720	5,656	6,720	5,921
43,950	44,000	6,733	5,664	6,733	5,929
44,000					
44,000	44,050	6,745	5,671	6,745	5,936
44,050	44,100	6,758	5,679	6,758	5,944
44,100	44,150	6,770	5,686	6,770	5,951
44,150	44,200	6,783	5,694	6,783	5,959
44,200	44,250	6,795	5,701	6,795	5,966
44,250	44,300	6,808	5,709	6,808	5,974
44,300	44,350	6,820	5,716	6,820	5,981
44,350	44,400	6,833	5,724	6,833	5,989
44,400	44,450	6,845	5,731	6,845	5,996
44,450	44,500	6,858	5,739	6,858	6,004
44,500	44,550	6,870	5,746	6,870	6,011
44,550	44,600	6,883	5,754	6,883	6,019
44,600	44,650	6,895	5,761	6,895	6,026
44,650	44,700	6,908	5,769	6,908	6,034
44,700	44,750	6,920	5,770	6,920	6,041
44,750	44,800	6,933	5,784	6,933	6,049
44,800	44,850	6,945	5,791	6,945	6,056
44,850	44,900	6,958	5,799	6,958	6,064
44,900	44,950	6,970	5,806	6,970	6,071
44,950	45,000	6,983	5,814	6,983	6,079

45,000 – 47,000

At least	But less than	Single	Married filing jointly *	Married filing separately	Head of a household
		Your tax is—			
45,000					
45,000	45,050	6,995	5,821	6,995	6,086
45,050	45,100	7,008	5,829	7,008	6,094
45,100	45,150	7,020	5,836	7,020	6,101
45,150	45,200	7,033	5,844	7,033	6,109
45,200	45,250	7,045	5,851	7,045	6,116
45,250	45,300	7,058	5,859	7,058	6,124
45,300	45,350	7,070	5,866	7,070	6,131
45,350	45,400	7,083	5,874	7,083	6,139
45,400	45,450	7,095	5,881	7,095	6,146
45,450	45,500	7,108	5,889	7,108	6,154
45,500	45,550	7,120	5,896	7,120	6,161
45,550	45,600	7,133	5,904	7,133	6,169
45,600	45,650	7,145	5,911	7,145	6,176
45,650	45,700	7,158	5,919	7,158	6,184
45,700	45,750	7,170	5,926	7,170	6,191
45,750	45,800	7,183	5,934	7,183	6,199
45,800	45,850	7,195	5,941	7,195	6,206
45,850	45,900	7,208	5,949	7,208	6,214
45,900	45,950	7,220	5,956	7,220	6,221
45,950	46,000	7,233	5,964	7,233	6,229
46,000					
46,000	46,050	7,245	5,971	7,245	6,236
46,050	46,100	7,258	5,979	7,258	6,244
46,100	46,150	7,270	5,986	7,270	6,251
46,150	46,200	7,283	5,994	7,283	6,259
46,200	46,250	7,295	6,001	7,295	6,266
46,250	46,300	7,308	6,009	7,308	6,274
46,300	46,350	7,320	6,016	7,320	6,281
46,350	46,400	7,333	6,024	7,333	6,289
46,400	46,450	7,345	6,031	7,345	6,296
46,450	46,500	7,358	6,039	7,358	6,304
46,500	46,550	7,370	6,046	7,370	6,311
46,550	46,600	7,383	6,054	7,383	6,319
46,600	46,650	7,395	6,061	7,395	6,326
46,650	46,700	7,408	6,069	7,408	6,334
46,700	46,750	7,420	6,076	7,420	6,341
46,750	46,800	7,433	6,084	7,433	6,349
46,800	46,850	7,445	6,091	7,445	6,356
46,850	46,900	7,458	6,099	7,458	6,364
46,900	46,950	7,470	6,106	7,470	6,371
46,950	47,000	7,483	6,114	7,483	6,379
47,000					
47,000	47,050	7,495	6,121	7,495	6,386
47,050	47,100	7,508	6,129	7,508	6,394
47,100	47,150	7,520	6,136	7,520	6,401
47,150	47,200	7,533	6,144	7,533	6,409
47,200	47,250	7,545	6,151	7,545	6,416
47,250	47,300	7,558	6,159	7,558	6,424
47,300	47,350	7,570	6,166	7,570	6,431
47,350	47,400	7,583	6,174	7,583	6,439
47,400	47,450	7,595	6,181	7,595	6,446
47,450	47,500	7,608	6,189	7,608	6,454
47,500	47,550	7,620	6,196	7,620	6,461
47,550	47,600	7,633	6,204	7,633	6,469
47,600	47,650	7,645	6,211	7,645	6,476
47,650	47,700	7,658	6,219	7,658	6,484
47,700	47,750	7,670	6,226	7,670	6,491
47,750	47,800	7,683	6,234	7,683	6,499
47,800	47,850	7,695	6,241	7,695	6,506
47,850	47,900	7,708	6,249	7,708	6,514
47,900	47,950	7,720	6,256	7,720	6,521
47,950	48,000	7,733	6,264	7,733	6,529

(Continued)

* This column must also be used by a qualifying widow(er).

Need more information or forms? Visit IRS.gov.

If line 43 (taxable income) is—		And you are—				If line 43 (taxable income) is—		And you are—				If line 43 (taxable income) is—		And you are—			
At least	But less than	Single	Married filing jointly *	Married filing separately	Head of a household	At least	But less than	Single	Married filing jointly *	Married filing separately	Head of a household	At least	But less than	Single	Married filing jointly *	Married filing separately	Head of a household
		Your tax is—						Your tax is—						Your tax is—			

48,000 **51,000** **54,000**

At least	But less than	Single	MFJ*	MFS	HoH	At least	But less than	Single	MFJ*	MFS	HoH	At least	But less than	Single	MFJ*	MFS	HoH
48,000	48,050	7,745	6,271	7,745	6,536	51,000	51,050	8,495	6,721	8,495	7,009	54,000	54,050	9,245	7,171	9,245	7,759
48,050	48,100	7,758	6,279	7,758	6,544	51,050	51,100	8,508	6,729	8,508	7,021	54,050	54,100	9,258	7,179	9,258	7,771
48,100	48,150	7,770	6,286	7,770	6,551	51,100	51,150	8,520	6,736	8,520	7,034	54,100	54,150	9,270	7,186	9,270	7,784
48,150	48,200	7,783	6,294	7,783	6,559	51,150	51,200	8,533	6,744	8,533	7,046	54,150	54,200	9,283	7,194	9,283	7,796
48,200	48,250	7,795	6,301	7,795	6,566	51,200	51,250	8,545	6,751	8,545	7,059	54,200	54,250	9,295	7,201	9,295	7,809
48,250	48,300	7,808	6,309	7,808	6,574	51,250	51,300	8,558	6,759	8,558	7,071	54,250	54,300	9,308	7,209	9,308	7,821
48,300	48,350	7,820	6,316	7,820	6,581	51,300	51,350	8,570	6,766	8,570	7,084	54,300	54,350	9,320	7,216	9,320	7,834
48,350	48,400	7,833	6,324	7,833	6,589	51,350	51,400	8,583	6,774	8,583	7,096	54,350	54,400	9,333	7,224	9,333	7,846
48,400	48,450	7,845	6,331	7,845	6,596	51,400	51,450	8,595	6,781	8,595	7,109	54,400	54,450	9,345	7,231	9,345	7,859
48,450	48,500	7,858	6,339	7,858	6,604	51,450	51,500	8,608	6,789	8,608	7,121	54,450	54,500	9,358	7,239	9,358	7,871
48,500	48,550	7,870	6,346	7,870	6,611	51,500	51,550	8,620	6,796	8,620	7,134	54,500	54,550	9,370	7,246	9,370	7,884
48,550	48,600	7,883	6,354	7,883	6,619	51,550	51,600	8,633	6,804	8,633	7,146	54,550	54,600	9,383	7,254	9,383	7,896
48,600	48,650	7,895	6,361	7,895	6,626	51,600	51,650	8,645	6,811	8,645	7,159	54,600	54,650	9,395	7,261	9,395	7,909
48,650	48,700	7,908	6,369	7,908	6,634	51,650	51,700	8,658	6,819	8,658	7,171	54,650	54,700	9,408	7,269	9,408	7,921
48,700	48,750	7,920	6,376	7,920	6,641	51,700	51,750	8,670	6,826	8,670	7,184	54,700	54,750	9,420	7,276	9,420	7,934
48,750	48,800	7,933	6,384	7,933	6,649	51,750	51,800	8,683	6,834	8,683	7,196	54,750	54,800	9,433	7,284	9,433	7,946
48,800	48,850	7,945	6,391	7,945	6,656	51,800	51,850	8,695	6,841	8,695	7,209	54,800	54,850	9,445	7,291	9,445	7,959
48,850	48,900	7,958	6,399	7,958	6,664	51,850	51,900	8,708	6,849	8,708	7,221	54,850	54,900	9,458	7,299	9,458	7,971
48,900	48,950	7,970	6,406	7,970	6,671	51,900	51,950	8,720	6,856	8,720	7,234	54,900	54,950	9,470	7,306	9,470	7,984
48,950	49,000	7,983	6,414	7,983	6,679	51,950	52,000	8,733	6,864	8,733	7,246	54,950	55,000	9,483	7,314	9,483	7,996

49,000 **52,000** **55,000**

At least	But less than	Single	MFJ*	MFS	HoH	At least	But less than	Single	MFJ*	MFS	HoH	At least	But less than	Single	MFJ*	MFS	HoH
49,000	49,050	7,995	6,421	7,995	6,686	52,000	52,050	8,745	6,871	8,745	7,259	55,000	55,050	9,495	7,321	9,495	8,009
49,050	49,100	8,008	6,429	8,008	6,694	52,050	52,100	8,758	6,879	8,758	7,271	55,050	55,100	9,508	7,329	9,508	8,021
49,100	49,150	8,020	6,436	8,020	6,701	52,100	52,150	8,770	6,886	8,770	7,284	55,100	55,150	9,520	7,336	9,520	8,034
49,150	49,200	8,033	6,444	8,033	6,709	52,150	52,200	8,783	6,894	8,783	7,296	55,150	55,200	9,533	7,344	9,533	8,046
49,200	49,250	8,045	6,451	8,045	6,716	52,200	52,250	8,795	6,901	8,795	7,309	55,200	55,250	9,545	7,351	9,545	8,059
49,250	49,300	8,058	6,459	8,058	6,724	52,250	52,300	8,808	6,909	8,808	7,321	55,250	55,300	9,558	7,359	9,558	8,071
49,300	49,350	8,070	6,466	8,070	6,731	52,300	52,350	8,820	6,916	8,820	7,334	55,300	55,350	9,570	7,366	9,570	8,084
49,350	49,400	8,083	6,474	8,083	6,739	52,350	52,400	8,833	6,924	8,833	7,346	55,350	55,400	9,583	7,374	9,583	8,096
49,400	49,450	8,095	6,481	8,095	6,746	52,400	52,450	8,845	6,931	8,845	7,359	55,400	55,450	9,595	7,381	9,595	8,109
49,450	49,500	8,108	6,489	8,108	6,754	52,450	52,500	8,858	6,939	8,858	7,371	55,450	55,500	9,608	7,389	9,608	8,121
49,500	49,550	8,120	6,496	8,120	6,761	52,500	52,550	8,870	6,946	8,870	7,384	55,500	55,550	9,620	7,396	9,620	8,134
49,550	49,600	8,133	6,504	8,133	6,769	52,550	52,600	8,883	6,954	8,883	7,396	55,550	55,600	9,633	7,404	9,633	8,146
49,600	49,650	8,145	6,511	8,145	6,776	52,600	52,650	8,895	6,961	8,895	7,409	55,600	55,650	9,645	7,411	9,645	8,159
49,650	49,700	8,158	6,519	8,158	6,784	52,650	52,700	8,908	6,969	8,908	7,421	55,650	55,700	9,658	7,419	9,658	8,171
49,700	49,750	8,170	6,526	8,170	6,791	52,700	52,750	8,920	6,976	8,920	7,434	55,700	55,750	9,670	7,426	9,670	8,184
49,750	49,800	8,183	6,534	8,183	6,799	52,750	52,800	8,933	6,984	8,933	7,446	55,750	55,800	9,683	7,434	9,683	8,196
49,800	49,850	8,195	6,541	8,195	6,806	52,800	52,850	8,945	6,991	8,945	7,459	55,800	55,850	9,695	7,441	9,695	8,209
49,850	49,900	8,208	6,549	8,208	6,814	52,850	52,900	8,958	6,999	8,958	7,471	55,850	55,900	9,708	7,449	9,708	8,221
49,900	49,950	8,220	6,556	8,220	6,821	52,900	52,950	8,970	7,006	8,970	7,484	55,900	55,950	9,720	7,456	9,720	8,234
49,950	50,000	8,233	6,564	8,233	6,829	52,950	53,000	8,983	7,014	8,983	7,496	55,950	56,000	9,733	7,464	9,733	8,246

50,000 **53,000** **56,000**

At least	But less than	Single	MFJ*	MFS	HoH	At least	But less than	Single	MFJ*	MFS	HoH	At least	But less than	Single	MFJ*	MFS	HoH
50,000	50,050	8,245	6,571	8,245	6,836	53,000	53,050	8,995	7,021	8,995	7,509	56,000	56,050	9,745	7,471	9,745	8,259
50,050	50,100	8,258	6,579	8,258	6,844	53,050	53,100	9,008	7,029	9,008	7,521	56,050	56,100	9,758	7,479	9,758	8,271
50,100	50,150	8,270	6,586	8,270	6,851	53,100	53,150	9,020	7,036	9,020	7,534	56,100	56,150	9,770	7,486	9,770	8,284
50,150	50,200	8,283	6,594	8,283	6,859	53,150	53,200	9,033	7,044	9,033	7,546	56,150	56,200	9,783	7,494	9,783	8,296
50,200	50,250	8,295	6,601	8,295	6,866	53,200	53,250	9,045	7,051	9,045	7,559	56,200	56,250	9,795	7,501	9,795	8,309
50,250	50,300	8,308	6,609	8,308	6,874	53,250	53,300	9,058	7,059	9,058	7,571	56,250	56,300	9,808	7,509	9,808	8,321
50,300	50,350	8,320	6,616	8,320	6,881	53,300	53,350	9,070	7,066	9,070	7,584	56,300	56,350	9,820	7,516	9,820	8,334
50,350	50,400	8,333	6,624	8,333	6,889	53,350	53,400	9,083	7,074	9,083	7,596	56,350	56,400	9,833	7,524	9,833	8,346
50,400	50,450	8,345	6,631	8,345	6,896	53,400	53,450	9,095	7,081	9,095	7,609	56,400	56,450	9,845	7,531	9,845	8,359
50,450	50,500	8,358	6,639	8,358	6,904	53,450	53,500	9,108	7,089	9,108	7,621	56,450	56,500	9,858	7,539	9,858	8,371
50,500	50,550	8,370	6,646	8,370	6,911	53,500	53,550	9,120	7,096	9,120	7,634	56,500	56,550	9,870	7,546	9,870	8,384
50,550	50,600	8,383	6,654	8,383	6,919	53,550	53,600	9,133	7,104	9,133	7,646	56,550	56,600	9,883	7,554	9,883	8,396
50,600	50,650	8,395	6,661	8,395	6,926	53,600	53,650	9,145	7,111	9,145	7,659	56,600	56,650	9,895	7,561	9,895	8,409
50,650	50,700	8,408	6,669	8,408	6,934	53,650	53,700	9,158	7,119	9,158	7,671	56,650	56,700	9,908	7,569	9,908	8,421
50,700	50,750	8,420	6,676	8,420	6,941	53,700	53,750	9,170	7,126	9,170	7,684	56,700	56,750	9,920	7,576	9,920	8,434
50,750	50,800	8,433	6,684	8,433	6,949	53,750	53,800	9,183	7,134	9,183	7,696	56,750	56,800	9,933	7,584	9,933	8,446
50,800	50,850	8,445	6,691	8,445	6,959	53,800	53,850	9,195	7,141	9,195	7,709	56,800	56,850	9,945	7,591	9,945	8,459
50,850	50,900	8,458	6,699	8,458	6,971	53,850	53,900	9,208	7,149	9,208	7,721	56,850	56,900	9,958	7,599	9,958	8,471
50,900	50,950	8,470	6,706	8,470	6,984	53,900	53,950	9,220	7,156	9,220	7,734	56,900	56,950	9,970	7,606	9,970	8,484
50,950	51,000	8,483	6,714	8,483	6,996	53,950	54,000	9,233	7,164	9,233	7,746	56,950	57,000	9,983	7,614	9,983	8,496

(Continued)

* This column must also be used by a qualifying widow(er).

If line 43 (taxable income) is—		And you are—			
At least	But less than	Single	Married filing jointly *	Married filing separately	Head of a household
		Your tax is—			

57,000

At least	But less than	Single	Married filing jointly *	Married filing separately	Head of a household
57,000	57,050	9,995	7,621	9,995	8,509
57,050	57,100	10,008	7,629	10,008	8,521
57,100	57,150	10,020	7,636	10,020	8,534
57,150	57,200	10,033	7,644	10,033	8,546
57,200	57,250	10,045	7,651	10,045	8,559
57,250	57,300	10,058	7,659	10,058	8,571
57,300	57,350	10,070	7,666	10,070	8,584
57,350	57,400	10,083	7,674	10,083	8,596
57,400	57,450	10,095	7,681	10,095	8,609
57,450	57,500	10,108	7,689	10,108	8,621
57,500	57,550	10,120	7,696	10,120	8,634
57,550	57,600	10,133	7,704	10,133	8,646
57,600	57,650	10,145	7,711	10,145	8,659
57,650	57,700	10,158	7,719	10,158	8,671
57,700	57,750	10,170	7,726	10,170	8,684
57,750	57,800	10,183	7,734	10,183	8,696
57,800	57,850	10,195	7,741	10,195	8,709
57,850	57,900	10,208	7,749	10,208	8,721
57,900	57,950	10,220	7,756	10,220	8,734
57,950	58,000	10,233	7,764	10,233	8,746

58,000

At least	But less than	Single	Married filing jointly *	Married filing separately	Head of a household
58,000	58,050	10,245	7,771	10,245	8,759
58,050	58,100	10,258	7,779	10,258	8,771
58,100	58,150	10,270	7,786	10,270	8,784
58,150	58,200	10,283	7,794	10,283	8,796
58,200	58,250	10,295	7,801	10,295	8,809
58,250	58,300	10,308	7,809	10,308	8,821
58,300	58,350	10,320	7,816	10,320	8,834
58,350	58,400	10,333	7,824	10,333	8,846
58,400	58,450	10,345	7,831	10,345	8,859
58,450	58,500	10,358	7,839	10,358	8,871
58,500	58,550	10,370	7,846	10,370	8,884
58,550	58,600	10,383	7,854	10,383	8,896
58,600	58,650	10,395	7,861	10,395	8,909
58,650	58,700	10,408	7,869	10,408	8,921
58,700	58,750	10,420	7,876	10,420	8,934
58,750	58,800	10,433	7,884	10,433	8,946
58,800	58,850	10,445	7,891	10,445	8,959
58,850	58,900	10,458	7,899	10,458	8,971
58,900	58,950	10,470	7,906	10,470	8,984
58,950	59,000	10,483	7,914	10,483	8,996

59,000

At least	But less than	Single	Married filing jointly *	Married filing separately	Head of a household
59,000	59,050	10,495	7,921	10,495	9,009
59,050	59,100	10,508	7,929	10,508	9,021
59,100	59,150	10,520	7,936	10,520	9,034
59,150	59,200	10,533	7,944	10,533	9,046
59,200	59,250	10,545	7,951	10,545	9,059
59,250	59,300	10,558	7,959	10,558	9,071
59,300	59,350	10,570	7,966	10,570	9,084
59,350	59,400	10,583	7,974	10,583	9,096
59,400	59,450	10,595	7,981	10,595	9,109
59,450	59,500	10,608	7,989	10,608	9,121
59,500	59,550	10,620	7,996	10,620	9,134
59,550	59,600	10,633	8,004	10,633	9,146
59,600	59,650	10,645	8,011	10,645	9,159
59,650	59,700	10,658	8,019	10,658	9,171
59,700	59,750	10,670	8,026	10,670	9,184
59,750	59,800	10,683	8,034	10,683	9,196
59,800	59,850	10,695	8,041	10,695	9,209
59,850	59,900	10,708	8,049	10,708	9,221
59,900	59,950	10,720	8,056	10,720	9,234
59,950	60,000	10,733	8,064	10,733	9,246

60,000

At least	But less than	Single	Married filing jointly *	Married filing separately	Head of a household
60,000	60,050	10,745	8,071	10,745	9,259
60,050	60,100	10,758	8,079	10,758	9,271
60,100	60,150	10,770	8,086	10,770	9,284
60,150	60,200	10,783	8,094	10,783	9,296
60,200	60,250	10,795	8,101	10,795	9,309
60,250	60,300	10,808	8,109	10,808	9,321
60,300	60,350	10,820	8,116	10,820	9,334
60,350	60,400	10,833	8,124	10,833	9,346
60,400	60,450	10,845	8,131	10,845	9,359
60,450	60,500	10,858	8,139	10,858	9,371
60,500	60,550	10,870	8,146	10,870	9,384
60,550	60,600	10,883	8,154	10,883	9,396
60,600	60,650	10,895	8,161	10,895	9,409
60,650	60,700	10,908	8,169	10,908	9,421
60,700	60,750	10,920	8,176	10,920	9,434
60,750	60,800	10,933	8,184	10,933	9,446
60,800	60,850	10,945	8,191	10,945	9,459
60,850	60,900	10,958	8,199	10,958	9,471
60,900	60,950	10,970	8,206	10,970	9,484
60,950	61,000	10,983	8,214	10,983	9,496

61,000

At least	But less than	Single	Married filing jointly *	Married filing separately	Head of a household
61,000	61,050	10,995	8,221	10,995	9,509
61,050	61,100	11,008	8,229	11,008	9,521
61,100	61,150	11,020	8,236	11,020	9,534
61,150	61,200	11,033	8,244	11,033	9,546
61,200	61,250	11,045	8,251	11,045	9,559
61,250	61,300	11,058	8,259	11,058	9,571
61,300	61,350	11,070	8,266	11,070	9,584
61,350	61,400	11,083	8,274	11,083	9,596
61,400	61,450	11,095	8,281	11,095	9,609
61,450	61,500	11,108	8,289	11,108	9,621
61,500	61,550	11,120	8,296	11,120	9,634
61,550	61,600	11,133	8,304	11,133	9,646
61,600	61,650	11,145	8,311	11,145	9,659
61,650	61,700	11,158	8,319	11,158	9,671
61,700	61,750	11,170	8,326	11,170	9,684
61,750	61,800	11,183	8,334	11,183	9,696
61,800	61,850	11,195	8,341	11,195	9,709
61,850	61,900	11,208	8,349	11,208	9,721
61,900	61,950	11,220	8,356	11,220	9,734
61,950	62,000	11,233	8,364	11,233	9,746

62,000

At least	But less than	Single	Married filing jointly *	Married filing separately	Head of a household
62,000	62,050	11,245	8,371	11,245	9,759
62,050	62,100	11,258	8,379	11,258	9,771
62,100	62,150	11,270	8,386	11,270	9,784
62,150	62,200	11,283	8,394	11,283	9,796
62,200	62,250	11,295	8,401	11,295	9,809
62,250	62,300	11,308	8,409	11,308	9,821
62,300	62,350	11,320	8,416	11,320	9,834
62,350	62,400	11,333	8,424	11,333	9,846
62,400	62,450	11,345	8,431	11,345	9,859
62,450	62,500	11,358	8,439	11,358	9,871
62,500	62,550	11,370	8,446	11,370	9,884
62,550	62,600	11,383	8,454	11,383	9,896
62,600	62,650	11,395	8,461	11,395	9,909
62,650	62,700	11,408	8,469	11,408	9,921
62,700	62,750	11,420	8,476	11,420	9,934
62,750	62,800	11,433	8,484	11,433	9,946
62,800	62,850	11,445	8,491	11,445	9,959
62,850	62,900	11,458	8,499	11,458	9,971
62,900	62,950	11,470	8,506	11,470	9,984
62,950	63,000	11,483	8,514	11,483	9,996

63,000

At least	But less than	Single	Married filing jointly *	Married filing separately	Head of a household
63,000	63,050	11,495	8,521	11,495	10,009
63,050	63,100	11,508	8,529	11,508	10,021
63,100	63,150	11,520	8,536	11,520	10,034
63,150	63,200	11,533	8,544	11,533	10,046
63,200	63,250	11,545	8,551	11,545	10,059
63,250	63,300	11,558	8,559	11,558	10,071
63,300	63,350	11,570	8,566	11,570	10,084
63,350	63,400	11,583	8,574	11,583	10,096
63,400	63,450	11,595	8,581	11,595	10,109
63,450	63,500	11,608	8,589	11,608	10,121
63,500	63,550	11,620	8,596	11,620	10,134
63,550	63,600	11,633	8,604	11,633	10,146
63,600	63,650	11,645	8,611	11,645	10,159
63,650	63,700	11,658	8,619	11,658	10,171
63,700	63,750	11,670	8,626	11,670	10,184
63,750	63,800	11,683	8,634	11,683	10,196
63,800	63,850	11,695	8,641	11,695	10,209
63,850	63,900	11,708	8,649	11,708	10,221
63,900	63,950	11,720	8,656	11,720	10,234
63,950	64,000	11,733	8,664	11,733	10,246

64,000

At least	But less than	Single	Married filing jointly *	Married filing separately	Head of a household
64,000	64,050	11,745	8,671	11,745	10,259
64,050	64,100	11,758	8,679	11,758	10,271
64,100	64,150	11,770	8,686	11,770	10,284
64,150	64,200	11,783	8,694	11,783	10,296
64,200	64,250	11,795	8,701	11,795	10,309
64,250	64,300	11,808	8,709	11,808	10,321
64,300	64,350	11,820	8,716	11,820	10,334
64,350	64,400	11,833	8,724	11,833	10,346
64,400	64,450	11,845	8,731	11,845	10,359
64,450	64,500	11,858	8,739	11,858	10,371
64,500	64,550	11,870	8,746	11,870	10,384
64,550	64,600	11,883	8,754	11,883	10,396
64,600	64,650	11,895	8,761	11,895	10,409
64,650	64,700	11,908	8,769	11,908	10,421
64,700	64,750	11,920	8,776	11,920	10,434
64,750	64,800	11,933	8,784	11,933	10,446
64,800	64,850	11,945	8,791	11,945	10,459
64,850	64,900	11,958	8,799	11,958	10,471
64,900	64,950	11,970	8,806	11,970	10,484
64,950	65,000	11,983	8,814	11,983	10,496

65,000

At least	But less than	Single	Married filing jointly *	Married filing separately	Head of a household
65,000	65,050	11,995	8,821	11,995	10,509
65,050	65,100	12,008	8,829	12,008	10,521
65,100	65,150	12,020	8,836	12,020	10,534
65,150	65,200	12,033	8,844	12,033	10,546
65,200	65,250	12,045	8,851	12,045	10,559
65,250	65,300	12,058	8,859	12,058	10,571
65,300	65,350	12,070	8,866	12,070	10,584
65,350	65,400	12,083	8,874	12,083	10,596
65,400	65,450	12,095	8,881	12,095	10,609
65,450	65,500	12,108	8,889	12,108	10,621
65,500	65,550	12,120	8,896	12,120	10,634
65,550	65,600	12,133	8,904	12,133	10,646
65,600	65,650	12,145	8,911	12,145	10,659
65,650	65,700	12,158	8,919	12,158	10,671
65,700	65,750	12,170	8,926	12,170	10,684
65,750	65,800	12,183	8,934	12,183	10,696
65,800	65,850	12,195	8,941	12,195	10,709
65,850	65,900	12,208	8,949	12,208	10,721
65,900	65,950	12,220	8,956	12,220	10,734
65,950	66,000	12,233	8,964	12,233	10,746

(Continued)

* This column must also be used by a qualifying widow(er).

Need more information or forms? Visit IRS.gov.

66,000

If line 43 (taxable income) is—		And you are—			
At least	But less than	Single	Married filing jointly *	Married filing separately	Head of a household
		Your tax is—			
66,000	66,050	12,245	8,971	12,245	10,759
66,050	66,100	12,258	8,979	12,258	10,771
66,100	66,150	12,270	8,986	12,270	10,784
66,150	66,200	12,283	8,994	12,283	10,796
66,200	66,250	12,295	9,001	12,295	10,809
66,250	66,300	12,308	9,009	12,308	10,821
66,300	66,350	12,320	9,016	12,320	10,834
66,350	66,400	12,333	9,024	12,333	10,846
66,400	66,450	12,345	9,031	12,345	10,859
66,450	66,500	12,358	9,039	12,358	10,871
66,500	66,550	12,370	9,046	12,370	10,884
66,550	66,600	12,383	9,054	12,383	10,896
66,600	66,650	12,395	9,061	12,395	10,909
66,650	66,700	12,408	9,069	12,408	10,921
66,700	66,750	12,420	9,076	12,420	10,934
66,750	66,800	12,433	9,084	12,433	10,946
66,800	66,850	12,445	9,091	12,445	10,959
66,850	66,900	12,458	9,099	12,458	10,971
66,900	66,950	12,470	9,106	12,470	10,984
66,950	67,000	12,483	9,114	12,483	10,996

67,000

At least	But less than	Single	Married filing jointly *	Married filing separately	Head of a household
67,000	67,050	12,495	9,121	12,495	11,009
67,050	67,100	12,508	9,129	12,508	11,021
67,100	67,150	12,520	9,136	12,520	11,034
67,150	67,200	12,533	9,144	12,533	11,046
67,200	67,250	12,545	9,151	12,545	11,059
67,250	67,300	12,558	9,159	12,558	11,071
67,300	67,350	12,570	9,166	12,570	11,084
67,350	67,400	12,583	9,174	12,583	11,096
67,400	67,450	12,595	9,181	12,595	11,109
67,450	67,500	12,608	9,189	12,608	11,121
67,500	67,550	12,620	9,196	12,620	11,134
67,550	67,600	12,633	9,204	12,633	11,146
67,600	67,650	12,645	9,211	12,645	11,159
67,650	67,700	12,658	9,219	12,658	11,171
67,700	67,750	12,670	9,226	12,670	11,184
67,750	67,800	12,683	9,234	12,683	11,196
67,800	67,850	12,695	9,241	12,695	11,209
67,850	67,900	12,708	9,249	12,708	11,221
67,900	67,950	12,720	9,256	12,720	11,234
67,950	68,000	12,733	9,264	12,733	11,246

68,000

At least	But less than	Single	Married filing jointly *	Married filing separately	Head of a household
68,000	68,050	12,745	9,271	12,745	11,259
68,050	68,100	12,758	9,279	12,758	11,271
68,100	68,150	12,770	9,286	12,770	11,284
68,150	68,200	12,783	9,294	12,783	11,296
68,200	68,250	12,795	9,301	12,795	11,309
68,250	68,300	12,808	9,309	12,808	11,321
68,300	68,350	12,820	9,316	12,820	11,334
68,350	68,400	12,833	9,324	12,833	11,346
68,400	68,450	12,845	9,331	12,845	11,359
68,450	68,500	12,858	9,339	12,858	11,371
68,500	68,550	12,870	9,346	12,870	11,384
68,550	68,600	12,883	9,354	12,883	11,396
68,600	68,650	12,895	9,361	12,895	11,409
68,650	68,700	12,908	9,369	12,908	11,421
68,700	68,750	12,920	9,376	12,920	11,434
68,750	68,800	12,933	9,384	12,933	11,446
68,800	68,850	12,945	9,391	12,945	11,459
68,850	68,900	12,958	9,399	12,958	11,471
68,900	68,950	12,970	9,406	12,970	11,484
68,950	69,000	12,983	9,414	12,983	11,496

69,000

At least	But less than	Single	Married filing jointly *	Married filing separately	Head of a household
69,000	69,050	12,995	9,421	12,995	11,509
69,050	69,100	13,008	9,429	13,008	11,521
69,100	69,150	13,020	9,436	13,020	11,534
69,150	69,200	13,033	9,444	13,033	11,546
69,200	69,250	13,045	9,451	13,045	11,559
69,250	69,300	13,058	9,459	13,058	11,571
69,300	69,350	13,070	9,466	13,070	11,584
69,350	69,400	13,083	9,474	13,083	11,596
69,400	69,450	13,095	9,481	13,095	11,609
69,450	69,500	13,108	9,489	13,108	11,621
69,500	69,550	13,120	9,496	13,120	11,634
69,550	69,600	13,133	9,504	13,133	11,646
69,600	69,650	13,145	9,511	13,145	11,659
69,650	69,700	13,158	9,519	13,158	11,671
69,700	69,750	13,170	9,526	13,170	11,684
69,750	69,800	13,183	9,534	13,183	11,696
69,800	69,850	13,195	9,541	13,195	11,709
69,850	69,900	13,208	9,549	13,208	11,721
69,900	69,950	13,220	9,556	13,220	11,734
69,950	70,000	13,233	9,564	13,233	11,746

70,000

At least	But less than	Single	Married filing jointly *	Married filing separately	Head of a household
70,000	70,050	13,245	9,571	13,245	11,759
70,050	70,100	13,258	9,579	13,258	11,771
70,100	70,150	13,270	9,586	13,270	11,784
70,150	70,200	13,283	9,594	13,283	11,796
70,200	70,250	13,295	9,601	13,295	11,809
70,250	70,300	13,308	9,609	13,308	11,821
70,300	70,350	13,320	9,616	13,320	11,834
70,350	70,400	13,333	9,624	13,333	11,846
70,400	70,450	13,345	9,631	13,345	11,859
70,450	70,500	13,358	9,639	13,358	11,871
70,500	70,550	13,370	9,646	13,370	11,884
70,550	70,600	13,383	9,654	13,383	11,896
70,600	70,650	13,395	9,661	13,395	11,909
70,650	70,700	13,408	9,669	13,408	11,921
70,700	70,750	13,420	9,676	13,420	11,934
70,750	70,800	13,433	9,684	13,433	11,946
70,800	70,850	13,445	9,691	13,445	11,959
70,850	70,900	13,458	9,699	13,458	11,971
70,900	70,950	13,470	9,706	13,470	11,984
70,950	71,000	13,483	9,714	13,483	11,996

71,000

At least	But less than	Single	Married filing jointly *	Married filing separately	Head of a household
71,000	71,050	13,495	9,721	13,495	12,009
71,050	71,100	13,508	9,729	13,508	12,021
71,100	71,150	13,520	9,736	13,520	12,034
71,150	71,200	13,533	9,744	13,533	12,046
71,200	71,250	13,545	9,751	13,545	12,059
71,250	71,300	13,558	9,759	13,558	12,071
71,300	71,350	13,570	9,766	13,570	12,084
71,350	71,400	13,583	9,774	13,583	12,096
71,400	71,450	13,595	9,781	13,595	12,109
71,450	71,500	13,608	9,789	13,608	12,121
71,500	71,550	13,620	9,796	13,620	12,134
71,550	71,600	13,633	9,804	13,633	12,146
71,600	71,650	13,645	9,811	13,645	12,159
71,650	71,700	13,658	9,819	13,658	12,171
71,700	71,750	13,670	9,826	13,670	12,184
71,750	71,800	13,683	9,834	13,683	12,196
71,800	71,850	13,695	9,841	13,695	12,209
71,850	71,900	13,708	9,849	13,708	12,221
71,900	71,950	13,720	9,856	13,720	12,234
71,950	72,000	13,733	9,864	13,733	12,246

72,000

At least	But less than	Single	Married filing jointly *	Married filing separately	Head of a household
72,000	72,050	13,745	9,871	13,745	12,259
72,050	72,100	13,758	9,879	13,758	12,271
72,100	72,150	13,770	9,886	13,770	12,284
72,150	72,200	13,783	9,894	13,783	12,296
72,200	72,250	13,795	9,901	13,795	12,309
72,250	72,300	13,808	9,909	13,808	12,321
72,300	72,350	13,820	9,916	13,820	12,334
72,350	72,400	13,833	9,924	13,833	12,346
72,400	72,450	13,845	9,931	13,845	12,359
72,450	72,500	13,858	9,939	13,858	12,371
72,500	72,550	13,870	9,946	13,870	12,384
72,550	72,600	13,883	9,954	13,883	12,396
72,600	72,650	13,895	9,961	13,895	12,409
72,650	72,700	13,908	9,969	13,908	12,421
72,700	72,750	13,920	9,976	13,920	12,434
72,750	72,800	13,933	9,984	13,933	12,446
72,800	72,850	13,945	9,991	13,945	12,459
72,850	72,900	13,958	9,999	13,958	12,471
72,900	72,950	13,970	10,006	13,970	12,484
72,950	73,000	13,983	10,014	13,983	12,496

73,000

At least	But less than	Single	Married filing jointly *	Married filing separately	Head of a household
73,000	73,050	13,995	10,021	13,995	12,509
73,050	73,100	14,008	10,029	14,008	12,521
73,100	73,150	14,020	10,036	14,020	12,534
73,150	73,200	14,033	10,044	14,033	12,546
73,200	73,250	14,045	10,051	14,045	12,559
73,250	73,300	14,058	10,059	14,058	12,571
73,300	73,350	14,070	10,066	14,070	12,584
73,350	73,400	14,083	10,074	14,083	12,596
73,400	73,450	14,095	10,081	14,095	12,609
73,450	73,500	14,108	10,089	14,108	12,621
73,500	73,550	14,120	10,096	14,120	12,634
73,550	73,600	14,133	10,104	14,133	12,646
73,600	73,650	14,145	10,111	14,145	12,659
73,650	73,700	14,158	10,119	14,158	12,671
73,700	73,750	14,170	10,126	14,170	12,684
73,750	73,800	14,183	10,134	14,183	12,696
73,800	73,850	14,195	10,141	14,195	12,709
73,850	73,900	14,208	10,149	14,208	12,721
73,900	73,950	14,220	10,156	14,220	12,734
73,950	74,000	14,233	10,164	14,233	12,746

74,000

At least	But less than	Single	Married filing jointly *	Married filing separately	Head of a household
74,000	74,050	14,245	10,171	14,245	12,759
74,050	74,100	14,258	10,179	14,258	12,771
74,100	74,150	14,270	10,186	14,270	12,784
74,150	74,200	14,283	10,194	14,283	12,796
74,200	74,250	14,295	10,201	14,295	12,809
74,250	74,300	14,308	10,209	14,308	12,821
74,300	74,350	14,320	10,216	14,320	12,834
74,350	74,400	14,333	10,224	14,333	12,846
74,400	74,450	14,345	10,231	14,345	12,859
74,450	74,500	14,358	10,239	14,358	12,871
74,500	74,550	14,370	10,246	14,370	12,884
74,550	74,600	14,383	10,254	14,383	12,896
74,600	74,650	14,395	10,261	14,395	12,909
74,650	74,700	14,408	10,269	14,408	12,921
74,700	74,750	14,420	10,276	14,420	12,934
74,750	74,800	14,433	10,284	14,433	12,946
74,800	74,850	14,445	10,291	14,445	12,959
74,850	74,900	14,458	10,299	14,458	12,971
74,900	74,950	14,470	10,306	14,470	12,984
74,950	75,000	14,483	10,314	14,483	12,996

(Continued)

* This column must also be used by a qualifying widow(er).

2017 Tax Table — Continued

If line 43 (taxable income) is— At least	But less than	And you are— Single	Married filing jointly *	Married filing separately	Head of a household
		Your tax is—			

75,000

At least	But less than	Single	Married filing jointly *	Married filing separately	Head of a household
75,000	75,050	14,495	10,321	14,495	13,009
75,050	75,100	14,508	10,329	14,508	13,021
75,100	75,150	14,520	10,336	14,520	13,034
75,150	75,200	14,533	10,344	14,533	13,046
75,200	75,250	14,545	10,351	14,545	13,059
75,250	75,300	14,558	10,359	14,558	13,071
75,300	75,350	14,570	10,366	14,570	13,084
75,350	75,400	14,583	10,374	14,583	13,096
75,400	75,450	14,595	10,381	14,595	13,109
75,450	75,500	14,608	10,389	14,608	13,121
75,500	75,550	14,620	10,396	14,620	13,134
75,550	75,600	14,633	10,404	14,633	13,146
75,600	75,650	14,645	10,411	14,645	13,159
75,650	75,700	14,658	10,419	14,658	13,171
75,700	75,750	14,670	10,426	14,670	13,184
75,750	75,800	14,683	10,434	14,683	13,196
75,800	75,850	14,695	10,441	14,695	13,209
75,850	75,900	14,708	10,449	14,708	13,221
75,900	75,950	14,720	10,459	14,720	13,234
75,950	76,000	14,733	10,471	14,733	13,246

76,000

At least	But less than	Single	Married filing jointly *	Married filing separately	Head of a household
76,000	76,050	14,745	10,484	14,745	13,259
76,050	76,100	14,758	10,496	14,758	13,271
76,100	76,150	14,770	10,509	14,770	13,284
76,150	76,200	14,783	10,521	14,783	13,296
76,200	76,250	14,795	10,534	14,795	13,309
76,250	76,300	14,808	10,546	14,808	13,321
76,300	76,350	14,820	10,559	14,820	13,334
76,350	76,400	14,833	10,571	14,833	13,346
76,400	76,450	14,845	10,584	14,845	13,359
76,450	76,500	14,858	10,596	14,858	13,371
76,500	76,550	14,870	10,609	14,870	13,384
76,550	76,600	14,883	10,621	14,883	13,396
76,600	76,650	14,895	10,634	14,897	13,409
76,650	76,700	14,908	10,646	14,911	13,421
76,700	76,750	14,920	10,659	14,925	13,434
76,750	76,800	14,933	10,671	14,939	13,446
76,800	76,850	14,945	10,684	14,953	13,459
76,850	76,900	14,958	10,696	14,967	13,471
76,900	76,950	14,970	10,709	14,981	13,484
76,950	77,000	14,983	10,721	14,995	13,496

77,000

At least	But less than	Single	Married filing jointly *	Married filing separately	Head of a household
77,000	77,050	14,995	10,734	15,009	13,509
77,050	77,100	15,008	10,746	15,023	13,521
77,100	77,150	15,020	10,759	15,037	13,534
77,150	77,200	15,033	10,771	15,051	13,546
77,200	77,250	15,045	10,784	15,065	13,559
77,250	77,300	15,058	10,796	15,079	13,571
77,300	77,350	15,070	10,809	15,093	13,584
77,350	77,400	15,083	10,821	15,107	13,596
77,400	77,450	15,095	10,834	15,121	13,609
77,450	77,500	15,108	10,846	15,135	13,621
77,500	77,550	15,120	10,859	15,149	13,634
77,550	77,600	15,133	10,871	15,163	13,646
77,600	77,650	15,145	10,884	15,177	13,659
77,650	77,700	15,158	10,896	15,191	13,671
77,700	77,750	15,170	10,909	15,205	13,684
77,750	77,800	15,183	10,921	15,219	13,696
77,800	77,850	15,195	10,934	15,233	13,709
77,850	77,900	15,208	10,946	15,247	13,721
77,900	77,950	15,220	10,959	15,261	13,734
77,950	78,000	15,233	10,971	15,275	13,746

78,000

At least	But less than	Single	Married filing jointly *	Married filing separately	Head of a household
78,000	78,050	15,245	10,984	15,289	13,759
78,050	78,100	15,258	10,996	15,303	13,771
78,100	78,150	15,270	11,009	15,317	13,784
78,150	78,200	15,283	11,021	15,331	13,796
78,200	78,250	15,295	11,034	15,345	13,809
78,250	78,300	15,308	11,046	15,359	13,821
78,300	78,350	15,320	11,059	15,373	13,834
78,350	78,400	15,333	11,071	15,387	13,846
78,400	78,450	15,345	11,084	15,401	13,859
78,450	78,500	15,358	11,096	15,415	13,871
78,500	78,550	15,370	11,109	15,429	13,884
78,550	78,600	15,383	11,121	15,443	13,896
78,600	78,650	15,395	11,134	15,457	13,909
78,650	78,700	15,408	11,146	15,471	13,921
78,700	78,750	15,420	11,159	15,485	13,934
78,750	78,800	15,433	11,171	15,499	13,946
78,800	78,850	15,445	11,184	15,513	13,959
78,850	78,900	15,458	11,196	15,527	13,971
78,900	78,950	15,470	11,209	15,541	13,984
78,950	79,000	15,483	11,221	15,555	13,996

79,000

At least	But less than	Single	Married filing jointly *	Married filing separately	Head of a household
79,000	79,050	15,495	11,234	15,569	14,009
79,050	79,100	15,508	11,246	15,583	14,021
79,100	79,150	15,520	11,259	15,597	14,034
79,150	79,200	15,533	11,271	15,611	14,046
79,200	79,250	15,545	11,284	15,625	14,059
79,250	79,300	15,558	11,296	15,639	14,071
79,300	79,350	15,570	11,309	15,653	14,084
79,350	79,400	15,583	11,321	15,667	14,096
79,400	79,450	15,595	11,334	15,681	14,109
79,450	79,500	15,608	11,346	15,695	14,121
79,500	79,550	15,620	11,359	15,709	14,134
79,550	79,600	15,633	11,371	15,723	14,146
79,600	79,650	15,645	11,384	15,737	14,159
79,650	79,700	15,658	11,396	15,751	14,171
79,700	79,750	15,670	11,409	15,765	14,184
79,750	79,800	15,683	11,421	15,779	14,196
79,800	79,850	15,695	11,434	15,793	14,209
79,850	79,900	15,708	11,446	15,807	14,221
79,900	79,950	15,720	11,459	15,821	14,234
79,950	80,000	15,733	11,471	15,835	14,246

80,000

At least	But less than	Single	Married filing jointly *	Married filing separately	Head of a household
80,000	80,050	15,745	11,484	15,849	14,259
80,050	80,100	15,758	11,496	15,863	14,271
80,100	80,150	15,770	11,500	15,877	14,284
80,150	80,200	15,783	11,521	15,891	14,296
80,200	80,250	15,795	11,534	15,905	14,309
80,250	80,300	15,808	11,546	15,919	14,321
80,300	80,350	15,820	11,559	15,933	14,334
80,350	80,400	15,833	11,571	15,947	14,346
80,400	80,450	15,845	11,584	15,961	14,359
80,450	80,500	15,858	11,596	15,975	14,371
80,500	80,550	15,870	11,609	15,989	14,384
80,550	80,600	15,883	11,621	16,003	14,396
80,600	80,650	15,895	11,634	16,017	14,409
80,650	80,700	15,908	11,646	16,031	14,421
80,700	80,750	15,920	11,659	16,045	14,434
80,750	80,800	15,933	11,671	16,059	14,446
80,800	80,850	15,945	11,684	16,073	14,459
80,850	80,900	15,958	11,696	16,087	14,471
80,900	80,950	15,970	11,709	16,101	14,484
80,950	81,000	15,983	11,721	16,115	14,496

81,000

At least	But less than	Single	Married filing jointly *	Married filing separately	Head of a household
81,000	81,050	15,995	11,734	16,129	14,509
81,050	81,100	16,008	11,746	16,143	14,521
81,100	81,150	16,020	11,759	16,157	14,534
81,150	81,200	16,033	11,771	16,171	14,546
81,200	81,250	16,045	11,784	16,185	14,559
81,250	81,300	16,058	11,796	16,199	14,571
81,300	81,350	16,070	11,809	16,213	14,584
81,350	81,400	16,083	11,821	16,227	14,596
81,400	81,450	16,095	11,834	16,241	14,609
81,450	81,500	16,108	11,846	16,255	14,621
81,500	81,550	16,120	11,859	16,269	14,634
81,550	81,600	16,133	11,871	16,283	14,646
81,600	81,650	16,145	11,884	16,297	14,659
81,650	81,700	16,158	11,896	16,311	14,671
81,700	81,750	16,170	11,909	16,325	14,684
81,750	81,800	16,183	11,921	16,339	14,696
81,800	81,850	16,195	11,934	16,353	14,709
81,850	81,900	16,208	11,946	16,367	14,721
81,900	81,950	16,220	11,959	16,381	14,734
81,950	82,000	16,233	11,971	16,395	14,746

82,000

At least	But less than	Single	Married filing jointly *	Married filing separately	Head of a household
82,000	82,050	16,245	11,984	16,409	14,759
82,050	82,100	16,258	11,996	16,423	14,771
82,100	82,150	16,270	12,009	16,437	14,784
82,150	82,200	16,283	12,021	16,451	14,796
82,200	82,250	16,295	12,034	16,465	14,809
82,250	82,300	16,308	12,046	16,479	14,821
82,300	82,350	16,320	12,059	16,493	14,834
82,350	82,400	16,333	12,071	16,507	14,846
82,400	82,450	16,345	12,084	16,521	14,859
82,450	82,500	16,358	12,096	16,535	14,871
82,500	82,550	16,370	12,109	16,549	14,884
82,550	82,600	16,383	12,121	16,563	14,896
82,600	82,650	16,395	12,134	16,577	14,909
82,650	82,700	16,408	12,146	16,591	14,921
82,700	82,750	16,420	12,159	16,605	14,934
82,750	82,800	16,433	12,171	16,619	14,946
82,800	82,850	16,445	12,184	16,633	14,959
82,850	82,900	16,458	12,196	16,647	14,971
82,900	82,950	16,470	12,209	16,661	14,984
82,950	83,000	16,483	12,221	16,675	14,996

83,000

At least	But less than	Single	Married filing jointly *	Married filing separately	Head of a household
83,000	83,050	16,495	12,234	16,689	15,009
83,050	83,100	16,508	12,246	16,703	15,021
83,100	83,150	16,520	12,259	16,717	15,034
83,150	83,200	16,533	12,271	16,731	15,046
83,200	83,250	16,545	12,284	16,745	15,059
83,250	83,300	16,558	12,296	16,759	15,071
83,300	83,350	16,570	12,309	16,773	15,084
83,350	83,400	16,583	12,321	16,787	15,096
83,400	83,450	16,595	12,334	16,801	15,109
83,450	83,500	16,608	12,346	16,815	15,121
83,500	83,550	16,620	12,359	16,829	15,134
83,550	83,600	16,633	12,371	16,843	15,146
83,600	83,650	16,645	12,384	16,857	15,159
83,650	83,700	16,658	12,396	16,871	15,171
83,700	83,750	16,670	12,400	16,885	15,184
83,750	83,800	16,683	12,421	16,899	15,196
83,800	83,850	16,695	12,434	16,913	15,209
83,850	83,900	16,708	12,446	16,927	15,221
83,900	83,950	16,720	12,459	16,941	15,234
83,950	84,000	16,733	12,471	16,955	15,246

* This column must also be used by a qualifying widow(er).

(Continued)

- 87 -

Need more information or forms? Visit IRS.gov.

If line 43 (taxable income) is—		And you are—			
At least	But less than	Single	Married filing jointly *	Married filing separately	Head of a household
		Your tax is—			

84,000

At least	But less than	Single	Married filing jointly *	Married filing separately	Head of a household
84,000	84,050	16,745	12,484	16,969	15,259
84,050	84,100	16,758	12,496	16,983	15,271
84,100	84,150	16,770	12,509	16,997	15,284
84,150	84,200	16,783	12,521	17,011	15,296
84,200	84,250	16,795	12,534	17,025	15,309
84,250	84,300	16,808	12,546	17,039	15,321
84,300	84,350	16,820	12,559	17,053	15,334
84,350	84,400	16,833	12,571	17,067	15,346
84,400	84,450	16,845	12,584	17,081	15,359
84,450	84,500	16,858	12,596	17,095	15,371
84,500	84,550	16,870	12,609	17,109	15,384
84,550	84,600	16,883	12,621	17,123	15,396
84,600	84,650	16,895	12,634	17,137	15,409
84,650	84,700	16,908	12,646	17,151	15,421
84,700	84,750	16,920	12,659	17,165	15,434
84,750	84,800	16,933	12,671	17,179	15,446
84,800	84,850	16,945	12,684	17,193	15,459
84,850	84,900	16,958	12,696	17,207	15,471
84,900	84,950	16,970	12,709	17,221	15,484
84,950	85,000	16,983	12,721	17,235	15,496

85,000

At least	But less than	Single	Married filing jointly *	Married filing separately	Head of a household
85,000	85,050	16,995	12,734	17,249	15,509
85,050	85,100	17,008	12,746	17,263	15,521
85,100	85,150	17,020	12,759	17,277	15,534
85,150	85,200	17,033	12,771	17,291	15,546
85,200	85,250	17,045	12,784	17,305	15,559
85,250	85,300	17,058	12,796	17,319	15,571
85,300	85,350	17,070	12,809	17,333	15,584
85,350	85,400	17,083	12,821	17,347	15,596
85,400	85,450	17,095	12,834	17,361	15,609
85,450	85,500	17,108	12,846	17,375	15,621
85,500	85,550	17,120	12,859	17,389	15,634
85,550	85,600	17,133	12,871	17,403	15,646
85,600	85,650	17,145	12,884	17,417	15,659
85,650	85,700	17,158	12,896	17,431	15,671
85,700	85,750	17,170	12,909	17,445	15,684
85,750	85,800	17,183	12,921	17,459	15,696
85,800	85,850	17,195	12,934	17,473	15,709
85,850	85,900	17,208	12,946	17,487	15,721
85,900	85,950	17,220	12,959	17,501	15,734
85,950	86,000	17,233	12,971	17,515	15,746

86,000

At least	But less than	Single	Married filing jointly *	Married filing separately	Head of a household
86,000	86,050	17,245	12,984	17,529	15,759
86,050	86,100	17,258	12,996	17,543	15,771
86,100	86,150	17,270	13,009	17,557	15,784
86,150	86,200	17,283	13,021	17,571	15,796
86,200	86,250	17,295	13,034	17,585	15,809
86,250	86,300	17,308	13,046	17,599	15,821
86,300	86,350	17,320	13,059	17,613	15,834
86,350	86,400	17,333	13,071	17,627	15,846
86,400	86,450	17,345	13,084	17,641	15,859
86,450	86,500	17,358	13,096	17,655	15,871
86,500	86,550	17,370	13,109	17,669	15,884
86,550	86,600	17,383	13,121	17,683	15,896
86,600	86,650	17,395	13,134	17,697	15,909
86,650	86,700	17,408	13,146	17,711	15,921
86,700	86,750	17,420	13,159	17,725	15,934
86,750	86,800	17,433	13,171	17,739	15,946
86,800	86,850	17,445	13,184	17,753	15,959
86,850	86,900	17,458	13,196	17,767	15,971
86,900	86,950	17,470	13,209	17,781	15,984
86,950	87,000	17,483	13,221	17,795	15,996

87,000

At least	But less than	Single	Married filing jointly *	Married filing separately	Head of a household
87,000	87,050	17,495	13,234	17,809	16,009
87,050	87,100	17,508	13,246	17,823	16,021
87,100	87,150	17,520	13,259	17,837	16,034
87,150	87,200	17,533	13,271	17,851	16,046
87,200	87,250	17,545	13,284	17,865	16,059
87,250	87,300	17,558	13,296	17,879	16,071
87,300	87,350	17,570	13,309	17,893	16,084
87,350	87,400	17,583	13,321	17,907	16,096
87,400	87,450	17,595	13,334	17,921	16,109
87,450	87,500	17,608	13,346	17,935	16,121
87,500	87,550	17,620	13,359	17,949	16,134
87,550	87,600	17,633	13,371	17,963	16,146
87,600	87,650	17,645	13,384	17,977	16,159
87,650	87,700	17,658	13,396	17,991	16,171
87,700	87,750	17,670	13,409	18,005	16,184
87,750	87,800	17,683	13,421	18,019	16,196
87,800	87,850	17,695	13,434	18,033	16,209
87,850	87,900	17,708	13,446	18,047	16,221
87,900	87,950	17,720	13,459	18,061	16,234
87,950	88,000	17,733	13,471	18,075	16,246

88,000

At least	But less than	Single	Married filing jointly *	Married filing separately	Head of a household
88,000	88,050	17,745	13,484	18,089	16,259
88,050	88,100	17,758	13,496	18,103	16,271
88,100	88,150	17,770	13,509	18,117	16,284
88,150	88,200	17,783	13,521	18,131	16,296
88,200	88,250	17,795	13,534	18,145	16,309
88,250	88,300	17,808	13,546	18,159	16,321
88,300	88,350	17,820	13,559	18,173	16,334
88,350	88,400	17,833	13,571	18,187	16,346
88,400	88,450	17,845	13,584	18,201	16,359
88,450	88,500	17,858	13,596	18,215	16,371
88,500	88,550	17,870	13,609	18,229	16,384
88,550	88,600	17,883	13,621	18,243	16,396
88,600	88,650	17,895	13,634	18,257	16,409
88,650	88,700	17,908	13,646	18,271	16,421
88,700	88,750	17,920	13,659	18,285	16,434
88,750	88,800	17,933	13,671	18,299	16,446
88,800	88,850	17,945	13,684	18,313	16,459
88,850	88,900	17,958	13,696	18,327	16,471
88,900	88,950	17,970	13,709	18,341	16,484
88,950	89,000	17,983	13,721	18,355	16,496

89,000

At least	But less than	Single	Married filing jointly *	Married filing separately	Head of a household
89,000	89,050	17,995	13,734	18,369	16,509
89,050	89,100	18,008	13,746	18,383	16,521
89,100	89,150	18,020	13,759	18,397	16,534
89,150	89,200	18,033	13,771	18,411	16,546
89,200	89,250	18,045	13,784	18,425	16,559
89,250	89,300	18,058	13,796	18,439	16,571
89,300	89,350	18,070	13,809	18,453	16,584
89,350	89,400	18,083	13,821	18,467	16,596
89,400	89,450	18,095	13,834	18,481	16,609
89,450	89,500	18,108	13,846	18,495	16,621
89,500	89,550	18,120	13,859	18,509	16,634
89,550	89,600	18,133	13,871	18,523	16,646
89,600	89,650	18,145	13,884	18,537	16,659
89,650	89,700	18,158	13,896	18,551	16,671
89,700	89,750	18,170	13,909	18,565	16,684
89,750	89,800	18,183	13,921	18,579	16,696
89,800	89,850	18,195	13,934	18,593	16,709
89,850	89,900	18,208	13,946	18,607	16,721
89,900	89,950	18,220	13,959	18,621	16,734
89,950	90,000	18,233	13,971	18,635	16,746

90,000

At least	But less than	Single	Married filing jointly *	Married filing separately	Head of a household
90,000	90,050	18,245	13,984	18,649	16,759
90,050	90,100	18,258	13,996	18,663	16,771
90,100	90,150	18,270	14,009	18,677	16,784
90,150	90,200	18,283	14,021	18,691	16,796
90,200	90,250	18,295	14,034	18,705	16,809
90,250	90,300	18,308	14,046	18,719	16,821
90,300	90,350	18,320	14,059	18,733	16,834
90,350	90,400	18,333	14,071	18,747	16,846
90,400	90,450	18,345	14,084	18,761	16,859
90,450	90,500	18,358	14,096	18,775	16,871
90,500	90,550	18,370	14,109	18,789	16,884
90,550	90,600	18,383	14,121	18,803	16,896
90,600	90,650	18,395	14,134	18,817	16,909
90,650	90,700	18,408	14,146	18,831	16,921
90,700	90,750	18,420	14,159	18,845	16,934
90,750	90,800	18,433	14,171	18,859	16,946
90,800	90,850	18,445	14,184	18,873	16,959
90,850	90,900	18,458	14,196	18,887	16,971
90,900	90,950	18,470	14,209	18,901	16,984
90,950	91,000	18,483	14,221	18,915	16,996

91,000

At least	But less than	Single	Married filing jointly *	Married filing separately	Head of a household
91,000	91,050	18,495	14,234	18,929	17,009
91,050	91,100	18,508	14,246	18,943	17,021
91,100	91,150	18,520	14,259	18,957	17,034
91,150	91,200	18,533	14,271	18,971	17,046
91,200	91,250	18,545	14,284	18,985	17,059
91,250	91,300	18,558	14,296	18,999	17,071
91,300	91,350	18,570	14,309	19,013	17,084
91,350	91,400	18,583	14,321	19,027	17,096
91,400	91,450	18,595	14,334	19,041	17,109
91,450	91,500	18,608	14,346	19,055	17,121
91,500	91,550	18,620	14,359	19,069	17,134
91,550	91,600	18,633	14,371	19,083	17,146
91,600	91,650	18,645	14,384	19,097	17,159
91,650	91,700	18,658	14,396	19,111	17,171
91,700	91,750	18,670	14,409	19,125	17,184
91,750	91,800	18,683	14,421	19,139	17,196
91,800	91,850	18,695	14,434	19,153	17,209
91,850	91,900	18,708	14,446	19,167	17,221
91,900	91,950	18,721	14,459	19,181	17,234
91,950	92,000	18,735	14,471	19,195	17,246

92,000

At least	But less than	Single	Married filing jointly *	Married filing separately	Head of a household
92,000	92,050	18,749	14,484	19,209	17,259
92,050	92,100	18,763	14,496	19,223	17,271
92,100	92,150	18,777	14,509	19,237	17,284
92,150	92,200	18,791	14,521	19,251	17,296
92,200	92,250	18,805	14,534	19,265	17,309
92,250	92,300	18,819	14,546	19,279	17,321
92,300	92,350	18,833	14,559	19,293	17,334
92,350	92,400	18,847	14,571	19,307	17,346
92,400	92,450	18,861	14,584	19,321	17,359
92,450	92,500	18,875	14,596	19,335	17,371
92,500	92,550	18,889	14,609	19,349	17,384
92,550	92,600	18,903	14,621	19,363	17,396
92,600	92,650	18,917	14,634	19,377	17,409
92,650	92,700	18,931	14,646	19,391	17,421
92,700	92,750	18,945	14,659	19,405	17,434
92,750	92,800	18,959	14,671	19,419	17,446
92,800	92,850	18,973	14,684	19,433	17,459
92,850	92,900	18,987	14,696	19,447	17,471
92,900	92,950	19,001	14,709	19,461	17,484
92,950	93,000	19,015	14,721	19,475	17,496

(Continued)

* This column must also be used by a qualifying widow(er).

93,000

At least	But less than	Single	Married filing jointly *	Married filing separately	Head of a household
93,000	93,050	19,029	14,734	19,489	17,509
93,050	93,100	19,043	14,746	19,503	17,521
93,100	93,150	19,057	14,759	19,517	17,534
93,150	93,200	19,071	14,771	19,531	17,546
93,200	93,250	19,085	14,784	19,545	17,559
93,250	93,300	19,099	14,796	19,559	17,571
93,300	93,350	19,113	14,809	19,573	17,584
93,350	93,400	19,127	14,821	19,587	17,596
93,400	93,450	19,141	14,834	19,601	17,609
93,450	93,500	19,155	14,846	19,615	17,621
93,500	93,550	19,169	14,859	19,629	17,634
93,550	93,600	19,183	14,871	19,643	17,646
93,600	93,650	19,197	14,884	19,657	17,659
93,650	93,700	19,211	14,896	19,671	17,671
93,700	93,750	19,225	14,909	19,685	17,684
93,750	93,800	19,239	14,921	19,699	17,696
93,800	93,850	19,253	14,934	19,713	17,709
93,850	93,900	19,267	14,946	19,727	17,721
93,900	93,950	19,281	14,959	19,741	17,734
93,950	94,000	19,295	14,971	19,755	17,746

94,000

At least	But less than	Single	Married filing jointly *	Married filing separately	Head of a household
94,000	94,050	19,309	14,984	19,769	17,759
94,050	94,100	19,323	14,996	19,783	17,771
94,100	94,150	19,337	15,009	19,797	17,784
94,150	94,200	19,351	15,021	19,811	17,796
94,200	94,250	19,365	15,034	19,825	17,809
94,250	94,300	19,379	15,046	19,839	17,821
94,300	94,350	19,393	15,059	19,853	17,834
94,350	94,400	19,407	15,071	19,867	17,846
94,400	94,450	19,421	15,084	19,881	17,859
94,450	94,500	19,435	15,096	19,895	17,871
94,500	94,550	19,449	15,109	19,909	17,884
94,550	94,600	19,463	15,121	19,923	17,896
94,600	94,650	19,477	15,134	19,937	17,909
94,650	94,700	19,491	15,146	19,951	17,921
94,700	94,750	19,505	15,159	19,965	17,934
94,750	94,800	19,519	15,171	19,979	17,946
94,800	94,850	19,533	15,184	19,993	17,959
94,850	94,900	19,547	15,196	20,007	17,971
94,900	94,950	19,561	15,209	20,021	17,984
94,950	95,000	19,575	15,221	20,035	17,996

95,000

At least	But less than	Single	Married filing jointly *	Married filing separately	Head of a household
95,000	95,050	19,589	15,234	20,049	18,009
95,050	95,100	19,603	15,246	20,063	18,021
95,100	95,150	19,617	15,259	20,077	18,034
95,150	95,200	19,631	15,271	20,091	18,046
95,200	95,250	19,645	15,284	20,105	18,059
95,250	95,300	19,659	15,296	20,119	18,071
95,300	95,350	19,673	15,309	20,133	18,084
95,350	95,400	19,687	15,321	20,147	18,096
95,400	95,450	19,701	15,334	20,161	18,109
95,450	95,500	19,715	15,346	20,175	18,121
95,500	95,550	19,729	15,359	20,189	18,134
95,550	95,600	19,743	15,371	20,203	18,146
95,600	95,650	19,757	15,384	20,217	18,159
95,650	95,700	19,771	15,396	20,231	18,171
95,700	95,750	19,785	15,409	20,245	18,184
95,750	95,800	19,799	15,421	20,259	18,196
95,800	95,850	19,813	15,434	20,273	18,209
95,850	95,900	19,827	15,446	20,287	18,221
95,900	95,950	19,841	15,459	20,301	18,234
95,950	96,000	19,855	15,471	20,315	18,246

96,000

At least	But less than	Single	Married filing jointly *	Married filing separately	Head of a household
96,000	96,050	19,869	15,484	20,329	18,259
96,050	96,100	19,883	15,496	20,343	18,271
96,100	96,150	19,897	15,509	20,357	18,284
96,150	96,200	19,911	15,521	20,371	18,296
96,200	96,250	19,925	15,534	20,385	18,309
96,250	96,300	19,939	15,546	20,399	18,321
96,300	96,350	19,953	15,559	20,413	18,334
96,350	96,400	19,967	15,571	20,427	18,346
96,400	96,450	19,981	15,584	20,441	18,359
96,450	96,500	19,995	15,596	20,455	18,371
96,500	96,550	20,009	15,609	20,469	18,384
96,550	96,600	20,023	15,621	20,483	18,396
96,600	96,650	20,037	15,634	20,497	18,409
96,650	96,700	20,051	15,646	20,511	18,421
96,700	96,750	20,065	15,659	20,525	18,434
96,750	96,800	20,079	15,671	20,539	18,446
96,800	96,850	20,093	15,684	20,553	18,459
96,850	96,900	20,107	15,696	20,567	18,471
96,900	96,950	20,121	15,709	20,581	18,484
96,950	97,000	20,135	15,721	20,595	18,496

97,000

At least	But less than	Single	Married filing jointly *	Married filing separately	Head of a household
97,000	97,050	20,149	15,734	20,609	18,509
97,050	97,100	20,163	15,746	20,623	18,521
97,100	97,150	20,177	15,759	20,637	18,534
97,150	97,200	20,191	15,771	20,651	18,546
97,200	97,250	20,205	15,784	20,665	18,559
97,250	97,300	20,219	15,796	20,679	18,571
97,300	97,350	20,233	15,809	20,693	18,584
97,350	97,400	20,247	15,821	20,707	18,596
97,400	97,450	20,261	15,834	20,721	18,609
97,450	97,500	20,275	15,846	20,735	18,621
97,500	97,550	20,289	15,859	20,749	18,634
97,550	97,600	20,303	15,871	20,763	18,646
97,600	97,650	20,317	15,884	20,777	18,659
97,650	97,700	20,331	15,896	20,791	18,671
97,700	97,750	20,345	15,909	20,805	18,684
97,750	97,800	20,359	15,921	20,819	18,696
97,800	97,850	20,373	15,934	20,833	18,709
97,850	97,900	20,387	15,946	20,847	18,721
97,900	97,950	20,401	15,959	20,861	18,734
97,950	98,000	20,415	15,971	20,875	18,746

98,000

At least	But less than	Single	Married filing jointly *	Married filing separately	Head of a household
98,000	98,050	20,429	15,984	20,889	18,759
98,050	98,100	20,443	15,996	20,903	18,771
98,100	98,150	20,457	16,009	20,917	18,784
98,150	98,200	20,471	16,021	20,931	18,796
98,200	98,250	20,485	16,034	20,945	18,809
98,250	98,300	20,499	16,046	20,959	18,821
98,300	98,350	20,513	16,059	20,973	18,834
98,350	98,400	20,527	16,071	20,987	18,846
98,400	98,450	20,541	16,084	21,001	18,859
98,450	98,500	20,555	16,096	21,015	18,871
98,500	98,550	20,569	16,109	21,029	18,884
98,550	98,600	20,583	16,121	21,043	18,896
98,600	98,650	20,597	16,134	21,057	18,909
98,650	98,700	20,611	16,146	21,071	18,921
98,700	98,750	20,625	16,159	21,085	18,934
98,750	98,800	20,639	16,171	21,099	18,946
98,800	98,850	20,653	16,184	21,113	18,959
98,850	98,900	20,667	16,196	21,127	18,971
98,900	98,950	20,681	16,209	21,141	18,984
98,950	99,000	20,695	16,221	21,155	18,996

99,000

At least	But less than	Single	Married filing jointly *	Married filing separately	Head of a household
99,000	99,050	20,709	16,234	21,169	19,009
99,050	99,100	20,723	16,246	21,183	19,021
99,100	99,150	20,737	16,259	21,197	19,034
99,150	99,200	20,751	16,271	21,211	19,046
99,200	99,250	20,765	16,284	21,225	19,059
99,250	99,300	20,779	16,296	21,239	19,071
99,300	99,350	20,793	16,309	21,253	19,084
99,350	99,400	20,807	16,321	21,267	19,096
99,400	99,450	20,821	16,334	21,281	19,109
99,450	99,500	20,835	16,346	21,295	19,121
99,500	99,550	20,849	16,359	21,309	19,134
99,550	99,600	20,863	16,371	21,323	19,146
99,600	99,650	20,877	16,384	21,337	19,159
99,650	99,700	20,891	16,396	21,351	19,171
99,700	99,750	20,905	16,409	21,365	19,184
99,750	99,800	20,919	16,421	21,379	19,196
99,800	99,850	20,933	16,434	21,393	19,209
99,850	99,900	20,947	16,446	21,407	19,221
99,900	99,950	20,961	16,459	21,421	19,234
99,950	100,000	20,975	16,471	21,435	19,246

$100,000
or over
use the Tax
Computation
Worksheet

* This column must also be used by a qualifying widow(er).

Need more information or forms? Visit IRS.gov.

2017 Tax Computation Worksheet—Line 44

 See the instructions for line 44 to see if you must use the worksheet below to figure your tax.

Note. If you are required to use this worksheet to figure the tax on an amount from another form or worksheet, such as the Qualified Dividends and Capital Gain Tax Worksheet, the Schedule D Tax Worksheet, Schedule J, Form 8615, or the Foreign Earned Income Tax Worksheet, enter the amount from that form or worksheet in column (a) of the row that applies to the amount you are looking up. Enter the result on the appropriate line of the form or worksheet that you are completing.

Section A—Use if your filing status is Single. Complete the row below that applies to you.

Taxable income. If line 43 is—	(a) Enter the amount from line 43	(b) Multiplication amount	(c) Multiply (a) by (b)	(d) Subtraction amount	Tax. Subtract (d) from (c). Enter the result here and on Form 1040, line 44.
At least $100,000 but not over $191,650	$	× 28% (0.28)	$	$ 7,018.25	$
Over $191,650 but not over $416,700	$	× 33% (0.33)	$	$ 16,600.75	$
Over $416,700 but not over $418,400	$	× 35% (0.35)	$	$ 24,934.75	$
Over $418,400	$	× 39.6% (0.396)	$	$ 44,181.15	$

Section B—Use if your filing status is Married filing jointly or Qualifying widow(er). Complete the row below that applies to you.

Taxable income. If line 43 is—	(a) Enter the amount from line 43	(b) Multiplication amount	(c) Multiply (a) by (b)	(d) Subtraction amount	Tax. Subtract (d) from (c). Enter the result here and on Form 1040, line 44.
At least $100,000 but not over $153,100	$	× 25% (0.25)	$	$ 8,522.50	$
Over $153,100 but not over $233,350	$	× 28% (0.28)	$	$ 13,115.50	$
Over $233,350 but not over $416,700	$	× 33% (0.33)	$	$ 24,783.00	$
Over $416,700 but not over $470,700	$	× 35% (0.35)	$	$ 33,117.00	$
Over $470,700	$	× 39.6% (0.396)	$	$ 54,769.20	$

Section C—Use if your filing status is Married filing separately. Complete the row below that applies to you.

Taxable income. If line 43 is—	(a) Enter the amount from line 43	(b) Multiplication amount	(c) Multiply (a) by (b)	(d) Subtraction amount	Tax. Subtract (d) from (c). Enter the result here and on Form 1040, line 44.
At least $100,000 but not over $116,675	$	× 28% (0.28)	$	$ 6,557.75	$
Over $116,675 but not over $208,350	$	× 33% (0.33)	$	$ 12,391.50	$
Over $208,350 but not over $235,350	$	× 35% (0.35)	$	$ 16,558.50	$
Over $235,350	$	× 39.6% (0.396)	$	$ 27,384.60	$

Section D—Use if your filing status is Head of household. Complete the row below that applies to you.

Taxable income. If line 43 is—	(a) Enter the amount from line 43	(b) Multiplication amount	(c) Multiply (a) by (b)	(d) Subtraction amount	Tax. Subtract (d) from (c). Enter the result here and on Form 1040, line 44.
At least $100,000 but not over $131,200	$	× 25% (0.25)	$	$ 5,747.50	$
Over $131,200 but not over $212,500	$	× 28% (0.28)	$	$ 9,683.50	$
Over $212,500 but not over $416,700	$	× 33% (0.33)	$	$ 20,308.50	$
Over $416,700 but not over $444,550	$	× 35% (0.35)	$	$ 28,642.50	$
Over $444,550	$	× 39.6% (0.396)	$	$ 49,091.80	$

General Information

How To Avoid Common Mistakes

Mistakes can delay your refund or result in notices being sent to you. One of the best ways to file an accurate return is to file electronically. Tax software does the math for you and will help you avoid mistakes. You may be eligible to use free tax software that will take the guesswork out of preparing your return. Free File makes available free brand-name software and free *e-file*. Visit *IRS.gov/FreeFile* for details. Join the eight in 10 taxpayers who get their refunds faster by using direct deposit and *e-file*.

• Make sure you entered the correct name and social security number (SSN) for each dependent you claim on line 6c. Check that each dependent's name and SSN agrees with his or her social security card. For each child under age 17 who is a qualifying child for the child tax credit, make sure you checked the box in line 6c, column (4).

• Check your math, especially for the child tax credit, earned income credit (EIC), taxable social security benefits, total income, itemized deductions or standard deduction, deduction for exemptions, taxable income, total tax, federal income tax withheld, and refund or amount you owe.

• Be sure you used the correct method to figure your tax. See the instructions for line 44.

• Be sure to enter your SSN in the space provided on page 1 of Form 1040. If you are married filing a joint or separate return, also enter your spouse's SSN. Be sure to enter your SSN in the space next to your name. Check that your name and SSN agree with your social security card.

• Make sure your name and address are correct. Enter your (and your spouse's) name in the same order as shown on your last return.

• If you live in an apartment, be sure to include your apartment number in your address.

• If you are taking the standard deduction, see the instructions for line 40 to be sure you entered the correct amount.

• If you received capital gain distributions but weren't required to file Schedule D, make sure you checked the box on line 13.

• If you are taking the EIC, be sure you used the correct column of the EIC Table for your filing status and the number of children you have.

• Remember to sign and date Form 1040 and enter your occupation(s).

• Attach your Form(s) W-2 and other required forms and schedules. Put all forms and schedules in the proper order. See *Assemble Your Return,* earlier.

• If you owe tax and are paying by check or money order, be sure to include all the required information on your payment. See the instructions for line 78 for details.

• Make sure to check *Where Do You File?* before mailing your return. Over the next several years, the IRS will be reducing the number of paper tax return processing sites from five down to two. Because of this, you may need to mail your return to a different address than you have in the past.

• Don't file more than one original return for the same year, even if you haven't gotten your refund or haven't heard from the IRS since you filed. Filing more than one original return for the same year, or sending in more than one copy of the same return (unless we ask you to do so), could delay your refund.

• Make sure you either indicate qualifying health care coverage for you, your spouse (if filing jointly), or anyone you can or do claim as a dependent by checking the box on line 61, claim an exemption from the requirement to have health care coverage by attaching Form 8965, or make a shared responsibility payment on line 61.

• Make sure that if you, your spouse, with whom you are filing a joint return, or your dependent was enrolled in Marketplace coverage and advance payments of the premium tax credit were made for the coverage, that you attach Form 8962. You may have to repay excess advance payments even if someone else enrolled you, your spouse, or your dependent in the Marketplace coverage. Excess advance payments may also have to be repaid if you enrolled someone in Marketplace coverage, you don't claim that individual as a dependent, and no one else claims that individual as a dependent. See the instructions for line 46 and the Instructions for Form 8962. You or whoever enrolled you should have received Form 1095-A from the Marketplace with information about who was covered and any advance payments of the premium tax credit.

• Make sure to check *Where Do You File?* before mailing your return. Over the next several years the IRS will be reducing the number of paper tax return processing sites from five down to two. Because of this, you may need to mail your return to a different address than you have in the past.

Innocent Spouse Relief

Generally, both you and your spouse are each responsible for paying the full amount of tax, interest, and penalties on your joint return. However, you may qualify for relief from liability for tax on a joint return if (a) there is an understatement of tax because your spouse omitted income or claimed false deductions or credits, (b) you are divorced, separated, or no longer living with your spouse, or (c) given all the facts and circumstances, it wouldn't be fair to hold you liable for the tax. You also may qualify for relief if you were a married resident of a community property state but didn't file a joint return and are now liable for an unpaid or understated tax. File Form 8857 to request relief. In some cases, Form 8857 may need to be filed within 2 years of the date on which the IRS first attempted to collect the tax from you. Don't file Form 8857 with your Form 1040. For more information, see Pub. 971 and Form 8857 or you can call the Innocent Spouse office toll-free at 1-855-851-2009.

Income Tax Withholding and Estimated Tax Payments for 2018

 You can use the IRS Withholding Calculator instead of Pub. 505 or the worksheets included with Form W-4 or W-4P, to determine whether you need to have your withholding increased or decreased.

In general, you don't have to make estimated tax payments if you expect that your 2018 Form 1040 will show a tax refund or a tax balance due of less than $1,000. If your total estimated tax for 2018 is $1,000 or more, see Form 1040-ES and Pub. 505 for a worksheet you can use to see if you have to make estimated tax payments. For more details, see Pub. 505.

Secure Your Tax Records From Identity Theft

Identity theft occurs when someone uses your personal information, such as your name, social security number (SSN), or other identifying information, without your permission, to commit fraud or other crimes. An identity thief may use your SSN to get a job or may file a tax return using your SSN to receive a refund.

To reduce your risk:
- Protect your SSN,
- Ensure your employer is protecting your SSN, and
- Be careful when choosing a tax preparer.

If your tax records are affected by identity theft and you receive a notice from the IRS, respond right away to the name and phone number printed on the IRS notice or letter. For more information, see Pub. 5027.

If your SSN has been lost or stolen or you suspect you are a victim of tax-related identity theft, visit *IRS.gov/ IdentityTheft* to learn what steps you should take.

Victims of identity theft who are experiencing economic harm or a systemic problem, or are seeking help in resolv-

ing tax problems that haven't been resolved through normal channels, may be eligible for Taxpayer Advocate Service (TAS) assistance. You can reach TAS by calling the National Taxpayer Advocate helpline at 1-877-777-4778. People who are deaf, hard of hearing, or have a speech disability and who have access to TTY/TDD equipment can call 1-800-829-4059. Deaf or hard-of-hearing individuals also can contact the IRS through relay services such as the Federal Relay Service available at *www.gsa.gov/fedrelay.*

Protect yourself from suspicious emails or phishing schemes. Phishing is the creation and use of email and websites designed to mimic legitimate business emails and websites. The most common form is sending an email to a user falsely claiming to be an established legitimate enterprise in an attempt to scam the user into surrendering private information that will be used for identity theft.

The IRS doesn't initiate contacts with taxpayers via emails. Also, the IRS doesn't request detailed personal information through email or ask taxpayers for the PIN numbers, passwords, or similar secret access information for their credit card, bank, or other financial accounts.

If you receive an unsolicited email claiming to be from the IRS, forward the message to *phishing@irs.gov.* You also may report misuse of the IRS name, logo, forms, or other IRS property to the Treasury Inspector General for Tax Administration toll-free at 1-800-366-4484. People who are deaf, hard of hearing, or have a speech disability and who have access to TTY/TDD equipment can call 1-800-877-8339. You can forward suspicious emails to the Federal Trade Commission (FTC) at *spam@uce.gov* or report them at *ftc.gov/complaint.* You can contact them at *www.ftc.gov/idtheft* or 1-877-IDTHEFT (1-877-438-4338). If you have been the victim of identity theft, see *www.IdentityTheft.gov* and Pub. 5027. People who are deaf, hard of hearing, or have a speech disability and who have access to TTY/TDD equipment can call 1-866-653-4261.

Visit IRS.gov and enter "identity theft" in the search box to learn more about identity theft and how to reduce your risk.

How Do You Make a Gift To Reduce Debt Held By the Public?

If you wish to do so, make a check payable to "Bureau of the Fiscal Service." You can send it to: Bureau of the Fiscal Service, Attn: Dept G, P.O. Box 2188, Parkersburg, WV 26106-2188. Or you can enclose the check with your income tax return when you file. In the memo section of the check, make a note that it is a gift to reduce the debt held by the public. Don't add your gift to any tax you may owe. See the instructions for line 78 for details on how to pay any tax you owe. For information on how to make this type of gift online, go to *www.treasurydirect.gov* and click on "How To Make a Contribution to Reduce the Debt."

 You may be able to deduct this gift on your 2018 tax return.

How Long Should Records Be Kept?

Keep a copy of your tax return, worksheets you used, and records of all items appearing on it (such as Forms W-2 and 1099) until the statute of limitations runs out for that return. Usually, this is 3 years from the date the return was due or filed or 2 years from the date the tax was paid, whichever is later. You should keep some records longer. For example, keep property records (including those on your home) as long as they are needed to figure the basis of the original or replacement property. For more details, see chapter 1 of Pub. 17.

Amended Return

File Form 1040X to change a return you already filed. Generally, Form 1040X must be filed within 3 years after the date the original return was filed or within 2 years after the date the tax was paid, whichever is later. But you may have more time to file Form 1040X if you live in a federally declared disaster area or you are physically or mentally unable to manage your financial affairs. See Pub. 556 for details.

Use the *Where's My Amended Return* application on IRS.gov to track the status of your amended return. It can take up to 3 weeks from the date you mailed it to show up in our system.

Need a Copy of Your Tax Return Information?

Tax return transcripts are free and generally are used to validate income and tax filing status for mortgage applications, student and small business loan applications, and during tax preparation. To get a free transcript:

- Visit *IRS.gov/Transcript*,
- Use Form 4506-T or 4506T-EZ, or
- Call us at 1-800-908-9946.

If you need a copy of your actual tax return, use Form 4506. There is a fee for each return requested. See Form 4506 for the current fee. If your main home, principal place of business, or tax records are located in a federally declared disaster area, this fee will be waived.

Death of a Taxpayer

If a taxpayer died before filing a return for 2017, the taxpayer's spouse or personal representative may have to file and sign a return for that taxpayer. A personal representative can be an executor, administrator, or anyone who is in charge of the deceased taxpayer's property. If the deceased taxpayer didn't have to file a return but had tax withheld, a return must be filed to get a refund. The person who files the return must enter "Deceased," the deceased taxpayer's name, and the date of death across the top of the return. If this information isn't provided, it may delay the processing of the return.

If your spouse died in 2017 and you didn't remarry in 2017, or if your spouse died in 2018 before filing a return for 2017, you can file a joint return. A joint return should show your spouse's 2017 income before death and your income for all of 2017. Enter "Filing as surviving spouse" in the area where you sign the return. If someone else is the personal representative, he or she also must sign.

The surviving spouse or personal representative should promptly notify all payers of income, including financial institutions, of the taxpayer's death. This will ensure the proper reporting of income earned by the taxpayer's estate or heirs. A deceased taxpayer's social security number shouldn't be used for tax years after the year of death, except for estate tax return purposes.

Claiming a Refund for a Deceased Taxpayer

If you are filing a joint return as a surviving spouse, you only need to file the tax return to claim the refund. If you are a court-appointed representative, file the return and include a copy of the certificate that shows your appointment. All other filers requesting the deceased taxpayer's refund must file the return and attach Form 1310.

For more details, use *Tax Topic 356* or see Pub. 559.

Past Due Returns

If you or someone you know needs to file past due tax returns, use *Tax Topic 153* or go to *IRS.gov/Individuals* for help in filing those returns. Send the return to the address that applies to you in the latest Form 1040 instructions. For example, if you are filing a 2014 return in 2018, use the address at the end of these instructions. However, if you got an IRS notice, mail the return to the address in the notice.

How To Get Tax Help

If you have questions about a tax issue, need help preparing your tax return, or want to download free publications, forms, or instructions, go to IRS.gov and find resources that can help you right away.

Preparing and filing your tax return. Find free options to prepare and file your return on IRS.gov or in your local community if you qualify.

The Volunteer Income Tax Assistance (VITA) program offers free tax help to people who generally make $54,000 or less, persons with disabilities, and limited-English-speaking taxpayers who need help preparing their own tax returns. The Tax Counseling for the Elderly (TCE) program offers free tax help for all taxpayers, particularly those who are 60 years of age and older. TCE volunteers specialize in answering questions about pensions and retirement-related issues unique to seniors.

You can go to IRS.gov to see your options for preparing and filing your return which include the following.

- **Free File.** Go to *IRS.gov/FreeFile*. See if you qualify to use brand-name software to prepare and *e-file* your federal tax return for free.
- **VITA.** Go to *IRS.gov/VITA*, download the free IRS2Go app, or call 1-800-906-9887 to find the nearest VITA location for free tax preparation.
- **TCE.** Go to *IRS.gov/TCE*, download the free IRS2Go app, or call 1-888-227-7669 to find the nearest TCE location for free tax preparation.

Getting answers to your tax law questions. On IRS.gov get answers to your tax questions anytime, anywhere.

- Go to *IRS.gov/Help* for a variety of tools that will help you get answers to some of the most common tax questions.
- Go to *IRS.gov/ITA* for the Interactive Tax Assistant, a tool that will ask you questions on a number of tax law topics and provide answers. You can print the entire interview and the final response for your records.
- Go to *IRS.gov/Pub17* to get Pub. 17, Your Federal Income Tax for Individuals, which features details on tax-saving opportunities, 2017 tax changes, and thousands of interactive links to help you find answers to your questions. View it online in HTML, as a PDF, or download it to your mobile device as an eBook.
- You also may be able to access tax law information in your electronic filing software.

Getting tax forms and publications. Go to *IRS.gov/Forms* to view, download, or print all of the forms and publications you may need. You also can download and view popular tax publications and instructions (including the 1040 instructions) on mobile devices as an eBook at no charge. Or, you can go to *IRS.gov/OrderForms* to place an order and have forms mailed to you within 10 business days.

Access your online account (Individual taxpayers only). Go to *IRS.gov/Account* to securely access information about your federal tax account.

- View the amount you owe, pay online or set up an online payment agreement.
- Access your tax records online.
- Review the past 18 months of your payment history.

• Go to *IRS.gov/SecureAccess* to review the required identity authentication process.

Using direct deposit. The fastest way to receive a tax refund is to combine direct deposit and IRS *e-file*. Direct deposit securely and electronically transfers your refund directly into your financial account. Eight in 10 taxpayers use direct deposit to receive their refund. IRS issues more than 90% of refunds in less than 21 days.

Delayed refund for returns claiming certain credits. The IRS can't issue refunds before mid-February 2018 for returns that properly claimed the earned income credit (EIC) or the additional child tax credit (ACTC). This applies to the entire refund, not just the portion associated with these credits. The IRS expects the earliest that earned income credit and/or additional child tax credit related refunds will be available in taxpayer bank accounts or on debit cards is February 27, 2018, if they chose direct deposit and there are no other issues with the tax return.

Getting a transcript or copy of a return. The quickest way to get a copy of your tax transcript is to go to *IRS.gov/Transcripts*. Click on either "Get Transcript Online" or "Get Transcript by Mail" to order a copy of your transcript. If you prefer, you can:

• Order your transcript by calling 1-800-908-9946.

• Mail Form 4506-T or Form 4506T-EZ (both available on IRS.gov).

Using online tools to help prepare your return. Go to *IRS.gov/Tools* for the following.

• The *Earned Income Tax Credit Assistant* (*IRS.gov/EIC*) determines if you are eligible for the EIC.

• The *Online EIN Application* (*IRS.gov/EIN*) helps you get an employer identification number.

• The *IRS Withholding Calculator* (*IRS.gov/W4App*) estimates the amount you should have withheld from your paycheck for federal income tax purposes.

• The *First Time Homebuyer Credit Account Look-up* (*IRS.gov/Homebuyer*) tool provides information on your repayments and account balance.

• The *Sales Tax Deduction Calculator* (*IRS.gov/SalesTax*) figures the amount you can claim if you itemize deductions on Schedule A (Form 1040), choose not to claim state and local income taxes, and you didn't save your receipts showing the sales tax you paid.

Resolving tax-related identity theft issues.

• The IRS doesn't initiate contact with taxpayers by email or telephone to request personal or financial information. This includes any type of electronic communication, such as text messages and social media channels.

• Go to *IRS.gov/IDProtection* for information and videos.

• If your SSN has been lost or stolen or you suspect you are a victim of tax-related identity theft, visit *IRS.gov/ID* to learn what steps you should take.

• See *Secure Your Tax Records From Identity Theft* under *General Information*, earlier.

Checking on the status of your refund.

• Go to *IRS.gov/Refunds*.

• The IRS can't issue refunds before mid-February 2018 for returns that properly claimed the EIC or ACTC. This applies to the entire refund, not just the portion associated with these credits. The IRS expects the earliest that earned income credit and/or additional child tax credit related refunds will be available in taxpayer bank accounts or on debit cards is February 27, 2018, if you chose direct deposit and there are no other issues with the tax return.

• Download the official IRS2Go app to your mobile device to check your refund status.

• Call the automated refund hotline at 1-800-829-1954. See *Refund Information*, later.

Making a tax payment. The IRS uses the latest encryption technology to ensure your electronic payments are safe and secure. You can make electronic payments online, by phone, and from a mobile device using the IRS2Go app. Paying electronically is quick, easy, and faster than mailing in a check or money order. Go to *IRS.gov/Payments* to make a payment using any of the following options.

• *IRS Direct Pay*: Pay your individual tax bill or estimated tax payment directly from your checking or savings account at no cost to you.

• **Debit or credit card:** Choose an approved payment processor to pay online, by phone, and by mobile device.

• **Electronic Funds Withdrawal:** Offered only when filing your federal taxes using tax preparation software or through a tax professional.

• **Electronic Federal Tax Payment System:** Best option for businesses. Enrollment is required.

• **Check or money order:** Mail your payment to the address listed on the notice or instructions.

• **Cash:** You may be able to pay your taxes with cash at a participating retail store.

What if I can't pay now? Go to *IRS.gov/Payments* for more information about your options.

• Apply for an *online payment agreement* (*IRS.gov/OPA*) to meet your tax obligation in monthly installments if you can't pay your taxes in full today. Once you complete the online process, you will receive immediate notification of whether your agreement has been approved.

• Use the *Offer in Compromise Pre-Qualifier* (*IRS.gov/OIC*) to see if you can settle your tax debt for less than the full amount you owe.

Checking the status of an amended return. Go to *IRS.gov/WMAR* to track the status of Form 1040X amended returns. Please note that it can take up to 3 weeks from the date you mailed your amended return for it to show up in our system and processing it can take up to 16 weeks.

Understanding an IRS notice or letter. Go to *IRS.gov/Notices* to find additional information about responding to an IRS notice or letter.

Contacting your local IRS office. Keep in mind, many questions can be answered on IRS.gov without visiting an IRS Tax Assistance Center (TAC). Go to *IRS.gov/LetUsHelp* for the topics people ask about most. If you still need help, IRS TACs provide help when a tax issue can't be handled online or by phone. All TACs now provide service by appointment so you'll know in advance that you can get the service you need without long wait times. Before you visit, go to *IRS.gov/TACLocator* to find the nearest TAC, check hours, available services, and appointment options.

Watching IRS videos. The IRS Video portal *IRSvideos.gov* contains video and audio presentations for individuals, small businesses, and tax professionals.

Getting tax information in other languages. For taxpayers whose native language isn't English, we have the following resources available. Taxpayers can find information on IRS.gov in the following languages.

- *Spanish* (*IRS.gov/Spanish*).
- *Chinese* (*IRS.gov/Chinese*).
- *Vietnamese* (*IRS.gov/Vietnamese*).
- *Korean* (*IRS.gov/Korean*).
- *Russian* (*IRS.gov/Russian*).

The IRS TACs provide over-the-phone interpreter service in over 170 languages, and the service is available free to taxpayers.

Interest and Penalties

You don't have to figure the amount of any interest or penalties you may owe. Because figuring these amounts can be complicated, we will do it for you if you want. We will send you a bill for any amount due.

If you include interest or penalties (other than the estimated tax penalty) with your payment, identify and enter the amount in the bottom margin of Form 1040, page 2. Don't include interest or penalties (other than the estimated tax penalty) in the amount you owe on line 78.

Interest

We will charge you interest on taxes not paid by their due date, even if an extension of time to file is granted. We also will charge you interest on penalties imposed for failure to file, negligence, fraud, substantial valuation misstatements, substantial understatements of tax, and reportable transaction understatements. Interest is charged on the penalty from the due date of the return (including extensions).

Penalties

Late filing. If you don't file your return by the due date (including extensions), the penalty is usually 5% of the amount due for each month or part of a month your return is late, unless you have a reasonable explanation. If you do, include it with your return. The penalty can be as much as 25% of the tax due. The penalty is 15% per month, up to a maximum of 75%, if the failure to file is fraudulent. If your return is more than 60 days late, the minimum penalty will be $210 or the amount of any tax you owe, whichever is smaller.

Late payment of tax. If you pay your taxes late, the penalty is usually ½ of 1% of the unpaid amount for each month or part of a month the tax isn't paid. The penalty can be as much as 25% of the unpaid amount. It applies to any unpaid tax on the return. This penalty is in addition to interest charges on late payments.

Frivolous return. In addition to any other penalties, the law imposes a penalty of $5,000 for filing a frivolous return. A frivolous return is one that doesn't contain information needed to figure the correct tax or shows a substantially incorrect tax because you take a frivolous position or desire to delay or interfere with the tax laws. This includes altering or striking out the preprinted language above the space where you sign. For a list of positions identified as frivolous, see Notice 2010-33, 2010-17 I.R.B. 609, available at *IRS.gov/irb/2010-17_IRB/ar13.html*.

Other. Other penalties can be imposed for negligence, substantial understatement of tax, reportable transaction understatements, filing an erroneous refund claim, and fraud. Criminal penalties may be imposed for willful failure to file, tax evasion, making a false statement, or identity theft. See Pub. 17 for details on some of these penalties.

Taxpayer Bill of Rights

All taxpayers have fundamental rights they should be aware of when dealing with the IRS. The Taxpayer Bill of Rights, which the IRS adopted in June of 2014, takes existing rights in the tax code and groups them into the following 10 broad categories, making them easier to understand. Explore your rights and our obligations to protect them.

The right to be informed. Taxpayers have the right to know what they need to do to comply with the tax laws. They are entitled to clear explanations of the laws and IRS procedures in all tax forms, instructions, publications, notices, and correspondence. They have the right to be informed of IRS decisions about their tax accounts and to receive clear explanations of the outcomes.

The right to quality service. Taxpayers have the right to receive prompt, courteous, and professional assistance in their dealings with the IRS, to be spoken to in a way they can easily understand, to receive clear and easily understandable communications from the IRS, and to speak to a supervisor about inadequate service.

The right to pay no more than the correct amount of tax. Taxpayers have the right to pay only the amount of tax legally due, including interest and penalties, and to have the IRS apply all tax payments properly.

The right to challenge the IRS's position and be heard. Taxpayers have the right to raise objections and provide additional documentation in response to formal IRS actions or proposed actions, to expect that the IRS will consider their timely objections and documentation promptly and fairly, and to receive a response if the IRS does not agree with their position.

The right to appeal an IRS decision in an independent forum. Taxpayers are entitled to a fair and impartial administrative appeal of most IRS decisions, including many penalties, and have the right to receive a written response regarding the Office of Appeals' decision. Taxpayers generally have the right to take their cases to court.

The right to finality. Taxpayers have the right to know the maximum amount of time they have to challenge the IRS's position as well as the maximum amount of time the IRS has to audit a particular tax year or collect a tax debt. Taxpayers have the right to know when the IRS has finished an audit.

The right to privacy. Taxpayers have the right to expect that any IRS inquiry, examination, or enforcement action will comply with the law and be no more intrusive than necessary, and will respect all due process rights, including search and seizure protections and will provide, where applicable, a collection due process hearing.

The right to confidentiality. Taxpayers have the right to expect that any information they provide to the IRS will not be disclosed unless authorized by the taxpayer or by law. Taxpayers have the right to expect appropriate action will be taken against employees, return preparers, and others who wrongfully use or disclose taxpayer return information.

The right to retain representation. Taxpayers have the right to retain an authorized representative of their choice to represent them in their dealings with the IRS. Taxpayers have the right to seek assistance from a _Low Income Taxpayer Clinic_ if they can't afford representation.

The right to a fair and just tax system. Taxpayers have the right to expect the tax system to consider facts and circumstances that might affect their underlying liabilities, ability to pay, or ability to provide information timely. Taxpayers have the right to receive assistance from the _Taxpayer Advocate Service_ if they are experiencing financial difficulty or if the IRS has not resolved their tax issues properly and timely through its normal channels.

Learn more at _IRS.gov/TaxpayerRights_.

Refund Information

where's my refund? To check the status of your refund, go to *IRS.gov/Refunds* or use the free IRS2Go app, 24 hours a day, 7 days a week. Information about your refund generally will be available within 24 hours after the IRS receives your e-filed return, or 4 weeks after you mail a paper return. But if you filed Form 8379 with your return, allow 14 weeks (11 weeks if you filed electronically) before checking your refund status.

The IRS can't issue refunds before mid-February 2018 for returns that claim the earned income credit or the additional child tax credit. This delay applies to the entire refund, not just the portion associated with these credits.

The IRS expects the earliest that earned income credit and/or additional child tax credit related refunds will be available in taxpayer bank accounts or on debit cards is February 27, 2018, if they chose direct deposit and there are no other issues with the tax return.

To use *Where's My Refund*, have a copy of your tax return handy. You will need to enter the following information from your return:

- Your social security number (or individual taxpayer identification number),
- Your filing status, and
- The exact whole dollar amount of your refund.

Where's My Refund will provide an actual personalized refund date as soon as the IRS processes your tax return and approves your refund.

TIP *Updates to refund status are made once a day - usually at night.*

If you don't have Internet access, you can call 1-800-829-1954 24 hours a day, 7 days a week, for automated refund information. Our phone and walk-in assistors can research the status of your refund only if it's been 21 days or more since you filed electronically or more than 6 weeks since you mailed your paper return.

Don't send in a copy of your return unless asked to do so.

To get a refund, you generally must file your return within 3 years from the date the return was due (including extensions).

Where's My Refund doesn't track refunds that are claimed on an amended tax return.

Refund information also is available in Spanish at *IRS.gov/Spanish* and 1-800-829-1954.

Tax Topics

You can read these Tax Topics at *IRS.gov/TaxTopics*.

List of Tax Topics

All topics are available in Spanish (and most topics are available in Chinese, Korean, Vietnamese, and Russian).

Topic No.	Subject
	IRS Help Available
101	IRS services—Volunteer tax assistance, outreach programs, and identity theft
102	Tax assistance for individuals with disabilities
103	Tax help for small businesses and the self-employed
104	Taxpayer Advocate Service—Your voice at the IRS
105	Armed Forces tax information
107	Tax relief in disaster situations
	IRS Procedures
151	Your appeal rights
152	Refund information
153	What to do if you haven't filed your tax return
154	Form W-2 and Form 1099-R (What to do if incorrect or not received)
155	Obtaining forms and publications
156	Copy or transcript of your tax return—How to get one
157	Change your address—How to notify the IRS
158	Paying your taxes and ensuring proper credit of payments
159	How to get a transcript or copy of Form W-2
161	Returning an erroneous refund—Paper check or direct deposit
	Collection
201	The collection process
202	Tax payment options
203	Refund offsets for unpaid child support, certain federal and state debts, and unemployment compensation debts
204	Offers in compromise
205	Innocent spouse relief (Including separation of liability and equitable relief)
206	Dishonored payments
	Alternative Filing Methods
253	Substitute tax forms
254	How to choose a tax return preparer
255	Signing your return electronically
	General Information
301	When, how, and where to file

Topic No.	Subject
303	Checklist of common errors when preparing your tax return
304	Extensions of time to file your tax return
305	Recordkeeping
306	Penalty for underpayment of estimated tax
307	Backup withholding
308	Amended returns
309	Roth IRA contributions
310	Coverdell education savings accounts
311	Power of attorney information
312	Disclosure authorizations
313	Qualified tuition programs (QTPs)
	Which Forms to File
352	Which form—1040, 1040A, or 1040EZ?
356	Decedents
	Types of Income
401	Wages and salaries
403	Interest received
404	Dividends
407	Business income
409	Capital gains and losses
410	Pensions and annuities
411	Pensions—The general rule and the simplified method
412	Lump-sum distributions
413	Rollovers from retirement plans
414	Rental income and expenses
415	Renting residential and vacation property
416	Farming and fishing income
417	Earnings for clergy
418	Unemployment compensation
419	Gambling income and losses
420	Bartering income
421	Scholarships, fellowship grants, and other grants
423	Social security and equivalent railroad retirement benefits
424	401(k) plans
425	Passive activities—Losses and credits
427	Stock options
429	Traders in securities (Information for Form 1040 filers)
430	Receipt of stock in a demutualization
431	Canceled debt—Is it taxable or not?
432	Form 1099-A (Acquisition or Abandonment of Secured Property) and Form 1099-C (Cancellation of Debt)

Topic No.	Subject
	Adjustments to Income
451	Individual retirement arrangements (IRAs)
452	Alimony
453	Bad debt deduction
455	Moving expenses
456	Student loan interest deduction
458	Educator expense deduction
	Itemized Deductions
501	Should I itemize?
502	Medical and dental expenses
503	Deductible taxes
504	Home mortgage points
505	Interest expense
506	Charitable contributions
508	Miscellaneous expenses
509	Business use of home
510	Business use of car
511	Business travel expenses
512	Business entertainment expenses
513	Work-related education expenses
514	Employee business expenses
515	Casualty, disaster, and theft losses (including federally declared disaster areas)
	Tax Computation
551	Standard deduction
552	Tax and credits figured by the IRS
553	Tax on a child's investment and other unearned income (Kiddie tax)
554	Self-employment tax
556	Alternative minimum tax
557	Additional tax on early distributions from traditional and Roth IRAs
558	Additional tax on early distributions from retirement plans, other than IRAs
559	Net Investment Income Tax
560	Additional Medicare Tax
561	Individual shared responsibility provision
	Tax Credits
601	Earned income credit
602	Child and dependent care credit
607	Adoption credit and adoption assistance programs
608	Excess social security and RRTA tax withheld
610	Retirement savings contributions credit
611	Repayment of the first-time homebuyer credit
612	The premium tax credit

List of Tax Topics

(Continued)

Tax Topic numbers are effective January 2, 2018.

Disclosure, Privacy Act, and Paperwork Reduction Act Notice

The IRS Restructuring and Reform Act of 1998, the Privacy Act of 1974, and the Paperwork Reduction Act of 1980 require that when we ask you for information we must first tell you our legal right to ask for the information, why we are asking for it, and how it will be used. We must also tell you what could happen if we do not receive it and whether your response is voluntary, required to obtain a benefit, or mandatory under the law.

This notice applies to all papers you file with us, including this tax return. It also applies to any questions we need to ask you so we can complete, correct, or process your return; figure your tax; and collect tax, interest, or penalties.

Our legal right to ask for information is Internal Revenue Code sections 6001, 6011, and 6012(a), and their regulations. They say that you must file a return or statement with us for any tax you are liable for. Your response is mandatory under these sections. Code section 6109 requires you to provide your identifying number on the return. This is so we know who you are, and can process your return and other papers. You must fill in all parts of the tax form that apply to you. But you do not have to check the boxes for the Presidential Election Campaign Fund or for the third-party designee. You also do not have to provide your daytime phone number.

You are not required to provide the information requested on a form that is subject to the Paperwork Reduction Act unless the form displays a valid OMB control number. Books or records relating to a form or its instructions must be retained as long as their contents may become material in the administration of any Internal Revenue law.

We ask for tax return information to carry out the tax laws of the United States. We need it to figure and collect the right amount of tax.

If you do not file a return, do not provide the information we ask for, or provide fraudulent information, you may be charged penalties and be subject to criminal prosecution. We may also have to disallow the exemptions, exclusions, credits, deductions, or adjustments shown on the tax return. This could make the tax higher

or delay any refund. Interest may also be charged.

Generally, tax returns and return information are confidential, as stated in Code section 6103. However, Code section 6103 allows or requires the Internal Revenue Service to disclose or give the information shown on your tax return to others as described in the Code. For example, we may disclose your tax information to the Department of Justice to enforce the tax laws, both civil and criminal, and to cities, states, the District of Columbia, and U.S. commonwealths or possessions to carry out their tax laws. We may disclose your tax information to the Department of Treasury and contractors for tax administration purposes; and to other persons as necessary to obtain information needed to determine the amount of or to collect the tax you owe. We may disclose your tax information to the Comptroller General of the United States to permit the Comptroller General to review the Internal Revenue Service. We may disclose your tax information to committees of Congress; federal, state, and local child support agencies; and to other federal agencies for the purposes of determining entitlement for benefits or the eligibility for and the repayment of loans. We may also disclose this information to other countries under a tax treaty, to federal and state agencies to enforce federal nontax criminal laws, or to federal law enforcement and intelligence agencies to combat terrorism.

Please keep this notice with your records. It may help you if we ask you for other information. If you have questions about the rules for filing and giving information, please call or visit any Internal Revenue Service office.

We Welcome Comments on Forms

We try to create forms and instructions that can be easily understood. Often this is difficult to do because our tax laws are very complex. For some people with income mostly from wages, filling in the forms is easy. For others who have businesses, pensions, stocks, rental income, or other investments, it is more difficult.

If you have suggestions for making these forms simpler, we would be happy to hear from you. You can send us com-

ments from *IRS.gov/Forms*. Click on "More Information" and then on "Give us feedback." Or you can send your comments to Internal Revenue Service, Tax Forms and Publications Division, 1111 Constitution Ave. NW, IR-6526, Washington, DC 20224. Don't send your return to this address. Instead, see the addresses at the end of these instructions.

Although we can't respond individually to each comment received, we do appreciate your feedback and will consider your comments as we revise our tax forms and instructions.

Estimates of Taxpayer Burden

The following table shows burden estimates based on current statutory requirements as of September 2017, for taxpayers filing a 2017 Form 1040, 1040A, or 1040EZ tax return. Time spent and out-of-pocket costs are presented separately. Time burden is broken out by taxpayer activity, with recordkeeping representing the largest component. Out-of-pocket costs include any expenses incurred by taxpayers to prepare and submit their tax returns. Examples include tax return preparation and submission fees, postage and photocopying costs, and tax preparation software costs. While these estimates don't include burden associated with post-filing activities, IRS operational data indicate that electronically prepared and filed returns have fewer arithmetic errors, implying lower post-filing burden.

Reported time and cost burdens are national averages and don't necessarily reflect a "typical" case. Most taxpayers experience lower than average burden, with taxpayer burden varying considerably by taxpayer type. For instance, the estimated average time burden for all taxpayers filing a Form 1040, 1040A, or 1040EZ is 12 hours, with an average cost of $210 per return. This average includes all associated forms and schedules, across all preparation methods and taxpayer activities. The average burden for taxpayers filing Form 1040 is about 15 hours and $270; the average burden for taxpayers filing Form 1040A is about 7 hours and $90; and the average for Form 1040EZ filers is about 5 hours and $40.

Within each of these estimates there is significant variation in taxpayer activity. For example, nonbusiness taxpayers are expected to have an average burden of about 8 hours and $120, while business taxpayers are expected to have an average burden of about 21 hours and $410. Simi-larly, tax preparation fees and other out-of-pocket costs vary extensively depending on the tax situation of the taxpayer, the type of software or professional preparer used, and the geographic location.

If you have comments concerning the time and cost estimates below, you can contact us at either one of the addresses shown under *We Welcome Comments on Forms.*

Estimated Average Taxpayer Burden for Individuals by Activity

Primary Form Filed or Type of Taxpayer	Percentage of Returns	Average Burden					Average Cost (Dollars)**
		Average Time (Hours)					
		Total Time*	Record Keeping	Tax Planning	Form Completion and Submission	All Other	
All taxpayers	100	12	5	2	4	1	$210
Primary forms filed							
1040	68	15	7	2	4	1	270
1040A	20	7	2	1	3	1	90
1040EZ	12	5	1	***	2	1	40
Type of taxpayer							
Nonbusiness****	70	8	3	1	3	1	120
Business****	30	21	11	3	5	1	410

*Detail may not add to total time due to rounding.

**Dollars rounded to the nearest $10.

***Rounds to less than one hour.

****You are considered a "business" filer if you file one or more of the following with Form 1040: Schedule C, C-EZ, E, or F or Form 2106 or 2106-EZ. You are considered a "nonbusiness" filer if you don't file any of those schedules or forms with Form 1040 or if you file Form 1040A or 1040EZ.

Order Form for Forms and Publications

You can view and download the tax forms and publications you need at IRS.gov/Forms. You also can place an order for forms at IRS.gov/Order-Forms to avoid having to complete and mail the order form.

The most frequently ordered forms and publications are listed on the order form. You will receive two copies of each form, one copy of the instructions, and one copy of each publication you order. To help reduce waste, please order only the items you need to prepare your return.

How To Use the Order Form

Circle the items you need on the order form. Use the blank spaces to order items not listed. If you need more space, attach a separate sheet of paper.

Print or type your name and address accurately in the space provided on the order form to ensure delivery of your order. Enclose the order form in an envelope and mail it to the IRS address shown next. You should receive your order within 10 business days after we receive your request.

Don't send your tax return to the address shown here. Instead, see the addresses at the end of these instructions.

Mail Your Order Form To:

Internal Revenue Service
1201 N. Mitsubishi Motorway
Bloomington, IL 61705-6613

- - - - - - - - - - - - - - - - - - - ▲ *Cut here* ▲ - - - - - - - - - - - - - - - - - - -

Save Money and Time by Going Online!
Download or order these and other forms and publications at IRS.gov/Forms

Order Form

Please print.

Name

Postal mailing address — Apt./Suite/Room

City — State — ZIP code

Foreign country — International postal code

Daytime phone number
( )

Circle the forms and publications you need. The instructions for any form you order will be included.

Use the **blank spaces** to order items not listed.

Use your QR Reader app on your smartphone to scan this code and get connected to the IRS Forms and Publications homepage.

1040	Schedule F (1040)	1040-V	5405	8960	Pub. 523	Pub. 554	Pub. 970
Schedule A (1040)	Schedule H (1040)	1040X	6251	8962	Pub. 525	Pub. 575	Pub. 972
Schedule B (1040A or 1040)	Schedule J (1040)	2106	8283	8965	Pub. 526	Pub. 583	Pub. 4681
Schedule C (1040)	Schedule R (1040A or 1040)	2441	8606	Pub. 1	Pub. 527	Pub. 587	
Schedule C-EZ (1040)	Schedule SE (1040)	3903	8822	Pub. 334	Pub. 529	Pub. 590-A	
Schedule D (1040)	Schedule 8812 (1040A or 1040)	4506	8829	Pub. 463	Pub. 535	Pub. 590-B	
Form 8949	1040A	4562	8863	Pub. 501	Pub. 547	Pub. 596	
Schedule E (1040)	1040EZ	4684	8917	Pub. 502	Pub. 550	Pub. 915	
Schedule EIC (1040A or 1040)	1040-ES (2018)	4868	8959	Pub. 505	Pub. 551	Pub. 946	

Major Categories of Federal Income and Outlays for Fiscal Year 2016

Income and Outlays. These pie charts show the relative sizes of the major categories of federal income and outlays for fiscal year 2016.

Income

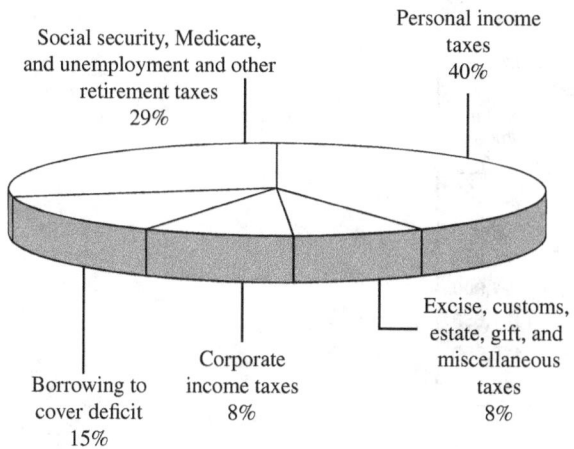

Social security, Medicare, and unemployment and other retirement taxes
29%

Personal income taxes
40%

Borrowing to cover deficit
15%

Corporate income taxes
8%

Excise, customs, estate, gift, and miscellaneous taxes
8%

Outlays*

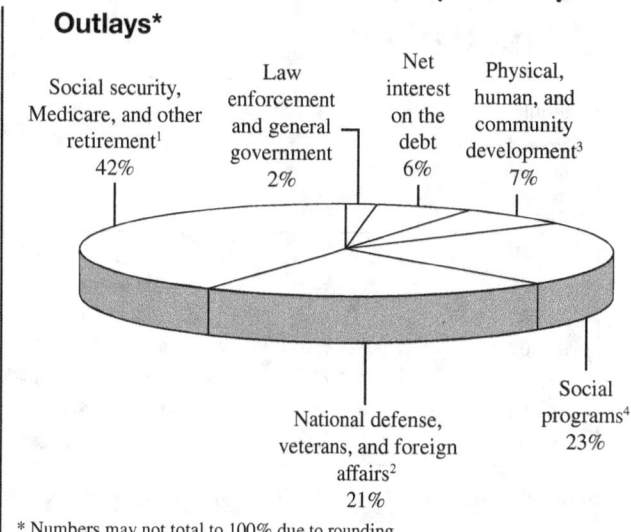

Social security, Medicare, and other retirement[1]
42%

Law enforcement and general government
2%

Net interest on the debt
6%

Physical, human, and community development[3]
7%

National defense, veterans, and foreign affairs[2]
21%

Social programs[4]
23%

* Numbers may not total to 100% due to rounding.

On or before the first Monday in February of each year, the President is required by law to submit to the Congress a budget proposal for the fiscal year that begins the following October. The budget plan sets forth the President's proposed receipts, spending, and the surplus or deficit for the federal government. The plan includes recommendations for new legislation as well as recommendations to change, eliminate, and add programs. After receipt of the President's proposal, the Congress reviews the proposal and makes changes. It first passes a budget resolution setting its own targets for receipts, outlays, and surplus or deficit. Next, individual spending and revenue bills that are consistent with the goals of the budget resolution are enacted.

In fiscal year 2016 (which began on October 1, 2015, and ended on September 30, 2016), federal income was $3.268 trillion and outlays were $3.853 trillion, leaving a deficit of $585 billion.

Footnotes for Certain Federal Outlays

1. **Social security, Medicare, and other retirement:** These programs provide income support for the retired and disabled and medical care for the elderly.

2. **National defense, veterans, and foreign affairs:** About 15% of outlays were to equip, modernize, and pay our armed forces and to fund national defense activities; about 4% were for veterans benefits and services; and about 1% were for international activities, including military and economic assistance to foreign countries and the maintenance of U.S. embassies abroad.

3. **Physical, human, and community development:** These outlays were for agriculture; natural resources; environment; transportation; aid for elementary and secondary education and direct assistance to college students; job training; deposit insurance, commerce and housing credit, and community development; and space, energy, and general science programs.

4. **Social programs:** About 16% of total outlays were for Medicaid, Supplemental Nutrition Assistance Program (formerly food stamps), temporary assistance for needy families, supplemental security income, and related programs; and 6% for health research and public health programs, unemployment compensation, assisted housing, and social services.

Note. The percentages shown here exclude undistributed offsetting receipts, which were $95 billion in fiscal year 2016. In the budget, these receipts are offset against spending in figuring the outlay totals shown above. These receipts are for the U.S. Government's share of its employee retirement programs, rents and royalties on the Outer Continental Shelf, and proceeds from the sale of assets.

2017 Tax Rate Schedules

The Tax Rate Schedules are shown so you can see the tax rate that applies to all levels of taxable income. Don't use them to figure your tax. Instead, see the instructions for line 44.

Schedule X—If your filing status is Single

If your taxable income is: Over—	But not over—	The tax is:	of the amount over—
$0	$9,325	--------- 10%	$0
9,325	37,950	$932.50 + 15%	9,325
37,950	91,900	5,226.25 + 25%	37,950
91,900	191,650	18,713.75 + 28%	91,900
191,650	416,700	46,643.75 + 33%	191,650
416,700	418,400	120,910.25 + 35%	416,700
418,400	---------	121,505.25 + 39.6%	418,400

Schedule Y-1—If your filing status is Married filing jointly or Qualifying widow(er)

If your taxable income is: Over—	But not over—	The tax is:	of the amount over—
$0	$18,650	--------- 10%	$0
18,650	75,900	$1,865.00 + 15%	18,650
75,900	153,100	10,452.50 + 25%	75,900
153,100	233,350	29,752.50 + 28%	153,100
233,350	416,700	52,222.50 + 33%	233,350
416,700	470,700	112,728.00 + 35%	416,700
470,700	---------	131,628.00 + 39.6%	470,700

Schedule Y-2—If your filing status is Married filing separately

If your taxable income is: Over—	But not over—	The tax is:	of the amount over—
$0	$9,325	--------- 10%	$0
9,325	37,950	$932.50 + 15%	9,325
37,950	76,550	5,226.25 + 25%	37,950
76,550	116,675	14,876.25 + 28%	76,550
116,675	208,350	26,111.25 + 33%	116,675
208,350	235,350	56,364.00 + 35%	208,350
235,350	---------	65,814.00 + 39.6%	235,350

Schedule Z—If your filing status is Head of household

If your taxable income is: Over—	But not over—	The tax is:	of the amount over—
$0	$13,350	--------- 10%	$0
13,350	50,800	$1,335.00 + 15%	13,350
50,800	131,200	6,952.50 + 25%	50,800
131,200	212,500	27,052.50 + 28%	131,200
212,500	416,700	49,816.50 + 33%	212,500
416,700	444,550	117,202.50 + 35%	416,700
444,550	---------	126,950.00 + 39.6%	444,550

Index to Instructions

Where Do You File? Mail your return to the address shown below that applies to you. If you want to use a private delivery service, see *Private Delivery Services* under *Filing Requirements*, earlier.

Envelopes without enough postage will be returned to you by the post office. Your envelope may need additional postage if it contains more than five pages or is oversized (for example, it is over ¼" thick). Also, include your complete return address.

IF you live in...	THEN use this address if you:	
	Are requesting a refund or are not enclosing a check or money order...	Are enclosing a check or money order...
Florida, Louisiana, Mississippi, Texas	Department of the Treasury Internal Revenue Service Austin, TX 73301-0002	Internal Revenue Service P.O. Box 1214 Charlotte, NC 28201-1214
Alaska, Arizona, California, Colorado, Hawaii, Idaho, Nevada, New Mexico, Oregon, Utah, Washington, Wyoming	Department of the Treasury Internal Revenue Service Fresno, CA 93888-0002	Internal Revenue Service P.O. Box 7704 San Francisco, CA 94120-7704
Arkansas, Illinois, Indiana, Iowa, Kansas, Michigan, Minnesota, Montana, Nebraska, North Dakota, Ohio, Oklahoma, South Dakota, Wisconsin	Department of the Treasury Internal Revenue Service Fresno, CA 93888-0002	Internal Revenue Service P.O. Box 802501 Cincinnati, OH 45280-2501
Alabama, Georgia, Kentucky, New Jersey, North Carolina, South Carolina, Tennessee, Virginia	Department of the Treasury Internal Revenue Service Kansas City, MO 64999-0002	Internal Revenue Service P.O. Box 931000 Louisville, KY 40293-1000
Delaware, Maine, Massachusetts, Missouri, New Hampshire, New York, Vermont	Department of the Treasury Internal Revenue Service Kansas City, MO 64999-0002	Internal Revenue Service P.O. Box 37008 Hartford, CT 06176-7008
Connecticut, District of Columbia, Maryland, Pennsylvania, Rhode Island, West Virginia	Department of the Treasury Internal Revenue Service Ogden, UT 84201-0002	Internal Revenue Service P.O. Box 37910 Hartford, CT 06176-7910
A foreign country, U.S. possession or territory*, or use an APO or FPO address, or file Form 2555, 2555-EZ, or 4563, or are a dual-status alien	Department of the Treasury Internal Revenue Service Austin, TX 73301-0215	Internal Revenue Service P.O. Box 1303 Charlotte, NC 28201-1303

*If you live in American Samoa, Puerto Rico, Guam, the U.S. Virgin Islands, or the Northern Mariana Islands, see Pub. 570.

www.ingramcontent.com/pod-product-compliance
Lightning Source LLC
Chambersburg PA
CBHW081734220526
45468CB00008B/2095

* 9 781984 172303 *